Contemporary Literature and the Body

T0281864

Contemporary Literature and the Body

A Critical Introduction

Edited by Alice Hall

BLOOMSBURY ACADEMIC

LONDON • NEW YORK • OXFORD • NEW DELHI • SYDNEY

BLOOMSBURY ACADEMIC
Bloomsbury Publishing Plc
50 Bedford Square, London, WC1B 3DP, UK
1385 Broadway, New York, NY 10018, USA
29 Earlsfort Terrace, Dublin 2, Ireland

BLOOMSBURY, BLOOMSBURY ACADEMIC and the Diana logo
are trademarks of Bloomsbury Publishing Plc

First published in Great Britain 2023

Cover design: Matt Beard
Cover image © Joanna Stawnicka, 'Self-Portrait in Autumn
and Self-Portrait in Winter 2021'

A catalogue record for this book is available from the British Library.

A catalog record for this book is available from the Library of Congress.

ISBN: HB: 978-1-3501-8016-1
         PB: 978-1-3501-8015-4
       ePDF: 978-1-3501-8022-2
      eBook: 978-1-3501-8017-8

Typeset by Integra Software Services Pvt. Ltd.
Printed and bound in Great Britain

To find out more about our authors and books visit www.bloomsbury.com
and sign up for our newsletters.

CONTENTS

CONTRIBUTORS

Boriana Alexandrova is Senior Lecturer of Women's Studies in the Centre for Women's Studies at the University of York, UK. She is the author of *Joyce, Multilingualism, and the Ethics of Reading* (2020) and has published articles on multilingual modernism, disability, trauma and translation in *Modernism/modernity*, *European Joyce Studies* and *Joyce Studies Annual*. She also served as reviews editor for *Modernism/modernity* from 2013 to 2016.

Marie Allitt is Early Career Teaching and Research Fellow in twentieth-century literature at the University of Edinburgh, specializing in life writing and literary medical humanities. Her research focuses on experiences and representations of caregiving, chronic illness, trauma, and health/care architectures and environments. Her first monograph, *Medical Caregiving Narratives of the First World War: Geographies of Care*, is published in 2023. She has previously published in the *BMJ Medical Humanities*, *The Polyphony* and in the edited collections *Re/Imagining Depression: Creative Approaches to 'Feeling Bad'* (2021) and *Diagnosing History: Medicine in Television Period Drama* (2022).

Timothy C. Baker is Personal Chair in Scottish and Contemporary Literature at the University of Aberdeen. He is the author of the five books, most recently *New Forms of Environmental Writing: Gleaning and Fragmentation* and *Reading My Mother Back: A Memoir in Childhood Animal Stories*, as well as numerous articles and book chapters.

J. Brooks Bouson is Professor Emerita of English at Loyola University Chicago. She is the author of *The Empathic Reader: A Study of the Narcissistic Character and the Drama of the Self* (1989); *Brutal Choreographies: Oppositional Strategies and Narrative Design in the Novels of Margaret Atwood* (1993); *Quiet As It's Kept: Shame,*

Trauma and Race in the Novels of Toni Morrison (2000); *Jamaica Kincaid: Writing Memory, Writing Back to the Mother* (2005); *Embodied Shame: Uncovering Female Shame in Contemporary Women's Writings* (2009) and *Shame and the Aging Woman: Confronting and Resisting Ageism in Contemporary Women's Writing* (2016).

She is also the editor of *Critical Insights: Margaret Atwood's The Handmaid's Tale* (2009); *Critical Insights: Margaret Atwood: The Robber Bride, The Blind Assassin, Oryx and Crake* (2011); *Critical Insights: Emily Dickinson* (2010); and *Critical Insights: Margaret Atwood* (2013).

Rebekah Cumpsty is Assistant Professor of Anglophone World Literature at Weber State University, Utah. She is the author of *Postsecular Poetics: Negotiating the Sacred and Secular in Contemporary African Fiction* (2022) and co-editor of 'The Body Now' (2020), a special issue of *Interventions: International Journal of Postcolonial Studies*. Her publications have appeared in the *Journal of Commonwealth Literature, Interventions, Wasafiri, Sikh Formations* and *Gothic Studies*, as well as in a collection for Edinburgh University Press.

Amelia DeFalco is Associate Professor of Medical Humanities in the School of English at the University of Leeds. She is Co-Investigator of the Wellcome-funded projects *Imagining Technologies for Disability Futures* and *LivingBodiesObjects: Technology and the Spaces of Health.* She is author of *Uncanny Subjects: Aging in Contemporary Narrative* (2010), *Imagining Care: Responsibility, Dependency, and Canadian Literature* (2016), *Curious Kin in Fictions of Posthuman Care* (2023) and co-editor of *Ethics and Affects in the Fiction of Alice Munro* (2018).

Luna Dolezal is Associate Professor of Philosophy and Medical Humanities at the University of Exeter, based in the Wellcome Centre for Cultures and Environments of Health. She is Principal Investigator on the *Shame and Medicine* Project and Co-I on the *Imagining Technologies for Disability Futures*, both funded by the Wellcome Trust. She is author of *The Body and Shame: Phenomenology, Feminism and the Socially Shaped Body* (2015) and co-editor of the books *Body/Self/Other: The Phenomenology* *of Social Encounters* (2017) and *New Feminist Perspectives on Embodiment* (2018).

Alice Hall is Lecturer of Contemporary and Global Literature in the Department of English and Related Literature at the University of York, UK. She is the author of *Disability and Modern Fiction: Faulkner, Morrison, Coetzee and the Nobel Prize for Literature* (2012) and *Literature and Disability: Contemporary Critical Thought* (2015). Alice is also editor of the *Routledge Companion to Literature and Disability* (2020).

Alexandra Kingston-Reese is Senior Lecturer of Modern and Contemporary Literature at the University of York. She is the author of *Contemporary Novelists and the Aesthetics of Twenty-First Century American Life* (2020) and the editor of *Art Essays* (2021). She is the editor of *ASAP/J*, the open-access platform of *ASAP/Journal*, the scholarly publication of the Association for the Study of the Arts of the Present. Her essays and reviews have recently appeared in *Literary Hub*, the *Los Angeles Review of Books*, *Post45*, and the *Times Literary Supplement*.

Elizabeth Losh is the Duane A. and Virginia S. Dittman Professor of American Studies and English at William & Mary with a specialization in New Media Ecologies. Before coming to William & Mary, she directed the Culture, Art, and Technology Program at the University of California, San Diego. She is the author of *Virtualpolitik: An Electronic History of Government Media-Making in a Time of War, Scandal, Disaster, Miscommunication, and Mistakes* (2009); *The War on Learning: Gaining Ground in the Digital University* (2014); *Hashtag* (2019); and *Selfie Democracy* (2022). She is the co-author with Jonathan Alexander of *Understanding Rhetoric: A Graphic Guide to Writing* (2013; second edition, 2017; third edition, 2020). She also produced *MOOCs and Their Afterlives: Experiments in Scale and Access in Higher Education* (2017) and co-edited *Bodies of Information: Intersectional Feminism and Digital Humanities* (2018).

Susannah Mintz is Professor of English at Skidmore College. She is the author of five books, including the memoir *Love Affair in the Garden of Milton: Poetry, Loss, and the Meaning of Unbelief* (2021) and four scholarly volumes on disability and literature, most recently *The Disabled Detective: Sleuthing Disability in*

Contemporary Crime Fiction (2019) and *Hurt and Pain: Literature and the Suffering Body* (2014). She has published extensively in the areas of disability representation and early modern literature, and as a writer of creative nonfiction, with work recognized by the South Loop National Essay Prize, the William Allen nonfiction prize, the Epiphany chapbook contest, the Cagibi essay prize, the *River Teeth* non-fiction prize, the notable list of *Best American Essays* and the *Pushcart Prize Anthology*. Current projects include a cultural history of hypochondria and an edited collection of essays about disability and place.

ACKNOWLEDGMENT

With thanks to Joanna Stawnicka for the cover image, 'Self-Portrait in Autumn and Self-Portrait in Winter 2021'.

Introduction

Alice Hall

Invisible bodies in contemporary culture

In Joanna Stawnicka's 'Self-Portrait in Autumn and Self-Portrait in Winter 2021', reproduced on the cover of this book, the artist's body is strikingly absent. Instead, viewers are presented with a skeleton-like structure, a chair, adorned with different clothing in each of the two different images. The framework of the chair remains the same but its meaning shifts according to the season (the title suggests) and the way in which it is dressed, illuminated and positioned. Stawnicka's images depict missing or invisible bodies but also suggest how identity and embodiment are constructed and mutable, processes that change over time and can be self-consciously restyled and reworked.

Stawnicka's artwork was made in 2021, a year in which the Covid-19 pandemic meant that the 'power to withdraw' one's body from public space became a new mark of privilege.[1] The high-vis jacket, gloves and parcel in the first image serve as a reminder of the kinds of jobs that cannot be done at a distance and 'the novel political cleavage' between 'the embodied and the remote worker' which defined that particular cultural moment.[2] It is unclear whether Stawnicka, as the subject of the self-portrait, is the recipient of the parcel or the one delivering it, but either way her body is implicated in a system of capital dependent on the physical labour of key workers, such as delivery drivers.

This idea of being able to withdraw or ignore one's body as a mark of privilege is articulated in other spheres too. Sinéad Gleeson's *Constellations: Reflections from Life* (2019), discussed in Chapter 3 of this collection, describes how the healthy body is often experienced as invisible: 'We don't stop to think of how the heart beats its steady rhythms; or watch our metatarsals fan out with every step. Unless it's involved in pleasure or pain, we pay this moving mass of vessel, blood and bone no mind.'[3] Simone de Beauvoir, writing much earlier in 1949, suggests that the privilege of an invisible body is a distinctly gendered one. She argues that while women are often constrained by forms of biological determinism, man 'superbly ignores the fact that his anatomy also includes glands, such as the testicles, and that they also secrete hormones. He thinks of his body as a direct and normal connection with the world, which he believes he apprehends objectively'.[4]

Stawnicka's playful artwork punctures this fantasy of rational objectivity: by removing her body from her self-portraits she highlights the ways in which we rely upon highly subjective processes of looking at the body to construct the identities of others and ourselves. Giddens, in *Modernity and Self-Identity* (1991), argues that a highly reflexive approach to the body is a particular characteristic of late modernity. Changes in the structures of family, work and religion at the second half of the twentieth century, he suggests, have led many people, especially in the Global North, to focus on the body as a marker of selfhood and the continuous aspect

of their identity: 'the reflexivity of the self', as a defining feature of
our age, 'extends to the body'.[5] Susan Bordo draws on Giddens
and Foucault to argue that this reflexivity results in 'bodies whose
forces are energies habituated to external regulation, subjection,
transformation, "improvement"'.[6] Women in particular, she argues,
are expected to work on their bodies through diet, fashion, make-up
and exercise. In consumer culture, Frederick Jameson points out that
the design of our public social space – open plan, with mirrors and
glass – is often structured around displays of the body. In this context,
the image, Rachel Bowlby argues, 'is useful for thinking about
consumer forms of subjectivity'.[7] Like the two images placed side
by side in Stawnicka's self-portraits, many contemporary theorists
of the body challenge ideas of singularity and fixedness, drawing on
this sense of bodies as being perpetually displayed, commodified and
transformed, to suggest a pluralistic view of 'the body multiple'.[8]

The financial freedom to withdraw one's body from the world
of in-person work and to be able to indulge in a fantasy of its
invisibility because of masculinity, whiteness, youth, ability or health
are all marks of privilege which imply individual agency and choice.
However, as many of the chapters in this collection discuss, inhabiting
a body that is considered by others to be invisible is a deeply
oppressive, even painful position. In her memoir, Gleeson recalls
how she internalized a sense of passivity and disgust associated with
her gender and disability: 'Ashamed of my bones and my scars and
the clunking way I walked … I wanted to make myself smaller, to
minimise the space I took up.'[9] J. Brooks Bouson, in Chapter 8 of this
book, raises issues of invisibility in relation to age and gender. She
cites Kate in Doris Lessing's *The Summer before Dark* (1973) who
asks, 'I'm here, can't you see? Why don't you look at me?' when she
walks down the street.[10] Timothy C. Baker, in Chapter 2, analyses
Jason Allen-Paisant's poem, 'On Property' (2021), to consider in/
visibility and race. The poem depicts a racist confrontation between
a white dog walker and a black bird watcher in New York's Central
Park which took place on the same day as the murder of George
Floyd in Minneapolis: 25 May 2020. It is, Baker notes, 'filled with
gaps and silences, large spaces between words and short lines':

How ordinary for her

to destroy

this body

How ordinary for her

to erase

this body

space[11]

The power of the poem lies, in part, in what is not said or made
visible on the page. Created in the same year as Allen-Paisant's
poem, in the aftermath of the #MeToo movement and at the
pinnacle of the Black Lives Matter protests, Stawnicka's work can
also be interpreted as a powerful reminder of how the politics of
public space, embodiment and invisibility dominate some of the
most explosive and important debates of our age.

Making the body visible: contemporary literature

How then, the authors in the collection ask, can literary writing
contribute to these highly charged social, political and ethical
debates about the body that dominate contemporary cultural
life? How do changing ideas about the body and technology shift
processes of reading, writing and thinking? And in what ways are
writers creating new languages and forms to represent the diversity,
messiness and shifting nature of our conceptions of embodiment
in the twenty-first century? David Hillman and Ulrike Maude
remind us that the body is, on one level, always invisible or absent
in literary writing:

The fact is that there are no bodies in literature. Not only there
is no obvious way for the concrete materiality of the body to be
fully present in or on the written page; even more profoundly,
there would seem on the face of it to be an apparent mutual

exclusivity of the body and language – the one all brute facticity, the other presupposing precisely the absence of matter.

'And yet,' they continue, 'over the last three or four decades, critics and theorists have found myriad ways of addressing the representation of the body and embodied experience in literature.'[12]

Literary writing can be understood as the attempt to conjure up an invisible, absent or missing body. Doireann Ní Ghríofa's *A Ghost in the Throat* (2020), for example, returns obsessively to an eighteenth-century Irish poem, *Caoineadh Airt Uí Laoghaire*, which sought to remember the narrator's dead lover: 'How powerful such a cataloguing must have felt in the aftermath of his murder, when each spoken detail conjured him back again, alive and impeccably dressed.'[13] For Ní Ghríofa, the poem offers the possibility of bringing the dead lover, momentarily, back to life through language, but its form also embodies the sense of grief that its narrator feels at his loss: 'She is in pain, as is the poem itself; this text is a text in pain.'[14] The act of reciting the poem is a highly physical act, 'an echo' which connects the reader and the writer across generations, 'I pick up my scruffy photocopy … inviting the voice of another woman to haunt my throat a while.'[15] Reading and writing are, Ní Ghríofa suggests, at once miraculous and also deeply embedded in the material and often mundane details of everyday life: 'This is a female text, composed while folding someone else's clothes … This is a female text and it is tiny miracle that it even exists, as it does in this moment, lifted to another consciousness by the ordinary wonder of type. Ordinary, too, the ricochet of thought that swoops, now, from my body to yours.'[16] Mind and body cannot be separated in Ní Ghríofa's writing; thought is embodied and, through textual and oral traditions, the poem itself 'ricochets' between bodies and across generations.

Baker, in Chapter 2, makes a similar point about the ways in which poetry can be used both to register physical experiences in its form and to discuss issues of embodiment. 'Contemporary ecopoetry is', he argues, 'able to address the complexities of entanglement: knowing the world through the body does not mean jettisoning culture and language, but seeing them in new ways'. Like Ní Ghríofa and many of the contributors to this collection, Baker is acutely attuned to the specificities of genre; he continues:

This is possible in poetry in a way it may not be in theory precisely because poems do not simply reflect on bodies, but are themselves bodies, bound in the environment of the page and yet able to reach the reader. These poets do not simply extol the virtues of nature, but emphasise the way historical conceptualisations of natural have privileged some bodies over others.

This book aims to celebrate the diversity of contemporary literature. Alongside analysis of poems, novels, short stories and film, it also engages with newer forms that expand and put pressure on existing notions of 'literature'. In Chapter 4, for example, Elizabeth Losh describes: 'the development of electronic literature written specifically for head mounted displays, tablets, smart phones, and – potentially – smart glasses and activity trackers'. Her analysis of 'how the body of the computer interacts with the body of the reader' in these experimental texts, 'complicate[s] the earlier screen/page paradigm that posits reading as a state of objective detachment in which the body is largely a passive participant in knowledge transfer'. Reading and writing are understood here as embodied processes which inspire experimentation with new literary forms, languages and technologies.

In Chapter 3, Marie Allitt also traces the emergence of a new genre: the pathography. She argues that these works, often categorized under the banner of creative non-fiction, call into question some established conceptions of what a narrative might be or what it might do: 'We no longer see narratives as primarily attempting to recover coherence, order, and chronology. Instead, recent pathographies consciously challenge representation, even disrupt coherence and chronology, and situate the body within histories and futures of experience.' Like Baker and Losh, she foregrounds the physical act of telling as practically, aesthetically and politically significant: 'In Frank's account, stories, and particularly illness stories, are not only or primarily *about* bodies as they are *told by* bodies, which testify values through their being and their presence.' While theorists such as Elaine Scarry have suggested that pain is a private, unshareable event which 'does not simply resist language but actively destroys it,'[17] Frank insists on the political and creative potential of putting bodies at the centre of storytelling and making pain public through illness narratives.[18] In Chapter 8, which is about aging and old age, Bouson also engages with the potential for storytelling to function as form of reclamation, making bodies present that have traditionally been absent from the history of representation.

As Boriana Alexandrova reminds us, in Chapter 5 on 'Gender and feminism', 'the concept of the body, like any theoretical framework, opens certain doors while simultaneously closing others; the inclusions it enables lead to parallel exclusions'. Writing about the body often brings us up against the limits, as well as the rich possibilities of language and literary forms. For example, Ato Quayson argues that the 'dominant protocols of representation' within a literary text are 'short-circuited in relation to disability'.[19] Yet the body persists as a central concern of contemporary literature: as a cultural battleground, as a metaphor, as a challenge to writers to create new ways of rendering material experiences in form and language, as a means of examining and challenging the ways in which bodies are 'written' by certain socio-historical forces but also how they can act as sites of resistance.

The geographical scope of this collection reflects another limitation. Much of the critical writing about literature and the body to date has focused on Anglo-American literature, although this volume also includes analysis of texts by writers from Zimbabwe, Cuba, Trinidad, India and Japan. The earliest literary examples discussed are from the 1960s, but many of the texts have been published in the last few years. In this sense, *Contemporary Literature and the Body: A Critical Introduction* aims to give a small snapshot of the possibilities of this rich, interdisciplinary field and to act a starting point, inspiring future discussion, debate and scholarship.

Body studies and the structure of this book

The structure of this book, comprising nine chapters organized according to their theme or theoretical focus, could suggest a false division between these various topics and approaches. Each chapter seeks to give a sense of a sub-field or area that is important in literary critical studies of the body and which has its own distinct history. However, all of the chapters can be seen as part of a broader, interdisciplinary field, body studies, which is founded on the very idea of challenging such divisions. Bryan S. Turner suggests that body studies, which emerged in the 1980s and became a major academic field in the 1990s, has at its core 'a determined critique of Cartesian dualism'.[20] Rene Descartes (1596–1650) is associated with a distinction between the mind and the body, the mental and the material, the soul and nature, in which the mind is privileged over, and seen as having an existence independent of, the body. Critics such as Gordon Baker and Katherine Morris have argued that these divisions are in fact a 'Cartesian legend' which do not account for the complex consideration of the body in Descartes's own texts (1996).[21] Nevertheless, the challenge to binaries between mind and body, and the insistence on the ways in which the body mediates all thought and experience, is a key starting point for many of the founding texts of body studies. For example, Maurice Merleau-Ponty, in his *Phenomenology of Perception* (1962), argued that '[t]he body is our general medium for having a world ... the precondition of having any experience at all'.[22] Michel Foucault (1926–1984) also placed the body at the centre of his analysis, arguing that through the training, individuation and micro-management of bodies, new forms of social control were constructed. So, for Foucault, the body is 'directly involved in the political field', and power relations 'have an immediate hold upon it; they invest it, mark it, train it, torture it, force it to carry out tasks, to perform ceremonies, to emit signs'.[23]

Turner argues that while many technological, scientific, environmental and social factors have inspired the formation of body studies as a field, four protest movements in particular have brought the body to social and political prominence: the women's movement; the gay and lesbian movement for recognition; the ability movement for social rights; and the geriatric movements around retirement, pensions and longevity.[24] The movements share a 'constructionist epistemology'[25] in the sense that they interrogate the ways in which gender, sexuality, disability and age are socially and culturally constructed as categories. Analysing the language, stereotypes and stories associated with these identities is an important part of the cultural work of challenging and re-imagining these constructions. In some senses, however, this approach can lead to another set of problematic dualisms, in which the social construction is seen as separate from the body itself, and the focus on language and narratives eclipses discussions of physical experiences such as pain or pleasure. Judith Butler's theory of 'materialization' is useful here: she suggests that constructionism itself is not fixed but rather a 'process of reiteration', an unstable, ongoing, repetitive process.[26]

Many of the chapters in this book are attuned to the dangers of interpreting bodies according to a single 'fixed' identity or boundary. In Chapter 1, for example, Alexandra Kingston-Reese suggests that '[i]f there has been a problem in affect studies, it is that it has tended to assume that the way in which affects, emotions and feelings cleave towards universality despite affect's inevitable impact from intersectional experiences like those of gender, class and race'. Similarly, in Chapter 5, Boriana Alexandrova describes how '[q]ueer and trans feminist theorists ... have widely interrogated the problems with delineating "the body" as a fixed, objective and hard-bounded entity'. Following Sara Ahmed, Alexandrova adopts an intersectional approach which 'evolves the body-as-object into *embodiment*: a relational, moving, and contextually and situationally specific process of being'.

So, despite the divisions implied by the structure of this book, the essays in this collection all explore the potential for literary writing and film to challenge fixed boundaries of the body and identity and to explore interconnectedness in different forms. Many are characterized by what Susannah Mintz, in her chapter which examines disability, chronic illness and care, describes as a 'radial interconnectedness'. In the final chapter of the collection, for example, Luna Dolezal and Amelia DeFalco describe how 'the posthuman subject is conceived of as radically relational', 'a malleable material entity interconnected and inter-related with a whole host of "others", human, animal, environmental and technological'. This radical interconnectedness works on many different levels in this collection, such as in the connection between human-animal environment relations in Mintz's reading of Petra Kuppers's *Gut Botany* (2020) and Timothy C. Baker's conception of 'entanglement' in ecopoetry and writing about the climate crisis. This examination of interconnectedness also works on a level of genre and form, such as in Allitt's discussion of the fluid relationship between creative non-fiction, autofiction and prose poetry in contemporary illness narratives in Chapter 3. These hybrid forms, Allitt argues, require an interdisciplinary approach and allow their writers to tell 'a history of bodies beyond the individual' which challenges neoliberal individualistic conceptions of healthcare. In Losh's chapter, this radical relationality is embedded within new forms of electronic literature, which is often considered a niche concern despite its creative potential: 'By incorporating certain machine vision technologies, the body of the reader can actually shape the body of the text.'

In Gleeson's *Constellations: Reflections from Life*, discussed in Chapter 3, the implanting of metal in the author's body through a hip replacement operation provides the author with structure and material for her physical body and the body of her writing: 'I have come to think of all the metal in my body as artificial stars, glistening beneath the skin, a constellation of old and new metal.'[27] 'Without those experiences', she continues, 'I would not be a person who picks up those shards and attempts to reshape them on the page. If I had been spared the complicated bones, I would be someone else entirely. Another self, a different map.'[28] Gleeson's memoir, which takes the form of a constellation, provides a metaphor of interconnectedness that is fitting for this collection of essays. She also explores the potential for storytelling to challenge and reshape ideas about embodiment and to make bodies that have been overlooked visible through the process of writing itself.

In many ways, the isolation created by the period of the Covid-19 pandemic has heightened awareness of the importance of understanding the relationships between bodies and environments, visibility and invisibility, control and self-determination. We live in an age of interconnectedness in which viruses, money, protest movements, refugees and human organs circulate around the globe. While we may be drawn to the digital and the posthuman, the body remains a persistent and enduring concern, even within these realms. By providing an overview of some of the scholarship that has shaped thinking about literature and embodiment in the past, and through the analysis of key literary examples, this book aims to reflect that enduring concern and to spark discussions about the future of the field.

Notes

1   Katrina Forrester and Moira Weigel, 'Bodies on the Line', *Dissent Magazine*, Autumn 2020, https://www.dissentmagazine.org/article/bodies-on-the-line.
2   Forrester and Weigel, 'Bodies on the Line'.

3 Sinéad Gleeson, *Constellations: Reflections from Life* (London: Picador, 2019), 1.

4 Simone de Beauvoir, *The Second Sex*, trans. H.M. Parshley (New York: Vintage, 1989), 27.

5 Anthony Giddens, *Modernity and Self-Identity* (Cambridge: Polity, 1991), 77.

6 Susan Bordo, *Unbearable Weight: Feminism, Western Culture and the Body* (Berkeley and Los Angeles: University of California Press, 1993), 166.

7 Rachel Bowlby, *Just Looking: Consumer Culture in Dreiser, Gissing and Zola* (Oxford and New York: Routledge, 1985), 29.

8 Annemarie Mol, *The Body Multiple: Ontology in Medical Practice* (Durham and London: Duke University Press, 2002).

9 Gleeson, *Constellations*, 6.

10 Doris Lessing, *The Summer before the Dark* (New York: Vintage-Random House, 1983), 180.

11 Jason Allen-Paisant, *Thinking with Trees* (Manchester: Carcanet, 2021), 53.

12 David Hillman and Ulrike Maude, 'Introduction', in *The Cambridge Companion to Literature and the Body*, ed. David Hillman and Ulrike Maude (Cambridge: Cambridge University Press, 2015), 3.

13 Doireann Ní Ghríofa, *A Ghost in the Throat* (Dublin: Tramp Press, 2020), 18.

14 Ibid., 19.

15 Ibid., 11.

16 Ibid., 3–4.

17 Scarry, Elaine, *The Body in Pain: The Making and Unmaking of the World* (Oxford: Oxford University Press, 1985), 4–5.

18 Arthur Frank, *The Wounded Storyteller: Body, Illness, and Ethics* (Chicago: The University of Chicago Press, 2013), 3.

19 Ato Quayson, *Aesthetic Nervousness: Disability and the Crisis of Representation* (New York: Columbia University Press, 2007), 14.

20 Bryan S. Turner, 'Introduction: The Turn of the Body', in *The Routledge Handbook of Body Studies*, ed. Bryan S. Turner (London and New York: Routledge, 2012), 10.

21 Gordon Baker and Katherine J. Morris, *Descartes' Dualism* (Oxford and New York: Routledge, 1996), 3.

22 Maurice Merleau-Ponty, *The Phenomenology of Perception*, trans. Colin Smith (London and New York: Routledge, 1992), 146.

23 Michel Foucault, *Discipline and Punish: The Birth of the Prison* (London: Vintage, 1995), 25.

24 Turner, 'Introduction', 6.

25 Ibid., 9.

26   Judith Butler, *Bodies that Matter: On the Discursive Limits of Sex* (London and New York: Routledge, 1993), 3.
27   Gleeson, *Constellations*, 17.
28   Ibid., 18.

Bibliography

Allen-Paisant, Jason. *Thinking with Trees*. Manchester: Carcanet, 2021.

Bordo, Susan. *Unbearable Weight: Feminism, Western Culture and the Body*. Berkeley and Los Angeles: University of California Press, 1993.

Butler, Judith. *Bodies That Matter: On the Discursive Limits of Sex*. London and New York: Routledge, 1993.

De Beauvoir, Simone. *The Second Sex*. Translated by H. M. Parshley. New York: Vintage, 1989.

Forrester, Katrina and Moira Weigel. 'Bodies on the Line'. *Dissent Magazine*, Autumn 2020. https://www.dissentmagazine.org/article/bodies-on-the-line.

Foucault, Michel. *Discipline and Punish: The Birth of the Prison*. London: Vintage, 1995.

Giddens, Anthony. *Modernity and Self-Identity*. Cambridge: Polity, 1991.

Gleeson, Sinéad. *Constellations: Reflections from Life*. London: Picador, 2019.

Hillman, David and Ulrike Maude. 'Introduction'. In *The Cambridge Companion to Literature and the Body*, edited by David Hillman and Ulrike Maude, 1–9. Cambridge: Cambridge University Press, 2015.

Lessing, Doris. *The Summer before the Dark*. New York: Vintage-Random House, 1983.

Merleau-Ponty, Maurice. *The Phenomenology of Perception*. Translated by Colin Smith. London and New York: Routledge, 1992.

Mol, Annemarie. *The Body Multiple: Ontology in Medical Practice*. Durham and London: Duke University Press, 2002.

Quayson, Ato. *Aesthetic Nervousness: Disability and the Crisis of Representation*. New York: Columbia University Press, 2007.

Scarry, Elaine. *The Body in Pain: The Making and the Unmaking of the World*. Oxford: Oxford University Press, 2010.

Turner, Bryan S. 'Introduction: The Turn of the Body'. In *The Routledge Handbook of Body Studies*, edited by Bryan S. Turner, 1–17. London and New York: Routledge, 2012.

1

Affect

Alexandra Kingston-Reese

Hearts and minds

It has become fashionable in recent cultural criticism to revisit our attachments, aesthetic, political, ethical and otherwise. From Rita Felski's *Hooked* (2020) to Arielle Zibrak's *Guilty Pleasures* (2021), being attached rejects a version of emotional life that cleaves towards detachment's cooler tendencies. It doesn't matter what you are attached to, Zibrak argues; there is intellectual power in redeeming what you are ashamed about enjoying. This most recent shift towards sentimentality has tended to describe such attachment as wholly *good*. Attachment, we're told, can yield productive critical affects of delight, love, disappointment, surprise and enchantment. For Sara Ahmed, however, attachment deserves a good dose of caution. Attachment derives from the Old French verb *atachier*, and its variant *estachier*, meaning 'to bind' and 'to stick'. Affect, she argues, 'is what sticks, or what sustains or preserves the connection between ideas, values, and objects'.[1] It is this inherent stickiness that means affect is unable to be detached from bodies and that means '[s]ome bodies are presumed to be the origin of bad feeling insofar as they disturb the promise of happiness ... Some bodies are blockage points, points where smooth communication stops'.[2] Too much stickiness congeals, frustrating 'the social pressure to maintain the signs of "getting along"'.[3] Being stuck spells affective trouble.

But what do we really talk about when we talk about the body and affect? Affect studies tends to be divided into two branches: the cultural arm – propelled by the work of Ahmed, Lauren Berlant, Sianne Ngai and Eve Kosofsky Sedgwick – and the philosophical arm – following Spinoza, and more closely associated with Gilles Deleuze, Félix Guattari and Brian Massumi. But even when reading for affect in the cultural arm of affect studies – as I will do in this chapter – it is useful to remember the core tenet upheld by the philosophical branch of affect: affect is both of the body and separate from it.[4] It both affects bodies and is the condition with which bodies affect; it both has and is form. With this in mind, this chapter attends to two specific conditions of the body's affective relationships. The first is *affectivity* – 'how one body affects another', as Mel Chen puts it in *Animacies* (2012) – which like affectability is problematized by the conditions the body is subject to, whether toxic, ill, intoxicated, sensitized, queered or utopian.[5] The second is *affectability*, which describes the extent to which a subject, a body, can be affected. Much of the recent work on affectability has been located around the subjects that problematize it, like Ahmed's 'affect aliens' – like the feminist killjoy, unhappy queer or melancholy migrant – and Christine Yao's 'disaffected', all of which 'threaten ... a break from affectability'.[6] If there has been a problem in affect studies, it is that it has tended to assume that the way in which affects, emotions and feelings cleave towards universality despite affect's inevitable impact from intersectional experiences like those of gender, class and race. Anger, happiness, shame and sadness – a subject's emotional or affective landscape – if not motivated for the same reasons, are assumed to look and feel the same no matter who you are. For philosopher Denise Ferreira da Silva, then, affectability is '[t]he condition of being subjected to both natural (in the scientific and lay sense) conditions and to others' power' but it also speaks to the construction of the racialized *affectable* 'I', defined as '[t]he scientific construction of non-European minds'.[7]

This chapter, therefore, speaks of characters as able and unable to be affected, and able and unable to affect. I have chosen my case studies to explore the body's affective relations in two ways: face to face and heart to heart. The first section of this chapter will move through analyses of the various ways in which the face and the head have been zoned by two very different contemporary American writers – Diane Williams and Ling Ma – and by recent work in affect studies that have theorized feeling via expression and animation. If central to reading a body for affect is distinguishing expression – what Rei Terada has called 'the expressive hypothesis' – then the face occupies a distinctive ontological, and sometimes aesthetic, role. Emmanuel Levinas's work on the face remains one of the most important and evocative examples of the genre. Take the following from *Totality and Infinity* (1961) as an example:

> The face resists possession, resists my powers. In its epiphany, in expression, the sensible, still graspable, turns into total resistance to the grasp. This mutation can occur only by the opening of a new dimension. For the resistance to the grasp is not produced as an insurmountable resistance, like the hardness of the rock against which the effort of the hand comes to naught, like the remoteness of a star in the immensity of space. The expression the face introduces into the world does not defy the feebleness of my powers, but my ability for power. The face, still a thing among things, breaks through the form that nevertheless delimits it. This means concretely: the face speaks to me and thereby invites me to a relation incommensurate with a power exercised, be it enjoyment or knowledge.[8]

The face and 'discourse', Levinas argues in later conversations with the French philosopher Philippe Nemo collected together in *Ethics and Infinity* (1985), are unbreakably interwoven: 'the face speaks'.[9] As site of affective meaning, the face in Levinas's formulation is 'signification without context', by which he means that the face does not capture 'a character within a context'.[10] Rejecting the idea that the face is a referent to 'everything that is in one's passport, the manner of dressing, of presenting oneself', 'the face is meaning all by itself. You are you.'[11] Unlike Levinas, though, Namwali Serpell treats the face as a sign, and like any sign, as divided between the sign and its referent, 'between the surface of the face itself and whatever we think that surface means: beauty, depth, a particular emotion, humanity'.[12] Knowing how trustworthy the sign can be, she is unconvinced by Levinas's deracinated face, insisting that '[s]igns can cease to point to referents because of wilful acts of deception, distortion, or erasure'. Faces are no exception to these interpretative failings. Indeed, '[s]tudies have shown that the average person correctly assesses another person's expressions (thinking, agreeing, confused, concentrating, interested, disagreeing) only 54% of the time'.[13] Even an impassive face, the absence of feeling can in fact suggest the opposite.

If the face signifies, the heart symbolizes. In the second part of the chapter, I consider the heart space of the body, attending to the ways in which both the heart and the breasts have been unsentimentally zoned by two further contemporary novelists – Margarita García Robayo and Mieko Kawakami – via recent work on desire and love. By constructing a heart not full of feeling or generosity, both authors reject the relationship the heart or breast has with the history of sentimentalism, which teaches us that cold prose and flat affect is an unsuitable form for dealing with the heart. Even in *Blues for Mister Charlie* (1964), James Baldwin in animated, expressive prose lambasted sentimentality, 'the ostentatious parading of excessive and spurious emotion', as 'the mark of dishonesty, the inability to feel; the wet eyes of the sentimentalist betray his aversion to experience, his fear of life, his arid heart; and it is always, therefore, the signal of secret and violent inhumanity, the mask of cruelty'. Here, the heart symbolizes danger – as heartache, heartburn, heart attacks – and the breast, not the chest full of feeling, but the most politicized and policed parts of the body. By attending to the face and to the heart, my aim is neither to debunk affect's relationship with them nor to affirm it. As the following discussion will show, the examples I have chosen take issue with expectation and anticipation, whether that be of the kind emitted by the face or communicated by the culturally produced biological clock. But perhaps unexpectedly, I don't suggest that it is Kosofsky Sedgwick's famous 'reparative reading' to which we must turn to read for the body's affective conditions.[14] The affective break need not always be repaired. And whether face to face or heart to heart, the following literary examples show how resisting repair and living in the break can bring about a form of affective and somatic revolution.[15]

Heads and faces

Dianne Williams seems to know the risks of misreading the face, erasing most of her characters of their expressions in *Fine, Fine, Fine, Fine, Fine* (2016), a collection that is animated by almost ecstatic levels of dispassion.[16] In 'Rhapsody Breeze', a salesman pressing his face against the mirror 'could not make it out, could not recognize the opportunity for bewitching himself'.[17] In 'The Great Passion and Its Context', a woman 'bears the problems inherent in her circumstance that are not suddenly in short supply and she sways while guessing who really looks at her impatiently while she faces all of the faces – the multiple rows of the pairs of persons – the prime examples in the train aisle'.[18] It is heads, not faces, that appear in titles, such as 'Head of a Naked Girl', in which a prostitute negotiates the extent to which comfort can be attained in the company of strangers who use her for sexual and emotional satisfaction, or 'Head of the Big Man', which examines the kind of living achieved by 'confident people [who] behave poorly by not being confident enough'.[19] Sometimes, these heads only infer faces – tea that is drunk or not drunk shapes the mouth; the acknowledgment of gaze suggests eyes with which to see: 'isn't looking into the near distance sometimes so quaint?'[20] In a story called 'A Gray Pottery Head', a woman 'tenderly' arranges on her mantelpiece a 'subtly revealed head of an archaic woman' before dying in a car crash.[21] But where the head 'exhibits some bumps and some splits',[22] after her own death the woman's 'facial features are remarkably symmetrical, expressing vigor and vulnerability'.[23]

A face with vigour in death animates oxymoronically. Williams's stories regularly skirt such surprising juxtaposition, particularly when thwarting affective and social convention. In the opening story of the collection, 'Beauty, Love, and Vanity Itself', we find this connection between life and death underplayed again in dispassionate style:

> I saw three women go into the pool and when they got to the rope, they kept on walking. One woman disappeared. The other two flapped their hands.
>   'They don't know what the rope is,' the lifeguard said. 'I mean everybody knows what a rope means.'

I said, 'Why didn't you tell them?' and he said, 'I don't speak Chinese.'

I said, 'They are drowning' and the lifeguard said, 'You know, I think you are right.'

Our eyes were on the surface of the water – the wobbling patterns of diagonals. It was a hash – nothing to look at – much like my situation – if you're not going to do anything about it.[24]

The inscrutability here is consistent with the inscrutability of all of Williams's characters; their faces cannot be read unless deceased, no longer animated. Rather than on the women's faces, presumably alight with distress at the imminence of death, the two onlookers look pensively on seemingly inconsequential elements of the scene ('the surface of the water', 'the wobbling patterns of diagonals'). But the damning reason there is 'nothing to look at' is precisely because, despite the threat of death, they decided not 'to do anything about it'.

With the power to save, the lifeguard's inability to perceive that they need saving, and the narrator's complicity in this inaction, 'Beauty, Love, and Vanity Itself', thus offers a brief allegory of how affect can be racialized. Asian Americans, as well as other ethnically marked subjects in America, as Christine Yao has argued, 'are not legible using dominant regimes of expression'.[25] Disaffected modes of feeling – which 'includes withholding, disregard, growing a thick skin, refusing to care, opacity, numbness, dissociation, inscrutability, frigidity, insensibility, obduracy, flatness, insensitivity, disinterest, coldness, heartlessness, fatigue, desensitization, and emotional unavailability' – model what she calls affect's 'antisocial turn'.[26] In this case, Asian-American feeling is inextricably interwoven with the social mythology of the model minority, in which Asian-American subjects are made assimilated, obedient, identical. As Cathy Park Hong has detailed recently in *Minor Feelings* (2020), such emotions are 'built from the sediments of everyday racial experience and the irritant of having one's perception of reality constantly questioned or dismissed'.[27] The women's unreported expressiveness taps into the genealogy of the American racial stereotype of 'Oriental inscrutability', in Yao's terms, which, as Sianne Ngai has argued, 'stands in noticeable contrast to what we might call the exaggeratedly emotional, hyperexpressive, and even "overscrutable" image of most racially or ethnically marked subjects in American culture'.[28] For Ngai, it is this *animatedness* that demonstrates affect's pernicious, racializing effect. Animatedness, which is 'the seemingly neutral state of "being moved", becomes twisted into the image of the overemotional racialized subject, abetting his or her construction as unusually receptive to external control'.[29] If the predominant story of American animatedness tends towards exaggerated expression, a story such as 'Beauty, Love, and Vanity Itself' – like Ngai's example of John Yau's poem cycle 'Genghis Chan: Private Eye' (1989–1996) – shows the extent to which animation remains central to the production of the racially marked subject, even when his or her difference is signalled by the pathos of emotional suppression rather than by emotional excess.[30] And here, just as Ngai describes, the lifeguard's refusal to engage (*I don't speak Chinese*) occurs at the cost of linguistic suppression, 'of having his or her speech acts controlled by another'.[31] Even if the women are not drowning, the narrator and lifeguard exert striking control over them: it is the lifeguard who claims the women speak Chinese; it is the narrator who claims them to be drowning. The figures of the women themselves actually give no indication of being Chinese – they do not speak – or of drowning, for waving arms are ambiguous, even in a pool.

There are many reasons why characters resist affect. As Sara Ahmed has argued, rebellious or errant characters commit disruptions to affect's seemingly universal affectability. 'Affect aliens' alienate and are alienated by feeling's broken promises but also feel emboldened by greater freedoms to not meet expectations. Unfeeling, she argues, can be construed

> as a form of antisocial discontent about, if not outright defiance of, the compulsory norms for expressing feeling along with susceptibility to the feelings of others. Unfeeling can signal skepticism and reluctance to signify the appropriate expressions of affect that are socially legible as human, which can rise to the refusal to care and sympathize as part of the expected cues of deference that maintain and structure biopolitical hierarchies of oppression.[32]

Employing Lauren Berlant, Yao's formulation of unfeeling celebrates how 'withholding can operate as a sign of civility for the privileged and is "often deemed good manners in the servant class," and for those so-called "problem populations," such disaffection signals the threat of the ungovernable'.[33] Many of Williams's characters – most of them women – lack the kind of universal affectability we tend to associate as socially acceptable. Stories are peppered with moderate characters feeling moderate feelings about everyday things – whether drowning or watching the water or unfeeling utterances elsewhere: 'I didn't cry some';[34] 'And after the last years were over, we were dead';[35] 'I am unemotional about the abrupt ending of friendship'[36] – all 'signal … a break from the emotional respectability required by the politics of recognition', all while couched in Williams's characteristic stylistic animation.[37] But while her style jumps off the page with abrupt syntax, unconventional registers, and non sequiturs, such energy doesn't originate from her characters, who, often finding themselves unmoved or unaffected, express only moderate feelings. In 'The Romantic Life', we find this connection between the epistemological and emotional aspects of being animated put to work by Williams in opening a gap, a quintessential feature of the short story genre. Here, a single young woman gestures towards what Teresa Brennan has called the 'transmission of affect',[38] often attributed as being the source of a room's atmosphere, noting that 'when I come into rooms, it's surely a relief to one and all that I am helpful'.[39] Feeling others to be affectable and herself to be able to affect, her impression is something she intuits rather than understands. 'I feel there is so much yet to explore', she notes, 'about how people experience a "pull" toward anyone'.

Affectability is intricately associated with animation, beyond those who are disaffected, unfeeling or alienated. Discussing the animation of the body in abolitionist movements, Ngai describes how it is 'surprisingly fostered through acts resembling the practice of puppeteering, involving either the body's ventriloquism or a physical manipulation of its parts', even in restorative situations that require reanimation – 'shifting the status of this body from thing to human' – 'to emphasize its personhood or subjectivity'.[40] Coercive animation or reanimation is not just the territory of pathologizing the racial or ethnic or (un)affected other, however. Ling Ma's 2018 debut novel *Severance* is another violator of affective habit, featuring the eradication of most of the world's population via a fungal infection originating in Shenzen, China.[41] Shen Fever is 'contracted by breathing in microscopic fungal spores. Once inhaled, they spread from the lungs and nasal area to other organs, most commonly to the brain' (148). As Eileen Ying has noted, though the novel compares the Fever to the West Nile virus, it is better associated with another set of illnesses, including the 2003 SARS coronavirus and the Covid-19 crisis, which 'represent a kind of sensational, medicalized, twenty-first-century Yellow Peril'.[42] As there is no cure, '[e]ventually Shen Fever results in a fatal loss of consciousness' as the body repeats over and over habitual action, like driving a cab or folding or stalking a mall, until the body decomposes.[43] Recalling Virginia Woolf's description in *Mrs Dalloway* wherein 'the skeleton of habit alone upholds the human frame', Shen Fever renders its victims animated without life.[44]

While still animated in the crudest sense, those infected with Shen Fever are no longer affectable. The fevered 'were creatures of habit, mimicking old routines and gestures they must have inhabited for years, decades', but docile. 'They could operate the mouse of a dead PC, they could drive stick in a jacked sedan, they could run an empty dishwater, they could look after dead houseplants', and they accept being pulled out of a taxi, carried down the stairs, tackled in a mall.[45] The fevered sit much lower than uninfected humans on the *animacy hierarchy*, which Mel Chen describes as measuring 'much more than the state of being animate'.[46] Animacy, he argues, 'is a craft of the senses; it endows our surroundings with life, death, and things in between'.[47] Between life and death, the fevered productively interrogate the hierarchy, which is strained by the continuous contestation of 'the coherence of the body'. What, Chen asks, 'is the line between the fetus (often categorized as "not yet living") and a rights-bearing infant-subject? How are those in persistent vegetative states deemed to be at, near, or beyond the threshold of death?'[48] The fevered, as 'not yet dead', have lost their ability to recognize language. Physically, they can be manipulated, puppeteered, but to speak in front of them incites no reaction. The loss of language is crucial in the loss of affectability. 'Words more than signify', Chen notes, 'they affect and effect. Whether read or heard, they complexly pulse through bodies (live or dead), rendering their effects in feeling and active response'.[49] They necessitate and require emotional and somatic reaction.

To alter a point of Chen's, animacy has the capacity to rewrite the conditions of affectability, intensifying the ethics of affect's socialization or, at least, how we might theorize them.[50] Recalling affect itself, Ying has noted, with the fever '[w]e see how something that's not really bodily at all maps so easily onto human subjects – for it's much more manageable to locate danger in corporeal form than it is to locate it, speaking metaphorically, in the air'.[51] During an event termed a 'live stalk', Candace Chen, the narrator, and the group of unfevered she has joined up with, shepherd the Gowers, a fevered family, into the dining room where some of them were rehearsing over and over having dinner around the table. Preparing to 'release' them (read: kill) – more humane to kill them straight away than let them degenerate – they are confronted with Levinas's claims that 'the relationship with the face is immediately ethical in nature'.[52] 'The first word of the face', he argues, 'is the "Thou shalt not kill." It is an order. There is a commandment in the appearance of the face, as if a master spoke to me'.[53] '[R]ecognizing their residual humanity', then, the protocol for Candace and the others is to shoot them 'in the heads but not the faces'.[54] Faces are important in the novel, and for Candace in particular, not only because the fungal infection takes root by inhaling it but because the face is a part of the body to be cherished, beautified, perfected. Her uncle and her father, both whom she's estranged from, share a face. She purchases Shu Uemera's Cleansing Beauty Oil in Hong Kong on a business trip from a saleslady who takes her 'face in her hands' to say '[y]ou have beautiful skin, it is just uncomfortable right now';[55] her mother, who had her moles and beauty marks removed in Hong Kong years earlier because her 'sisters used to call her a spotted leopard' only to return with white marks 'in the places she desired to be unmarked',[56] berates for not having 'a proper facial regimen' like her daily Clinique 3-Step facial routine.[57] When her recently fevered friend Ashley sneezes all over her face, Cadence's 'instinctive reaction' is to protect her face and run to wash it.[58] Here, though, Candace takes aim at Paige Gower's face: 'the sixth shot hit her in the cheek, and then the seventh reached the forehead ... the tenth in the eye, which spurted'.[59] The Gowers humanity, in their fevered state, is queered by surprising animality, looking at the group 'with crocodile eyes, knowing our difference'.[60] Severing the implicit moment of recognition that takes place in the face-to-face encounter Levinas takes to be so important, Candace takes aim at Paige Gower's face and does not stop shooting until she passes the 'death barrier' to something else.[61]

There is no doubt that the treatment of the fevered breaks the ultimate rules of ethics Levinas sets out across his works. But if Levinas says that the face is what protects the other, protects from harm, Ma's *Severance* asks what happens when that face no longer resembles life and what extremes will the subject go to eliminate it. What happens to our ethics when the face is a face with half a jaw missing, or a face with 'crocodile eyes', or a face like 'a birthday cake, covered in night cream, dripping onto the cable-knit sweater she wore'?[62] Speaking to the break between life and work, exploitation and care, love and control, *Severance* aestheticizes the erosion of humanity, something, the novel makes clear, capitalism has already done. And it does so with remarkable little feeling. As Dora Zhang has noted, '[e]ven as one loved object after another vanishes – country, father, mother, lover, job, city, friends – Candace Chen remains neutral, restrained, and matter of fact, not to say detached, numb, or even dissociated'.[63] We might say, in line with Yao, that Candace's disaffection stems from always not quite fitting the mould: of the college graduate who has moved to New York, of the Art Girl she so aspires to be. Or that floating through life, Candace could be read via David L. Eng and Shinhee Han's notion of 'racial dissociation' or via Hong's minor feelings.[64] Whichever way, Candace is okay with the elusiveness of feeling, okay with its minority:

> Every time we stalked, this feeling would come over me, imperceptible at first. It is hard to describe because it is close to nothing. Gradually, the din of other people's conversations or Todd's heavy footsteps, his ugly, flat gait on the floorboards would fall away. I would forget where I was or why I was there. I would get lost in the taking of inventory, with the categorizing and gathering, the packing of everything into space-efficient arrangements in the same boxes ... It was a trance. It was like burrowing underground, and the deeper I burrowed the warmer it became, and the more the nothing feeling subsumed me, snuffing out any worries and anxieties. It is the feeling I like best about working.[65]

Throughout the novel, Candace is worried that one could become fevered by living too nostalgically, by revisiting places that one had left, like a childhood home. But for Candace, repeatedly visiting her workplace offices in the dying days of New York City, this is where the mind of the capitalist subject, happy in this exploitative ecology, is allowed to thrive even as humanity dies. The 'rituals and customs' of her everyday life takes on the ergonomic tenor of aesthetic experience.[66] As Elizabeth Freeman has argued about choosing alternate temporalities to those insisted upon by the capitalist state, '[t]he point may be to trail behind actually existing social possibilities: to be interested in the tail end of things, to be willing to be bathed in the fading light of whatever has been declared useless'.[67] One wonders if the absolution of the trance feels comforting to the fevered, too.

Hearts and breasts

If the face animates or is animated by affect, from where in the body does affect originate? Even though emotion is brain chemistry, the mythology of the heart as the seat of feeling persists especially in Cuban novelist Margarita García Robayo's *Holiday Heart* (2017) and Japanese novelist Mieko Kawakami's *Breasts and Eggs* (2020). For both writers, the heart becomes the natural location for the body's ability to both affect and be affected. Like Williams and Ma, whose prose is stylistically energetic but whose characters only feel moderate feelings, when Robayo and Kawakami invoke the heart, it is not to dowse their characters with romantic or joyous emotion but to recast the heart's symbolic role in how desire impacts both conditions of the body's affective relationships I mentioned earlier, the body's *affectivity* and *affectability*.

Affective neologisms are perhaps my favourite moments of textual surprise. In *Severance*, it is Candace's 'Fuzhou Nighttime Feeling':

> It is not a cohesive thing, this feeling, it reaches out and bludgeons everything. It is excitement tinged by despair. It is despair heightened by glee. It is partly sexual in nature, though it precedes sexual knowledge. If Fuzhou Nighttime Feeling were a sound, it would be early/mid-nineties R&B. If it were a flavor, it would be the ice-cold Pepsi we drink as we turn down tiny alleyways where little kids defecate wildly. It is the feeling of drowning in a big hot open gutter, of crawling inside an undressed, unstanched wound that has never been cauterized.[68]

For Kojima, the teenage girl at the centre of Japanese novelist Mieko Kawakami's *Heaven* (2020), it is a trio of feelings: *happamine* ('it's, like, dopamine that comes out when you're really happy' [32]), *hurtamine* (for 'when you're really hurting' [33]) and *lonelamine* (for 'when you're lonely' [33]). The title of Robayo's *Holiday Heart*, translated into English by Charlotte Coombe, captures its own feeling, too.[69] Holiday heart (*tiempo muerto*) sounds like the full-to-bursting emotion of pure vacation bliss that turns quickly to sadness and nostalgia when returning home. To wife, mother and writer Lucía, whose husband Pablo has just been rushed to the hospital in cardiac distress, if it had corporeal form, it would sound like 'a sentimental love song' and would look like 'a roadside motel with blinking neon lights'.[70]

But, as Lucía learns, Holiday Heart is in fact a serious disease rather than a banal affective state. Unlike 'Fuzhou Nighttime Feeling' or *hurtamine*, Holiday Heart is not an affective condition but a disease that 'affects the cardiovascular system and is caused by excessive consumption of alcohol, red meat, salt, saturated fat and certain drugs'.[71] It is, Lucía's Chilean family doctor, Ignacio, tells her, 'an acquired disease rather than a congenital one, it occurs most commonly during the holiday season, when people get wasted and ignore their expanding waistlines'.[72] In her husband's case, it is nothing major – it caused a 'minor arterial obstruction', easily fixed with a stent that so many men of Pablo's age have – but his excessive eating and drinking has also been accompanied by 'excessive and, I presume, risky sexual activity'.[73] But what if this was an affective structure, as much as it is a bodily one? For the heart is of course one of the major metaphorical spaces of the body that directs and conjures up love and desire, as well as sadness, bereavement and betrayal. (One can die of a broken heart after all.) What if this affective structure didn't just block arteries but described the angst of heartbreak or failing marriages, the kinds of affective conditions that render relationship structures untenable? As it turns out, *Holiday Heart* takes up these questions to determine what such a disease feels like to those not actually suffering from it.

Immediately after the diagnosis, Lucía takes the children – six-year-old twins Tomás and Rosa – to Miami Beach. Pablo has been having an affair with Kelly J., one of his high school students. Increasingly alienated from his marriage to Lucía, he flirts with depressive inertia, complaining in analeptic episodes of his wife's cruelty. Lucía, before giving birth, he remarks at one point, had 'been both the most intelligent and the kindest person he knew', a mutually exclusive combination.[74] 'Therein lay her flaw', he details, 'though he didn't see it, or didn't want to see it: nobody could be both of those things to such a superlative degree at the same time. Plenty of evidence existed to back this up, in the form of evil geniuses, and foolish saints'.[75] To Pablo, his wife's kindness could thus only be false, to be 'expelled' when she became a mother 'along with the placenta'.[76] As with many men who fret about their status in the new family unit after a child enters the frame, Pablo saw Lucía becoming a mother as ultimately detrimental to emotion and feeling. 'What she was left with was a head full of knowledge which, outside of the Yale World Fellows Program, was of no interest to anyone.'[77] What was left was a triumph of intellection and of reason – of the head – over the heart.

Pablo, for his part, resents Lucía's academic successes, throwing her increasingly ruthless philosophy of motherhood and affection back at her during arguments. One essay on this subject, published in a XYZ magazine, led to 'confrontations':

> These didn't even turn into fights; he would just hurl snarky, underhanded reproaches at her, at inconvenient moments. In the morning rush, as they wolfed down croissants; or at night, as she was peeing and he was flossing: 'Have you thought about what you're going to tell Tommy the day he finds out that your love for him isn't innate, but rather' – he drew speech marks in the air – 'the product of social changes that impacted on your mental state?'[78]

Lucía, for her part – likely who the reader aligns themselves with most sympathetically – refuses to believe that such distinctions between head and heart are useful. She is under no illusions as to her imperfections, always viewing herself as 'selfish and irresponsible' 'deeply afraid'.[79] She carries around an 'unbearable weight' of death and failure, often seeing in front of her the ways in which she could die. But although she states that '[s]he goes to such great lengths not to show her family what she is really thinking that it exhausts her' – that it causes her tense facial muscles and jaw grinding – her writing becomes an outlet for working out her emotions.[80] In an article she is trying to write while on holiday, she spits out a 'collection of strained, resentful sentences': '*Mothers*

*shoulder too many images associated with their role: gentleness,
patience, resignation, altruism, worry, guilt, unconditional love, the
unspoken but irrefutable agreement to give up everything for their
children. What about the fathers?*'[81] Lucía mirrors the conditions of
Ahmed's affectively alienated and Yao's disaffected. The cooling of
emotion that Pablo perceives and critiques in her can just as easily
be accessed from the other direction: a symptom of the historical
burden of care, love and devotion falling on women and on the
mother. To be sure, Lucía's prose is often callously flippant: 'He was
having a breakdown, it was true, but then again, thought Lucía,
feeling suddenly furious, who wasn't?'[82] But what Pablo doesn't
understand is that when Lucía 'wrote about maternal love, she
wasn't referring to the love she had for her children' – '[i]t was a
category that contained them and went beyond them'.[83]

'Even in its most conventional form, as "love,"' Lauren Berlant
wrote, 'desire produces paradox'. In a small work, *Desire/Love*
(2012), in which they negotiated psychoanalytic accounts of desire,
Berlant describes how narratively powerful desire is: '[i]t is a
primary relay to individuated social identity, as in coupling, family,
reproduction, and other sites of personal history; yet it is also the
impulse that most destabilizes people, putting them into plots
beyond their control as it joins diverse lives and makes situations'.[84]
Inherent in love and desire is an affective complex that cleaves more
towards negative feelings than one tends to expect. As Pablo's heart
condition metaphorically reflects, Lucía and Pablo's marriage is
no great love story but his affective alienation – the falling out of
love – triggers bodily collapse. For Pablo, it 'started a year earlier'.[85]
Waking up home alone after a cocaine and alcohol fuelled party at
the neighbours' house – Lucía and the children were away visiting a
bear park – he notices bright purple mark on his neck, a bite mark
on his nipple and a note in the kitchen from Kelly J. telling him
she'd made coffee for him. As '[m]elancholia mirrors inversely the
idealizing narratives about merged souls more happily associated
with love', both husband and wife become a particular kind of affect
alien – the melancholic lover – whose connection with the other
has undergone a series of affective disturbances relating to all the
reasons Berlant enumerated: 'personal styles of seduction, anxious
or confident attachment, confusion, shame, dread, optimism, self-
or other-directed pleasure'.[86] Most of all, both have disembowelled
their marriage of fantasy, which love cannot be sustained without,

leaving them to navigate scenes and tableaux of interaction with attachments that can only be ambivalent.[87]

What are the bodily and affective conditions of attachment? 'All attachment is optimistic', Berlant argues elsewhere, so long as 'we describe optimism as the force that moves you out of yourself and into the world in order to bring closer the satisfying *something* that you cannot generate on your own'.[88] Drawing out a central distinction between what optimism is and what optimism feels like, they acknowledge that 'optimism might not *feel* optimistic' in part '[b]ecause optimism is ambitious, at any moment it might feel like anything, including nothing' – from the range of negative feeling to the 'sly neutrality' of anticipating change that's coming, or even, the change that never comes.[89] These complicated conditions of attachment describe what Berlant called 'cruel optimism' – that which 'exists when something you desire is actually an obstacle to your flourishing'.[90] Both Pablo and Lucía's desires – for a kind, soft wife or a more intellectually stable husband – fulfil this relation, where things we desire or are attached to become cruel 'when the object that draws your attachment actively impedes the aim that brought you to it initially'.[91] Kawakami's 2020 novel *Breasts and Eggs*, translated into English by Sam Bett and David Boyd, offers another rebellion against desire, populated by a series of interlinked women who flirt with the possibilities of being, as Sarah Chihaya calls it, 'post-desire'.[92] Though the novel circulates two stereotypical desires – to appear young and beautiful and to have a baby – the novel's women refuse sexual relationships and balk at conforming to societal norms perpetuated by 'the family romance'. The blunt words of Rika, friend to the narrator Natsuko Natsume, become a ringing trope of the novel: 'If you want a kid, there's no need to get wrapped up in a man's desire ... There's no need to involve women's desire, either. There's no need to get physical. All you need is the will, the will of a woman.'[93]

If the novel is a novel of ideas on female desire, *Breasts and Eggs* shows how much affective and ethical nuance can be explored by interrogating women's bodies from early puberty and adolescence, to sexuality; to motherhood, reproduction and birth; to beauty and ageing, to violence and murder. Carried off with an affective frankness Kawakami's work has come to be known for even in translation, Natsu drives the novel's attitudes towards women's bodies – organized, in the first part, around her sister Makiko's decision to get breast implants and, in the second, around assisted reproduction. It's become a cliché in contemporary literature – fiction and in essay form – that any narrative about a woman becoming a mother opens the door to meditations on her own mother. But any woman who has sisters, mothers and grandmothers knows the brutal coming-of-age sadness of seeing traits or attributes of an older generation being passed down. About Makiko, Natsu remarks cuttingly:

> I guess she was one of those people you see a lot these days who looked young from behind, but the second that she turned around ... Her fake teeth were noticeably yellow, and the metal made her gums look black. Her faded perm had thinned so much that you could see the perspiration on her scalp. She was wearing way too much foundation. It made her face look washed out and more wrinkly than it was. When she laughed, the sinews of her neck popped out. Her sunken eyes called attention to their sockets.

> She reminded me of Mom.[94]

Makiko surely knows this of herself, arriving in Tokyo from Osaka for a consultation at one of the best cosmetic surgery clinics. On the phone and now in Tokyo '[h]er speeches had two refrains: "I'm gonna do it, I'm gonna get big boobs," and "Can I really go through with this?"'[95] Natsu reports Makiko's clinical fascination with her three options – silicone, hyaluronic acid or the person's own fat – in careful detail. But listening to Makiko in person, rather than on the phone, made Natsu sad. 'It was the same feeling you get at a train station, or in a hospital, or on the street, when you stop at a safe distance away from someone who can't seem to help but talk and talk, whether or not anyone is there to listen.'[96] Watching a loved one argue with themselves over their own worth, the novel argues, is enough to break your heart.

By staging such debates about the desire and desirability of the body, *Breasts and Eggs* dramatizes value. The value of women's lives, their careers, their relationships and their choices, are picked over in moral and financial detail. At the clinic Makiko had chosen, silicone breasts cost only 1,500,000 yen, more than either sister had to spend. Expressing shock at the cost, Natsu worries that her reaction 'made it sound like it was too much for her breasts', as if she'd asked instead 'Are you really worth that much? Are your breasts worth that kind of an investment?'[97] As a backdrop to the main action, the sisters are aware of yet another woman's body being discovered discarded like trash in an alleyway. Later at a bathhouse, neck deep in water observing the other bodies of the women 'as if devouring them',[98] Makiko starts a conversation about the difference in colour of the nipples in the room, from the melanin-inducing dark ones to the chemically lightened pink ones. She had tried lightening hers, but it required too much upkeep, not to mention it hurt. Natsu, trying to find some common ground with Makiko, turns to her own adolescent expectations of what women's bodies were supposed to look like. Expecting all women grew up to have a body that 'provokes sexual fantasy', 'I never became the woman I imagined', she explains. To be denied this feels like betrayal: 'When you're pretty, everybody wants to look at you, they want to touch you.'[99]

Natsu's ruminations end up uncomfortably affirming Makiko's own reasoning. Having worked as a hostess in a run-down bar for most of her adult life, now forty, younger colleagues have greater earning potential. As Natsu remarks:

> Beauty meant that you were good. And being good meant being happy. Happiness can be defined all kinds of ways, but human beings, consciously or unconsciously, are always pulling for their own version of happiness. Even people who want to die see death as a kind of solace, and view ending their lives as the only way to make it there. Happiness is the base unit of consciousness, our single greatest motivator.[100]

There is something of Berlant's cruel optimism in Makiko's search for beautiful youthfulness unattainably gone. This popular narrative about happiness – 'as a kind of solace' – offers Natsu a moment of ontological resignation for bodily knowledge, accepting that there are some things the head can't understand that the body does. Natsu's evaluation – both as an assessment and as an attempt at valuing – echoes Ahmed's description of happiness. Arguing that 'to be affected by something is to evaluate that thing', she emphasizes how '[e]valuations are expressed in how bodies turn toward things. To give value to things is to shape what is near us'.[101] Bodies have the power to register and affect our happy attachments; their 'transformations' have the power to 'transform what is experienced as delightful. If our bodies change over time, then the world around us will create different impressions'.[102] And engineering such changes? In this position, Makiko in her desperation might just have cracked the solution to the happiness problem.

For what is in the heart is likely to be in the body. Makiko's desire to have breast implants, as an escape from inherited poverty and from the oblivion of ageing, is just one such example. In book one, we meet Natsu when she's thirty; in book two, she's nearing forty and is hit with the epiphany of wanting to have a child – not to conceive or give birth, but to meet them, as one would a soulmate. Single in Japan, where donor conception is uncommon and maligned, though legal, Natsu embarks on a process of reconciling this cerebral desire with the absence of sexual desire. 'Whenever we got naked and I let him start, the world went dark', she writes revealing her asexuality. 'It felt so wrong that I wanted to cry.'[103] Joining a raft of novels and collections of essays that seek to negotiate the uneasy emotional territory of becoming or not becoming a mother – from Maggie Nelson's *Argonauts* (2015) to Sheila Heti's *Motherhood* (2018) – Kawakami's *Breasts and Eggs* shows how wanting a baby need not be implicated in libidinal dramas.[104] Even to 'affect aliens', the family unit, Ahmed writes, 'sustains its place as a "happy object"'.[105] There ought to be, the novel argues, an option for the happy asexual, where passion and sex can be enthusiastically incompatible.

And there is: a girl is born in epiphanic splendour at the end of the novel. 'My head and body filled with blinding light, inside of which – I saw something expanding. Like a nebula, breathing without a sound, millions of years away.'[106] Though the journey of conception estranged the body from the mind, in birth the two unite ecstatically in what sounds uncannily orgasmic. But this shouldn't surprise us. Where the women of Kawakami, García Robayo, Ma, and Williams, view their bodies past and present with dispassion, there is always narrative and descriptive room for hopeful futures, even when they are also stuck in or to undesirable situations. Queer theory tells us this much about romance and family. Here, animated, alienated or not by compassion or by desire, such examples paint a picture of the contemporary body as running hot and running cold. Such examples show how contemporary fiction has mastered the art of turning the affect tap on and off, most of the time without consequence. Relationships fail, but sometimes they don't. Families are formed, but sometimes they're not. Worlds end, but sometimes they don't. Such examples give us a character of the body that can build various kinds of utopian futures. That these futures can be feeling or unfeeling or somewhere nebulous in between gifts us articulate literary models for something of which contemporary culture needs a good dose: freedom from affective expectation.

Notes

1   Sara Ahmed, 'Happy Objects', in *The Affect Theory Reader*, edited by Melissa Gregg and Gregory J. Seigworth (Durham, NC: Duke University Press, 2010), 29.

2   Ahmed, 'Happy Objects', 39.

3   Ibid., 39.

4   See Sara Ahmed, *The Cultural Politics of Emotion* (Abingdon: Routledge, 2004); Lauren Berlant, *Cruel Optimism* (Durham, NC: Duke University Press, 2011); Sianne Ngai, *Ugly Feelings* (Cambridge, MA: Harvard University Press, 2005); Eve Kosofsky Sedgwick, *Touching Feeling: Affect, Pedagogy, Performativity* (Durham, NC: Duke University Press, 2003); Spinoza, *Ethics* (London: Penguin, 1996 [1677]); Gilles Deleuze and Félix Guattari, *Thousand Plateaus: Capitalism and Schizophrenia*, trans. and foreword by Brian Massumi (Minneapolis and London: University of Minnesota Press, 1987 [1980]) and *What Is Philosophy*, trans. Hugh Tomlinson and Graham Burchell (New York: Columbia University Press, 1994); Brian Massumi, *Parables for the Virtual: Movement, Affect, Sensation* (Durham and London: Duke University Press, 2002) and *Politics of Affect* (Cambridge: Wiley, 2015).

5   Mel Y. Chen, *Animacies: Biopolitics, Racial Mattering, and Queer Affect* (Durham, NC: Duke University Press, 2012), 12.

6   Christine Yao, *Disaffected: The Cultural Politics of Unfeeling in Nineteenth-Century America* (Durham, NC: Duke University Press, 2021), 5.

7   Denise Ferreira da Silva, *Toward a Global Idea of Race* (Minneapolis: University of Minnesota Press, 2007), xv.

8   Emmanuel Levinas, *Totality and Infinity*, trans. Alphonso Lingis (Pittsburgh, PA: Duquesne University Press, 1961), 198–9.

9   Emmanuel Levinas, *Ethics and Infinity: Conversations with Philippe Nemo*, trans. Richard A. Cohen (Pittsburgh, PA: Duquesne University Press, 1985), 88.

10   Levinas, *Ethics and Infinity*, 88.

11 Ibid., 86.
12 Namwali Serpell, *Stranger Faces* (Oakland: Transit Books, 2020), 13.
13 Ibid.
14 This turn to repair is a common trope in affect studies – perhaps a sign of our sentimentality for piecing things back together.
15 I recall Jameson's suggestion in *Marxism and Form: Twentieth-Century Dialectical Theories of Literature* (1974) that we must make way for 'an art which might be prophetic rather than fantasy-oriented, one which might portend genuine solutions underway' (385).
16 Diane Williams, *Fine, Fine, Fine, Fine, Fine* (San Francisco: McSweeney's, 2016). All citations to this collection hereafter will appear parenthetically.
17 Williams, *Fine*, 33.
18 Ibid., 44.
19 Ibid., 52.
20 Ibid., 14.
21 Ibid., 17.
22 Ibid.
23 Ibid., 18.
24 Ibid., 14–15.
25 Yao, *Disaffected*, 11.
26 Ibid., 10.
27 Ibid., 11.
28 Ngai, *Ugly Feelings*, 93.
29 Ibid., 91.
30 Ibid., 95.
31 Ibid., 93.
32 Yao, *Disaffected*, 7.
33 Ibid.
34 Williams, *Fine*, 28.
35 Ibid., 75.
36 Ibid., 131.
37 Yao, *Disaffected*, 11.
38 Teressa Brennan, *The Transmission of Affect* (Ithaca, NY: Cornell University Press, 2014).
39 Williams, *Fine*, 41.
40 Ngai, *Ugly Feelings*, 93.
41 Ling Ma, *Severance* (Picador, 2016). All citations to this collection hereafter will appear parenthetically.
42 Eileen Ying, 'Coolie Pathology', *Post45* (13 October 2020), available online: https://post45.org/2020/10/coolie-pathology/.
43 Ma, *Severance*, 149.

44 I owe thanks to Dora Zhang for making this association with Woolf in her essay 'Staying Alive' in the Post45 cluster on *Severance*. Available online: https://post45.org/2020/10/staying-alive.
45 Ma, *Severance*, 28.
46 Chen, *Animacies*, 4.
47 Ibid., 55.
48 Ibid., 7.
49 Ibid., 46.
50 Chen's original point was about intimacy: 'animacy has the capacity to rewrite conditions of intimacy, engendering different communalisms and revising biopolitical spheres, or, at least, how we might theorize them' (*Animacies*, 3).
51 Ying, 'Coolie Pathology', available online: https://post45.org/2020/10/coolie-pathology/.
52 Levinas, *Ethics and Infinity*, 87.
53 Ibid., 89.
54 Ma, *Severance*, 28–9.
55 Ibid., 101.
56 Ibid.
57 Ibid., 63.
58 Ibid., 128.
59 Ibid., 71.
60 Ibid.
61 Ibid., 72.
62 Ibid., 61.
63 Zhang, 'Staying Alive'.
64 David L. Eng and Shinhee Han, *Racial Melancholia, Racial Dissociation* (Durham, NC: Duke University Press, 2019).
65 Ma, *Severance*, 65.
66 Ibid., 58.
67 Elizabeth Freeman, *Time Binds: Queer Temporalities, Queer Histories* (Durham, NC: Duke University Press, 2010), xiii.
68 Ma, *Severance*, 58.
69 Margarita García Robayo, *Holiday Heart*, trans. Charlotte Coombe (Edinburgh: Charco Press, 2017).
70 Robayo, *Holiday*, 9.
71 Ibid., 8.
72 Ibid., 8–9.
73 Ibid., 8.
74 Ibid., 18.
75 Ibid.
76 Ibid.
77 Ibid.
78 Ibid., 109–10.

79   Ibid., 64.
80   Ibid.
81   Ibid., 155.
82   Ibid., 7.
83   Ibid., 155.
84   Lauren Berlant, *Desire/Love* (Santa Barbara: Punctum Books, 2012), 13.
85   Robayo, *Holiday*, 13.
86   Berlant, *Desire/Love*, 29; 69.
87   Ibid., 69.
88   Berlant, *Cruel Optimism*, 1.
89   Ibid., 2.
90   Ibid., 1.
91   Ibid.
92   Sarah Chihaya, 'All over Desire', *New York Review of Books*, 29 April 2021, available online: https://www.nybooks.com/articles/2021/04/29/mieko-kawakami-all-over-desire/. Mieko Kawakami, *Breasts and Eggs*, trans. Sam Bett and David Boyd (Picador, 2020).
93   Kawakami, *Breasts*, 320.
94   Ibid.
95   Ibid., 36.
96   Ibid., 43.
97   Ibid., 41.
98   Ibid., 52.
99   Ibid., 55.
100   Ibid., 56.
101   Ahmed, 'Happy Objects', 31.
102   Ibid.
103   Kawakami, *Breasts*, 175.
104   See Lauren Elkin's essay on the subject 'Why All the Books about Motherhood', *Paris Review*, 17 July 2018, available online: https://www.theparisreview.org/blog/2018/07/17/why-all-the-books-about-motherhood/.
105   Ahmed, 'Happy Objects', 30.
106   Kawakami, *Breasts*, 429.

Bibliography

Ahmed, Sara. 'Happy Objects'. In *The Affect Theory Reader*, edited by Melissa Gregg and Gregory J. Seigworth. Durham, NC: Duke University Press, 2010.

Berlant, Lauren. *Cruel Optimism*. Durham, NC: Duke University Press, 2011.

Berlant, Lauren. *Desire/Love*. Santa Barbara: Punctum Books, 2012.

Brennan, Teressa. *The Transmission of Affect*. Ithaca, NY: Cornell University Press, 2014.

Chen, Mel Y. *Animacies: Biopolitics, Racial Mattering, and Queer Affect*. Durham, NC: Duke University Press, 2012.

Chihaya, Sarah. 'All over Desire'. *New York Review of Books*, 29 April 2021. Available online: https://www.nybooks.com/articles/2021/04/29/mieko-kawakami-all-over-desire/.

da Silva, Denise Ferreira. *Toward a Global Idea of Race*. Minneapolis: University of Minnesota Press, 2007.

Eng, David L. and Shinhee Han. *Racial Melancholia, Racial Dissociation*. Durham, NC: Duke University Press, 2019.

Freeman, Elizabeth. *Time Binds: Queer Temporalities, Queer Histories*. Durham, NC: Duke University Press, 2010.

García Robayo, Margarita. *Holiday Heart*. Translated by Charlotte Coombe. Edinburgh: Charco Press, 2017.

Kawakami, Mieko. *Breasts and Eggs*. Translated by Sam Bett and David Boyd. London: Picador, 2020.

Levinas, Emmanuel. *Ethics and Infinity: Conversations with Philippe Nemo*. Translated by Richard A. Cohen. Pittsburgh, PA: Duquesne University Press, 1985.

Levinas, Emmanuel. *Totality and Infinity*. Translated by Alphonso Lingis. Pittsburgh, PA: Duquesne University Press, 1961: 198–9.

Ma, Ling. *Severance*. London: Picador, 2016.

Ngai, Sianne. *Ugly Feelings*. Cambridge, MA: Harvard University Press, 2005.

Serpell, Namwali. *Stranger Faces*. Oakland: Transit Books, 2020.

Williams, Diane. *Fine, Fine, Fine, Fine, Fine*. San Francisco: McSweeney's, 2016.

Yao, Christine. *Disaffected: The Cultural Politics of Unfeeling in Nineteenth-Century America*. Durham, NC: Duke University Press, 2021.

Ying, Eileen. 'Coolie Pathology'. *Post45*. 13 October 2020. Available online: https://post45.org/2020/10/coolie-pathology/.

Zhang, Dora. 'Staying Alive'. 13 October 2020. Available online: https://post45.org/2020/10/staying-alive/.

2

Ecocriticism

Timothy C. Baker

In Zadie Smith's strange, disturbing story 'The Dialectic' (2019), a mother and daughter sit on a beach in Poland, eating fried chicken. The mother speaks of her desire to be on good terms with non-human animals, while the daughter ridicules her aspirations. The mother seeks the anonymity of the beach, where she can be one of many tourists, but keeps being reminded of her tense relationship with her family. The brief story then reaches its abrupt, climactic ending:

> As her daughter applied what looked like cooking oil to the taut skin of her tummy, the woman discreetly placed her chicken wing in the sand before quickly, furtively, kicking more sand over it, as if it were a turd she buried. And the little chicks, hundreds of thousands of them, perhaps millions, pass down an assembly line, every day of the week, and chicken sexers turn them over, and sweep all the males into huge grinding vats where they are minced alive.[1]

The first sentence provides a direct, if disquieting, relation between the daughter's body and that of the chicken. Bodies might be burnished or buried, but our knowledge of ourselves and of others begins, and ends, at the level of the body. In the second sentence, however, Smith highlights our ignorance of such embodiment: the factual account of industrial chicken farming that closes the story seems out of place in its horror. It is unthinkable, even as it must be thought. Smith, in four pages, raises many of the central questions of contemporary ecocriticism: the relation between human and non-human bodies, and between individual and collective forms of experience, which are difficult to enunciate, but ever more pressing.

Smith's concerns are paralleled in Daisy Hildyard's *The Second Body* (2017), where Hildyard develops a theory of embodiment that is as straightforward as it is radical. Most of us, she argues, are used to thinking of the body as materially constrained: human embodiment is singular, inviolable and stops, as it were, at the level of the skin. Our reality as individuals depends on having an individual body. In a time of climate crisis, however, this view is insufficient. Now, Hildyard writes, we must move to a view in which 'every animal body [is] implicated in the whole world'.[2] Hildyard initially couches her definition in terms of responsibility: each body, human or non-human, is responsible for each other body. As she clarifies, however, this is not a metaphorical stance: 'This second body is your own literal and physical biological existence – it is a version of you. It is not a concept, it is your own body.'[3] We are all, always, multiple; we are all, always, complicit in the changes going around us, at the level of the body.

Hildyard confesses that she finds it difficult to remember that she has two bodies: one that is, in a sense, hers, and one that might be on the other side of the planet. When I present Hildyard's ideas to my students, they are often confused or resistant. I often use the example of breath to explain Hildyard's idea. Sitting in a classroom, an environment no less real for being constructed, we each inhale and exhale, and the breath that has been in my body, and is a part of me, is moments later part of another person. Our embodiment as individuals is, at a fundamental level, not separable from our environment. We are, as a number of the thinkers discussed below affirm, co-constituted with other forms of life. While there are many different strands of contemporary ecocritical thought, including but not limited to the material ecocritical and ecofeminist approaches discussed here, perhaps the central theme of current scholarship is the idea that no one human body can be seen independently. Embodiment is not only a human concern, nor is it a matter of individuation: instead, embodiment is shared between multiple living creatures (and, indeed, for some critics, with non-living entities). Ecocritical approaches to the body do not, as in past decades, simply relate a knowable human body to a larger sphere of 'nature' but instead open up questions of how bodies relate or are entangled.

Hildyard's text is particularly notable for the way its discussion of entanglement and multiplicity is not simply argued but intrinsic to its form: the volume combines perspectives from the sciences and arts, memoir and criticism, conversations with experts and observation of non-human animals, all in order to argue against an easy assumption of individual or disciplinary authority. In different ways, this hybrid approach is common to many contemporary ecocritical writings. Consequently, this chapter looks at multiple ways of relating theoretical and creative work. The opening section briefly traces some of the key ideas in ecofeminism and material ecocriticism, drawing both on scholars squarely in the field of ecocriticism and those from other disciplines whose work has influenced ecocritical study. The following section looks at a number of recent poetry collections, including work by Seán Hewitt, Tishani Doshi, Elizabeth-Jane Burnett and Jason Allen-Paisant, published in 2020 and 2021. Rather than applying theoretical insights to literary texts, I argue that these poetic texts, like Smith's story, are themselves a way of theorizing or constructing ideas of the relation between body and environment. The chapter concludes with a discussion of Jesmyn Ward's novel *Salvage the Bones* (2011), which combines themes of climate crisis and human-animal relations in order to show the precarity and vulnerability that is central to human and non-human experience. Each of these texts works to address the fundamental question of how bodies are constituted in relation to their environment, and how a recognition of human entanglement in a more-than-human world requires new forms of thinking and expression.

Ecocriticism and entanglement

Summarizing the work of ecofeminist thinkers as diverse as Karen Barad, Joy Williams and Val Plumwood, Stacy Alaimo argues that human corporeality should be imagined as 'trans-corporeality'. This 'trans-corporeality', she suggests, acknowledges the ways in which humans are 'always enmeshed with the more-than-human world'.[4] Writing in 2010, Alaimo argues that thinking of humans and non-human, or more-than-human, agents as equally involved in, and constitutive of, the world, is a way to open the ethical and political questions that define our time. She stresses connection and integration rather than binary separations between humans and nature, where nature is defined simply as everything the human is not. Two years later, in a 2012 survey of the material turn in ecocriticism, Serenella Iovino makes a similar point, emphasizing that a focus on matter and materiality provides a way not only to think past binary oppositions 'but also to redraw the maps of ecological interactions, restructuring ethics and politics in the complex, nonlinear, co-evolutionary interplay of human and nonhuman agency'.[5] For both thinkers, and many others, the material turn in both ecocriticism and ecofeminism is also an ethical turn. If, as Cheryll Glotfelty argues in her influential definition of ecocriticism, literature 'plays a part in an immensely complex global system, in which energy, matter, *and ideas* interact', contemporary ecocriticism is particularly invested in the study of bodily interaction and its ethical outcomes.[6]

The importance of the material turn is, in part, that it not only provides a way to avoid familiar essentialisms where, for instance, nature is framed as 'feminine' and women are framed as 'natural', but that it allows thinkers to engage with the often racist, sexist and heteronormative assumptions about nature that have previously dominated discourse. Rather than positioning the human as a remote observer who is able to pronounce on nature, a materialist perspective reinforces that no separation is possible: 'nature' is itself a human construct, while the human is inseparable from its environment. As Jane Bennett argues, thinking of matter as inert and designed for human use 'feeds human hubris and our earth-destroying fantasies of conquest and consumption'.[7] In this sense, contemporary ecocriticism can be seen as an intervention into particularly destructive formulations and ontologies.

Material approaches invite new ways of thinking of what, or who, counts as a subject and what, or who, has a body. One of the foundational premises of critical animal studies, as seen in the work of thinkers ranging from Ralph R. Acampora to Sunaura Taylor, is that any ethical or compassionate relation with non-human animals begins at the level of the body. Pattrice Jones, for instance, claims that '[a]ctual animal liberation is all about bodies – theirs *and* ours – and is therefore all about eros'.[8] The treatment of non-human animals, such thinkers argue, should not be predicated on intelligence or sentience, any measurement of which is likely to be faulty and anthropocentric, but simply on the fact that non-human animals, like us, are embodied beings. These considerations extend far beyond non-human animals. Jeffrey Jerome Cohen, for instance, in a discussion of Alaimo's work, makes the case for stone as similarly trans-corporeal, insofar as stone 'enables movement and violence, extends cognition, and invites worldbuilding'.[9] Mel Y. Chen, on the other hand, argues for 'animacy', rather than life or liveliness, as a foundational term: while she explicitly denies stone agency, she argues for animacy as a term that undoes binary distinctions between, for instance, life and death, or dynamism and stasis.[10] What unites these thinkers, despite their significant differences, is a desire to unpick many of the foundational terms and ideas that have contributed to a sense of human supremacy. Bodies, life, agency and animacy are not restricted to human subjects alone but are shared across species and types of being.

For many theorists, this rethinking of the relation between self and nature is particularly urgent in the present context of the Anthropocene. The Anthropocene can most easily be defined as the period in which human activity has decisively altered the earth at a geological level. As Alaimo asks, '[w]hat can it mean to be human in this time when the human is something that has become sedimented in the geology of the planet?'[11] The Anthropocene requires new ways of thinking not simply about what humans do, or have done, but who and what humans are. Considering the Anthropocene requires us to recognize life not as something reserved for humans but as what Rosi Braidotti calls a 'transversal force that cuts across and reconnects previously segregated species, categories, and domains'.[12] Nature is no longer positioned as an externalized other; instead, humans must be seen as environmental and ecological agents, and life as a shared force.

As many Indigenous thinkers have noted, however, this perspective is only new if considered in a Eurocentric context. The Métis scholar Zoe Todd points to the Inuit term 'Sila', which is often translated simply as 'climate' but can also be understood as both the breath that moves through everything and a form of wisdom.[13] 'Sila' is a way of linking questions of environment, selfhood and knowledge that, in certain respects, parallels and prefigures some of the ideas above. The often-unacknowledged adoption of such ideas by Western thinkers is, as Todd shows, a form of colonial violence. This violence is experienced at the level of the body: if, as the Michi Saagiig Nishnaabeg writer Leanne Betasamosake Simpson argues, Indigenous bodies 'represented the lived alternative to heteronormative constructions of gender, political systems, and rules of descent', the removal of those bodies from the land has been a constant, and ongoing, form of erasure.[14] Thinking of bodies in new ways requires acknowledging those bodies that have been displaced or killed in pursuit of power and control. If, in Alaimo's words, a 'posthuman environmental ethics denies the human the sense of separation from the interconnected, mutually constitutive actions of material reality', it is imperative to understand how that sense of separation has been enforced.[15]

Alaimo, like many other contemporary thinkers, draws extensively on Karen Barad's *Meeting the Universe Halfway* (2007), where Barad proposes a form of 'agential realism' that states there are not pre-existing bodies, or things, but rather that all matter acts, and intra-acts, in relation. One does not know about a particular body; instead, knowing is a material engagement that reconfigures the world.[16] Barad's examples are largely taken from quantum physics: she explains at length that the act of observation changes the material that is observed. As such, bodies cannot be seen as fixed substances with inherent boundaries and properties, nor can a distinction between human and non-human bodies be sustained.[17] The implications for ecocriticism are clear. Considering humans as separate from their environment is not only a falsehood but a force of violence. As the theologian Catherine Keller writes, in reference to Barad: 'If the separateness of our lives is a sham, then the work of our civilization to produce us as discrete subjects vying to emulate, master, know, and consume external objects succeeds only through [...] systemic repression.'[18] Understanding either human or non-human bodies in terms of fixed properties, and focusing on individuation rather than relation, is a form of epistemological violence. While these perspectives are clearly not limited to ecocriticism, they suggest new ways of approaching the relation between humans and the environment and of reconsidering ecological ethics.

Astrida Neimanis offers an excellent example of such an approach, focusing on water. Humans are not, she writes, on the one hand embodied, and on the other comprised of water: instead, they are both at the same time. Humans are bodies of water at the same time that 'bodies of water undo the idea that bodies are necessarily or only human'.[19] Water's ability to connect different bodies, Neimanis argues, allows us to think of a different 'we' that is premised on interconnection. For Neimanis, the central question for theories of embodiment is not simply what a body is, but where – and when and why – it is.[20] If embodiment is a form of relation, then it cannot be approached as static but moves in and through space and time. A body does not simply inhabit an environment but absorbs it and transforms it. Thinking of the world as a planetary hydrocommons is a way to acknowledge that each body transforms water at the level of the flesh.[21] Neimanis, for instance, positions specific human bodily waters, such as breast milk or amniotic fluid, as metonyms for the planetary bodies of water. Human bodies are connected with, formed by, and formative of planetary environments at every level. Such an approach radically upturns traditions of environmental study that divide humans and the environment into a subject/object relationship. Like Hildyard's 'second body', Neimanis's bodies of water requires the reader to forge a new understanding of what it means to be embodied and insists that bodies are not individual or constrained.

If some of these approaches might strike readers as potentially abstract or opaque, the anthropologist Anna Lowenhaupt Tsing's formulation of encounter, precarity and assemblage in *The Mushroom at the End of the World* (2015) might provide more familiar examples. Tsing focuses on *matusake*, a mushroom harvested in the north-western United States by immigrant workers which is then sold in Japan. At the heart of Tsing's study is an emphasis on the transformative power of encounter between different people and different species. Focusing on mushrooms provides a new way of thinking about bodily indeterminacy: while human bodies often 'achieve a determinate form early in our lives', fungi change form all of their lives. As such, Tsing asks what it would mean 'if our indeterminate life form was not the shape of our bodies but rather the shape of our motions over time'.[22] Encounter is always transformative; it allows us, in a time of environmental and capitalist crisis, to recognize the precarity that is shared between different living beings – thinking about humans and environments in terms of assemblage, or gathering, rather than in terms of subject/object relations. Humans create, and are created by, new ecosystems; what is essential, for Tsing, is moving from accounts of division or separation to seeing human and non-human life in terms of what is held in common.

This is very much the approach taken in Donna Haraway's *Staying with the Trouble* (2016), where she approaches 'multispecies storytelling' in terms of 'partial recuperation and getting on together'.[23] Like Tsing, Haraway advocates ideas of assemblage including non-human or more-than-human agents. In a period not only of climate change but environmental devastation, genocide and system collapse, it is essential for humans to work with and in relation to non-human others. Haraway dismisses the idea of the Anthropocene precisely because it favours the human: instead, she argues for a world-building project that recognizes the entanglement and shared responsibility of all beings. Robin Wall Kimmerer, focusing specifically on plants, likewise argues that '[r]estoration is an opportunity for partnership'.[24] Environmental ethics and planetary flourishing, for both thinkers, requires cooperation between multiple species and forms of life.

The different theoretical perspectives discussed above overlap in several key areas. Each of them argues that humans are entangled or enmeshed in a broader, multispecies environment at the level of the body: bodies are not separate from their environment but known in relation to it. An historical and Eurocentric focus on bodies as divisible from the land, and from other species, has repeatedly worked to exclude marginalized bodies, whether in terms of race, gender or disability. Focusing on bodies in their corporeality, as Diana Coole and Samantha Frost argue, 'dislocates agency as the property of a discrete, self-knowing subject' in favour of understanding bodies as they move in space and time, and in relation to other bodies.[25] These formulations of embodiment are predicated on feminist, antiracist and anti-colonialist principles and share many key elements with posthuman philosophies, as discussed in the final chapter of this volume. In the context of ecocriticism specifically, contemporary theories of embodiment have been used to move away from anthropocentric or human supremacist conceptions of the body as divorced from or superior to nature. Instead, they move towards an understanding of bodies as, in various ways, co-constituted with their environment.

As Eva Haifa Giraud argues, however, this emphasis on connection and entanglement at times paints an overly harmonious picture that ignores the importance of exclusion. Placing relation as 'the fundamental unit of analysis' forecloses the possibility of other modes of ethics or politics.[26] Giraud does not deny the rhetorical force of arguments for multispecies entanglement but also notes the prominence of sentiment in many accounts: which species are attended to depends, in part, on charisma and popularity. An environmental or multispecies ethics that emphasizes relation and proximity might, in this sense, reinforce existing hierarchies between species. Focusing on care, for instance, as 'something that unfolds through proximal encounters and entanglements between bodies' can reinforce epistemic hierarchies, privileging perspectives that have already been deemed legitimate.[27] Giraud's concerns are paralleled in the work of thinkers such as Nicole Seymour and Jack Halberstam. Seymour, for instance, argues that environmental writing has long been seen as privileging sentiment over irony, arguing that rather than 'love and wonder', many humans are invested in the 'obscene, queer, and repulsive aspects of nonhumans'.[28] Halberstam opposes the division between wilderness and civilization to emphasize that '[w]ildness is all at once what we were, what we have become, and what we will be'.[29] Positing bodily relation and entanglement as central to environmental ethics does not entail, all three thinkers suggest, ignoring bodily diversity or measuring all creaturely life against an anthropocentric template.

Although the perspectives here come from a variety of disciplinary perspectives, in part revealing how diverse the field of ecocriticism has become in recent years, many scholars continue to privilege literature and storytelling as a way to approach these central questions. While Pieter Vermeulen cautions that the Anthropocene is not only a literary problem, he asserts that 'literature helps us see to what extent the Anthropocene is a matter of reading and writing, of decoding and inscription'.[30] Tsing begins her book with the claim that while Western philosophers have emphasized a separation between humans and nature, it 'was left to fabulists, including non-Western and non-civilizational storytellers, to remind us of the lively activities of all beings, human and not human'.[31] Literature is a way to provide new insights into human and more-than-human relations and to understand our own time. In particular, focusing on storytelling leads back to a focus on bodies. Citing influential early theorizations of ecocriticism from Glotfelty and Kate Rigby, Serenella Iovino and Serpil Oppermann analyse the interactions between nature and culture as 'material narratives': 'Bodies, both human and nonhuman, provide an eloquent example of the way matter can be read as a text.'[32] If ecocriticism has always, most simply, been defined as the study of the relation between literature and the world, contemporary ecocritical approaches emphasize the way matter itself can tell stories.

Rigby cautions, however, that stories 'can potentially obscure as much as they reveal'.[33] It matters, perhaps more than ever, who tells stories, and what stories are heeded. It matters how stories of environmental devastation are framed, and which bodies are made visible. As many BIPOC scholars have noted, the environmental devastation which drives many contemporary ecocritical approaches is not new but has been experienced by marginalized bodies for centuries. The very idea of the Anthropocene, Kathryn Yusoff argues, erases histories of racism just as much as the separation between humans and nature: the divisions between human and inhuman, and between life and nonlife, 'pertains not only to matter but to the racial organization of life as foundational to New World geographies'.[34] Likewise, as Catriona Mortimer-Sandilands and Bruce Erikson point out, accounts of nature as wilderness are frequently 'heterosexualized'; a queer ecological or ecocritical approach 'calls into question heteronormativity itself as part of its advocacy around issues of nature and environment'.[35] It is not only, as Amitav Ghosh has influentially claimed, that climate crisis and other environmental disasters have 'defie[d] both literary fiction and contemporary common sense'.[36] Accounts of entanglement also often privilege, if unintentionally, dominant voices at the expense of a focus on individual bodily relations. The literary texts that I explore in the section below each, in different ways, approach the questions of materiality and bodily entanglement at the level of the individual, as well as at social and planetary levels.

Corporeal ecopoetics

The four collections discussed in this section are all by poets who are currently or have been based in the UK and were all published between 2020 and 2021. As such they are not presented to offer a comprehensive or definitive approach to questions of how the body is presented in contemporary ecopoetical work; rather, their close similarities, as well as significant differences, indicate how poetry might consider the same ideas that have been discussed in relation to some of the works by the theorists and critics above. Each of these collections – Hewitt's *Tongues of Fire* (2020), Doshi's *A God at the Door* (2021), Burnett's *Of Sea* (2021) and Allen-Paisant's *Thinking with Trees* (2021) – raises key questions about what and who constitutes a body and about how human and non-human bodies can be understood in terms of enmeshment. While the four poets write from a variety of cultural perspectives, and are formally distinct, each presents a world that is known as and through bodily relation.

Tongues of Fire, the earliest collection discussed here, is filled with references to non-human bodies. A wych elm 'can sow from its body these translucent // frailties', a blackened fungus is 'a war-burnt body', and in 'Oak Glossary' the nature of arboreal time is expressed through sap that 'is produced / and is made to run from the body'.[37] Human bodies are known in relation to these non-human bodies; the speaker of 'Petition' describes walking through the trees at night, the darkness so overwhelming 'it is as though / I am leaving my body by the pond's // moonlit edge' and thinking of each of the bodies that surround them, whether trees, creatures, waters or other humans.[38] The world is populated and known through bodily immersion: each body is known as itself and in relation. The landscape of the poems is largely rural: the majority of poems are set in parks and wooded areas. Hewitt joins a long tradition of celebratory, observant nature poetry that focuses, in part, on the solaces of the natural world.

Hewitt's work is also marked by what might be called a queer ecopoetics. As Angela Hume and Samia Rahimtoola articulate, while the question of dwelling on the earth has long been a key concern of ecopoetics, queer ecopoetics 'orients us toward the affects, kinship practices, and erotic exchanges that shape dwelling as a relational endeavor'.[39] These erotic exchanges are clearly presented in the long poem 'Dryad', where the figure of a woman, 'carved from the bole of an oak', marks the path into the woods where the speaker encounters other men while cruising as a teenager.[40] The speaker describes an encounter with a man 'whose whole body / was muscled, as though he too had been carved / from a single trunk of wood'; kneeling in front of the man is not only a sexual act but one of connection with the earth, as the speaker remembers the land as a 'bed of all the plants // and trees', the groundwater spreading through his jeans.[41] The speaker briefly wonders if he has, somehow, despoiled the woods but concludes:

> what is a tree, or a plant, if not an act
> of kneeling to the earth, a way of bidding
>
> the water to move, of taking in the mouth
> the inner part of the world and coaxing it out.[42]

The world is full of bodies, human and non-human, and these bodies are known in relation to the speaker's own. To be in the world is not only an act of enmeshment, but immersion, a form of supplication. Flesh is wood, and wood flesh, and these bodies intertwine and penetrate each other. Dwelling, and eros, is above all a form of bodily relation.

As Allen-Paisant's collection reveals, however, such wooded spaces can also be hostile to bodies perceived as other. At times, Allen-Paisant gestures towards a similar corporeal relation to that found in Hewitt's work, writing: 'among the oaks / my skin is a type of bark', and envisioning a spring as 'skin coming / to cover the body'.[43] As in Hume's analysis of Claudia Rankine, however, Allen-Paisant's work 'concerns the difficulty of relating to or identifying with one's environment when one has been othered by the dominant white society'.[44] Many of the poems in *Thinking with Trees* describe the difficulty of walking in the woods as a Black man in England, where the speaker articulates that 'I never allowed my body / to occupy space / the way these people do'.[45] Allen-Paisant's poems document the way British nature poetry, specifically Wordsworth's, has centred white experience, and the differences between English and Jamaican environments. A number of poems also focus on the way white walkers position their dogs as more deserving of space than Black walkers, whereas in his encounters with dogs he is reminded of how 'his ancestors /were property / less than these animals'.[46] While the speakers of Allen-Paisant's poems often do find the sense of coexistence with trees portrayed in Hewitt's work, they are also always conscious of the way they are marked as other.

Two poems at the collection's centre typify Allen-Paisant's approach. 'On Property' depicts the well-publicized story of a racist confrontation between Amy Cooper, a white dog walker, and

Christian Cooper, a Black bird watcher, in Central Park on 25 May 2020 – the same day, as the poem notes, as the murder of George Floyd in Minneapolis. The poem is filled with gaps and silences, large spaces between words and short lines:

How ordinary for her

to destroy

this body

How ordinary for her

to erase

this body

space.[47] (53)

A public space, a space of connection between human and non-human life, is transformed into a space of racism and violence. There is, as many of the critics discussed above also note, no access to a 'nature' that is not already shaped by centuries of racism and colonialism. In the following poem, 'Behaviour (A Black Man Enters the Woods)', the speaker describes his need to place his body in relation to another walker. Walking slowly, in order to avoid the appearance of threat, draws his attention to the plants and animals around him: 'you share the land with squirrels / […] in this flourishing / life of leaves'.[48] The speaker is careful, aware of his body, and yet realizes, at the poem's end, that 'this shared constructed space // is all you have // to think & feel with'.[49] Even as his body is othered, encounters with a more-than-human world still allow a necessary form of relation and thinking. The speaker's marginalization and exclusion dominate the poems, and yet entanglement is still possible.

While Burnett also reflects on such exclusions in her previous work, *Of Sea* is a collection that largely focuses on the many invertebrates encountered while swimming in Dawlish Warren, in Devon. As a collection, *Of Sea* is more emphatically dedicated to what Burnett calls 'post-nature, the powers of the body'.[50] The many non-human animals Burnett describes are known in and as bodies – a bootlace worm is a '[b]ody within body, whirligig' – while the sea itself, as in Neimanis's theoretical writing, is 'a body without end'.[51] The bodies of the creatures, the speaker and the waters are 'post-nature' in the sense that there is no firm separation between nature and culture or between human and non-human: each body is known in its powers, its forms and its relation.

For Burnett, this form of knowing is a question of language. In 'Ragworm' the speaker notes how in an experience of bodily relation and enmeshment '[a]ll our lines break, all that's fixed shakes, when we nestle / in the worm's wake, all our meanings fumble'.[52] Yet even as meanings fumble, the strict metre and emphasis on rhyme here, unusual in Burnett's work, indicate the extent to which the poetic line is itself a body, entangled in the same sphere. Burnett's poems do not pronounce on bodily being so much as they bring beings to life. In various poems she uses a range of languages, including Kiembu, Kikuyu and Inuktuit, which are glossed at the back of the volume but positioned as equal with English in the poems themselves. She also uses a variety of experimental onomatopoetic devices, as in the poem 'Ground Beetle', which Burnett notes is to be 'sung/clicked/slicked':

> how to make such a little /////
> how to make such a little sOund that you /// know I'm talking //
> how to make such a little sOund that you /// know I'm talking to you.[53]

The strokes here simultaneously evoke line breaks and clicks; the extra spaces and unusual capitalization force the reader to disentangle, and re-entangle, the relation between sound and sense, human and non-human. By the end of the poem the text is given entirely to sound, 'tt-tt-tt-tt-tt' or 'p-LA-LA-LA-LA-LA', presented in a variety of sizes.[54] This is not simply a representation of the ground beetle's voice. Rather, the text is presented as a body, or a series of bodies, in the environment of the page. The reader's encounter with the text, whether or not they choose to perform it, is an echo of the encounter between speaker and beetle. Human language is not framed as superior but as a path towards relation.

Doshi's collection likewise uses a number of different formal approaches, including calligrams and other elements of concrete poetry, as well as more traditional stanzaic forms, to reflect on both human and non-human entanglement and on questions of racial and gender marginalization. The collection, published in April 2021, includes a number of references to the Covid-19 pandemic and very recent Indian political events: like Allen-Paisant's work, it reflects explicitly on its own moment. The opening poem, 'Mandala', juxtaposes political, bodily and environmental concerns:

> We talk of bodies
> as though we could not understand them,
> even though we've all gaped at the stump of a tree
> and understood that time moves outward in a circle.[55]

Trees are a path to understanding human bodies, at the same time that the natural world is framed as a form of escape, where leaving the house without a mask offers an opportunity 'to take a break / from who we are'.[56] The natural world, filled with trees and animals, offers solace and understanding; attention to that world changes the speaker's sense of time and offers a new ethical perspective. Human embodiment is consistently positioned as difficult but not unknowable: understanding human bodies instead requires understanding the wider world.

Like the poets above, however, Doshi also suggests that any discussion of the non-human world will always refer back to the human. The poem 'A Possible Explanation as to Why We Mutilate Women & Trees, which Tries to End on a Note of Hope' invites the reader to '[b]egin with trees' before looking at how trees are often framed in a 'heavily heteronormative fantasy'.[57] And yet, as in Allen-Paisant's work, the legacies of violence that shape experiences of nature can only be thought through by bodily immersion: the 'Note of Hope' on which the poem ends is an invitation to '[p]ut your mouth / to the flower, that wound'.[58] The natural world cannot be experienced unmediated, and is always shaped, and yet that very act of shaping becomes a path to bodily engagement. 'Tree of Life' includes references to Simone de Beauvoir and Satyajit Ray, as well as the story of seven Bengali men who self-quarantined in a tree when lockdown was declared in India in March 2020; Doshi invites the reader to 'adore the convoluted roots of our attachments'.[59]

Entanglement is presented both as bodily relation and as desire. The speaker of 'Roots', for instance, quotes Frida Kahlo: 'I too want to believe / in *the vegetable miracle* / *of my body's landscape*'.[60] Similarly, the speaker of 'Tigress Hugs Manchurian Fir' reflects on her own desire to hug trees in a time when 'hugging has been outlawed':

> I begin my diaries with *Chipko means to hug in Hindi.*
> And even though I know the history of the ecofeminist
> embrace is fierce, not cute, it helps me understand the gap
> between my life and the denuded hillside.[61]

Doshi's poems are filled with cultural reference points and mentions of contemporary political events precisely in order to break down an apparent separation between nature and culture. A binary division between material presence and intellectual contemplation is impossible. Instead, Doshi indicates how attention to the present, and to the complexities of interwoven cultures and histories, is a way of thinking that allows for new forms of bodily being.

Each of the poets discussed here is notable for the use of poetry to think through questions of body and nature, of self and other, of human and non-human. Contemporary ecopoetry is able to address the complexities of entanglement: knowing the world through the body does not mean jettisoning culture and language but seeing them in new ways. This is possible in poetry in a way it may not be in theory precisely because poems do not simply reflect on bodies but are themselves bodies, bound in the environment of the page and yet able to reach the reader. These poets do not simply extol the virtues of nature but emphasize the way historical conceptualizations of natural have privileged some bodies over others: attending to those bodies, human and non-human, that have been marginalized and excluded invites new forms and new ways of thinking.

'Bodies tell stories'

If ecopoetry provides a way of resituating human bodies in relation to a more-than-human world, contemporary literary fiction can also serve a similar function and offers an opportunity to represent the social construction of bodies. While contemporary ecocriticism's emphasis on the Anthropocene has often, in the past decade, focused on stories of environmental collapse, granting prominence to apocalyptic narratives, other work has looked at the similarities between sustainability and narrative, which both imply a form of 'narrative coherence'.[62] Fiction provides a means of 'reconceptualising environments', in John Parham's term, that provides readers with the possibility of agency to mitigate environmental disasters.[63] Any such reconceptualization also requires increased attention to the nuances of corporeal entanglement and marginalization. Ward's *Salvage the Bones* is a central text in this area: not only is it an important portrayal, in its focus on Hurricane Katrina, of environmental devastation, but it is also viewed by many critics as an exemplification of Rob Nixon's theory of slow violence. Nixon defines slow violence as 'neither spectacular nor instantaneous, but rather incremental and accretive', pointing specifically to climate change and other environmental catastrophes.[64] As Nixon notes in a brief discussion of Katrina, the structural failures that led to the hurricane's devastation were the product of racist discrimination over decades: rather than viewing the hurricane as a sudden 'natural' catastrophe, it is a product of ongoing violence. Like Yusoff, Simpson and many others, Nixon emphasizes the extent to which environmental devastation is disproportionately experienced by the poor and racial minorities.

In her non-fiction writing Ward uses environmental metaphors to discuss African American lives: 'Life is a hurricane, and we board up to save what we can and bow low to the earth to crouch in that small space above the dirt where the wind will not reach.'[65] Christina Sharpe makes a similar point in formulating the 'weather' of racism: 'In what I am calling the weather, antiblackness is pervasive *as* climate. The weather necessitates changeability and improvisation; it is the atmospheric condition of time and place; it produces new ecologies.'[66] For both writers, this is not simply a figure of speech: social and physical environments are inseparable. *Salvage the Bones* tells the story of Katrina's arrival in a small Mississippi town; set over twelve days, and focusing primarily on one family, it emphasizes both human enmeshment in an environment and the legacies of discrimination. The novel is also of particular interest from an ecocritical perspective, however, for its focus on non-human life: throughout the novel dogs are as central as humans and offer models of care and sustainability that humans must adopt to survive. In this sense, Ward's novel is a clear exemplar of the idea of a second body discussed in the Introduction: it is focused on the life of one teenage girl, Esch, but Esch's story can be understood at both local and planetary level and in relation to both human and more-than-human agents.

Salvage the Bones juxtaposes several different modes of relation with non-human or more-than-human life. Most notably, Esch's story closely parallels that of China, her brother Skeetah's dog. The novel begins with China giving birth, a scene which both allows Esch to remember her deceased mother and prefigures her own discovery of her pregnancy shortly afterwards. As Skeetah says, 'between man and dog is a relationship. [...] Equal'.[67] China is a fighting dog, and the source of the family's only income, but is not positioned as property. Instead, both her scenes with her puppies and her scenes of fighting are extremely violent and visceral, drawing attention to the way entanglement in the world is always felt at the level of the body. If, as Esch declares of her own pregnancy, '[b]odies tell stories', the positioning of canine and human stories as overlapping indicates the impossibility of separating humans from the rest of the environment.[68] Esch uses her knowledge of Greek mythology to inform the way she tells both China's story and her own: stories of motherhood and violence follow the same arc regardless of species.

The same sense of intimate relation is found in the presentation of the physical environment, both before and after the hurricane. The Pit, where Esch's family lives, is a microclimate filled with 'pines, oaks, birch, birds', while the nearby coast is filled with pelicans.[69] The physical environment is not simply a setting for human affairs but presented as a tangle of bodies: even their house is a 'drying animal skeleton' while the flood, when it comes, is a 'wide-nosed snake'.[70] The hurricane is presented, in a long run-on sentence, as a force that acts on bodies:

> Skeet is laying next to the hole in the attic floor, looking at us, his face sick, twisted, and he is reaching a hand down to Daddy, hoisting him, up, and the puppy must be dead in my shirt because it is not moving and I pull it out as I cough and cough up the water and the hurricane and the pit and I can't stop.[71]

Esch is transfigured by the hurricane, but it is felt in her own body as much as it is an external force. Katrina is herself a 'mother', creating a precarious community of bodies in relation.[72] Ward limits her discussion of any external overview of the disaster: instead, the hurricane is a body, indeed a second body, which is known through the way it acts on other bodies, human and non-human. Like both the poets and theorists discussed above, Ward suggests that human and non-human life must be seen in relation; this is not an intrinsically harmonious form of relation but rather one that shows the impossibility of separation.

Conclusion

The writers discussed in this chapter do not, of course, represent the only current approaches to the questions of the relation between environments and bodies. They suggest, however, the importance of challenging any separation between the two terms. The environment is known as and through bodies; humans can only be understood as they are entangled with more-than-human others. This approach allows for wide-ranging considerations of the legacies of colonialist, racist, heterosexist and misogynist thought in constructing our ideas of 'nature'. These works also suggest the bodily and environmental dimensions of thought itself. As Rebecca Tamás writes: 'With the death of different spaces, different environments, different histories and different bodily forms of moving through them, forms of thought die too.'[73] Thinking and writing are forms of bodily engagement. In a time of increasing and pervasive crisis, ecocritical work in all its forms demonstrates the necessity of finding different ways of knowing. Rejecting inherited, Eurocentric ideas of bodily individuation and human supremacy becomes, perhaps, the best way of ensuring that there are bodies, and stories, left to tell.

Notes

1   Zadie Smith, *Grand Union* (London: Hamish Hamilton, 2019), 4.
2   Daisy Hildyard, *The Second Body* (London: Fitzcarraldo, 2017), 13.

3   Hildyard, *The Second Body*, 25.
4   Stacy Alaimo, *Bodily Natures: Science, Environment, and the Material Self* (Bloomington: Indiana University Press, 2010), 2.
5   Serenella Iovino and Serpil Oppermann, 'Theorizing Material Ecocriticism: A Dipytch', *ISLE: Interdisciplinary Studies in Literature and Environment* 19, no. 3 (2012): 451.
6   Cheryll Glotfelty, 'Introduction: Literary Studies in an Age of Environmental Crisis', in *The Ecocriticism Reader: Landmarks in Literary Ecology*, ed. Cheryll Glotfelty and Harold Fromm (Athens and London: University of Georgia Press, 1996), xix.
7   Jane Bennett, *Vibrant Matter: A Political Ecology of Things* (Durham and London: Duke University Press, 2010), ix.
8   Pattrice Jones, 'Eros and the Mechanisms of Eco-Defense', in *Ecofeminism: Feminist Intersections with Other Animals and the Earth*, ed. Carol J. Adams and Lori Gruen (New York and London: Bloomsbury, 2014), 103.
9   Jeffrey Jerome Cohen, 'Introduction: Ecostitial', in *Inhuman* Nature, ed. Jeffrey Jerome Cohen (Washington, DC: Oliphaunt Books, 2014), iii.
10 Mel Y. Chen, *Animacies: Biopolitics, Racial Mattering, and Queer Affect* (Durham and London: Duke University Press, 2012), 3.
11 Stacy Alaimo, *Exposed: Environmental Politics and Pleasures in Posthuman Times* (Minneapolis and London: University of Minnesota Press, 2016), 1.
12 Rosi Braidotti, 'Four Theses on Posthuman Feminism', in *Anthropocene Feminism*, ed. Richard Grusin (Minneapolis and London: University of Minnesota Press, 2017), 32.
13 Zoe Todd, 'An Indigenous Feminist's Take on the Ontological Turn: "Ontology" Is Just Another Word for Colonialism', *Journal of Historical Sociology* 29, no. 1 (2016): 5.
14 Leanne Betasamosake Simpson, *As We Have Always Done: Indigenous Freedom through Radical Resistance* (Minneapolis and London: University of Minnesota Press, 2017), 41.
15 Alaimo, *Bodily Natures*, 157.
16 Karen Barad, *Meeting the Universe Halfway: Quantum Physics and the Entanglement of Matter and Meaning* (Durham and London: Duke University Press, 2007), 91.
17 Barad, *Meeting the Universe Halfway*, 153.
18 Catherine Keller, *Cloud of the Impossible: Negative Theology and Planetary Entanglement* (New York: Columbia University Press, 2015), 129.
19 Astrida Neimanis, *Bodies of Water: Posthuman Feminist Phenomenology* (London: Bloomsbury Academic, 2019), 2.
20 Neimanis, *Bodies of Water*, 29.

21 Ibid., 111.

22 Anna Lowenhaupt Tsing, *The Mushroom at the End of the World: On the Possibility of Life in Capitalist Ruins* (Princeton and Oxford: Princeton University Press, 2015), 47.

23 Donna J. Haraway, *Staying with the Trouble: Making Kin in the Chthulucene* (Durham and London: Duke University Press, 2016), 10.

24 Robin Wall Kimmerer, *Braiding Sweetgrass: Indigenous Wisdom, Scientific Knowledge, and the Teachings of Plants* (Minneapolis: Milkweed Editions, 2013), 333.

25 Diana H. Coole and Samantha Frost, 'Introducing the New Materialisms', in *New Materialisms: Ontology, Agency, and Politics*, ed. Diana H. Coole and Samantha Frost (Durham and London: Duke University Press, 2010), 20.

26 Eva Haifa Giraud, *What Comes after Entanglement? Activism, Anthropocentrism, and an Ethics of Exclusion* (Durham and London: Duke University Press, 2019), 177.

27 Giraud, *What Comes after Entanglement*, 100, 116.

28 Nicole Seymour, *Bad Environmentalism: Irony and Irreverence in the Ecological Age* (Minneapolis and London: University of Minnesota Press, 2018), 96.

29 Jack Halberstam, *Wild Things: The Disorder of Desire* (Durham and London: Duke University Press, 2020), 7.

30 Pieter Vermeulen, *Literature and the Anthropocene* (London and New York: Routledge, 2020), 26.

31 Tsing, *The Mushroom at the End of the World*, vii.

32 Serenella Iovino and Serpil Oppermann, 'Introduction: Stories Come to Matter', in *Material Ecocriticism*, ed. Serenella Iovino and Serpil Oppermann (Bloomington and Indianapolis: Indiana University Press, 2014), 6.

33 Kate Rigby, *Dancing with Disaster: Environmental Histories, Narratives, and Ethics for Perilous Times* (Charlottesville and London: University of Virginia Press, 2015), 2.

34 Kathryn Yusoff, *A Billion Black Anthropocenes or None* (Minneapolis: University of Minnesota Press, 2018), 5.

35 Catriona Mortimer-Sandilands and Bruce Erickson, 'Introduction: A Genealogy of Queer Ecologies', in *Queer Ecologies: Sex, Nature, Politics, Desire*, ed. Catriona Mortimer-Sandilands and Bruce Erickson (Bloomington and Indianapolis: Indiana University Press, 2010), 4–5.

36 Amitav Ghosh, *The Great Derangement: Climate Change and the Unthinkable* (Chicago and London: University of Chicago Press, 2016), 26.

37 Seán Hewitt, *Tongues of Fire* (London: Jonathan Cape, 2020), 13, 44, 15.

38 Hewitt, *Tongues of Fire*, 15.
39 Angela Hume, 'Introduction: Queering Ecopoetics', *ISLE: Interdisciplinary Studies in Literature and Environment* 25, no. 1 (2018): 139.
40 Hewitt, *Tongues of Fire*, 3.
41 Ibid., 4.
42 Ibid., 5.
43 Jason Allen-Paisant, *Thinking with Trees* (Manchester: Carcanet, 2021), 30, 2.
44 Angela Hume, 'Toward an Antiracist Ecopoetics: Waste and Wasting in the Poetry of Claudia Rankine', *Contemporary Literature* 57, no. 1 (2016): 80.
45 Allen-Paisant, *Thinking with Trees*, 34.
46 Ibid., 49.
47 Ibid., 53.
48 Ibid., 55.
49 Ibid., 56.
50 Elizabeth-Jane Burnett, *Of Sea* (London: Penned in the Margins, 2021), 64.
51 Ibid., 36, 46.
52 Ibid., 25.
53 Ibid., 65.
54 Ibid., 68.
55 Tishani Doshi, *A God at the Door* (Hexham: Bloodaxe, 2021), 11.
56 Ibid., 11.
57 Ibid., 80.
58 Ibid., 81.
59 Ibid., 43.
60 Ibid., 26.
61 Ibid., 50.
62 Karen Pinkus, 'The Risks of Sustainability', in *Criticism, Crisis, and Contemporary Narrative: Textual Horizons in an Age of Global Risk*, ed. Paul Crosthwaite (New York: Routledge, 2011), 74.
63 John Parham, 'Sustenance from the Past: Precedents to Sustainability in Nineteenth-Century Literature and Culture', in *Literature and Sustainability: Concept, Text and Culture*, ed. Adeline Johns-Putra, John Parham, and Louise Squire (Manchester: Manchester University Press, 2017), 40.
64 Rob Nixon, *Slow Violence and the Environmentalism of the Poor* (Cambridge, MA and London: Harvard University Press, 2011), 2.
65 Jesmyn Ward, *Men We Reaped: A Memoir* (2013; London: Bloomsbury, 2018), 250.

66 Christina Sharpe, *In the Wake: On Blackness and Being* (Durham and London: Duke University Press, 2016), 106.
67 Jesmyn Ward, *Salvage the Bones* (2011; London: Bloomsbury, 2017), 29.
68 Ibid., 83.
69 Ibid., 66.
70 Ibid., 58, 226.
71 Ibid., 236.
72 Ibid., 255.
73 Rebecca Tamás, *Strangers: Essays on the Human and Nonhuman* (London: Makina, 2020), 46.

Bibliography

Alaimo, Stacy. *Bodily Natures: Science, Environment, and the Material Self*. Bloomington: Indiana University Press, 2010.
Alaimo, Stacy. *Exposed: Environmental Politics and Pleasures in Posthuman Times*. Minneapolis and London: University of Minnesota Press, 2016.
Allen-Paisant, Jason. *Thinking with Trees*. Manchester: Carcanet, 2021.
Barad, Karen. *Meeting the Universe Halfway: Quantum Physics and the Entanglement of Matter and Meaning*. Durham and London: Duke University Press, 2007.
Bennett, Jane. *Vibrant Matter: A Political Ecology of Things*. Durham and London: Duke University Press, 2010.
Braidotti, Rosi. 'Four Theses on Posthuman Feminism'. In *Anthropocene Feminism*, edited by Richard Grusin, 21–48. Minneapolis and London: University of Minnesota Press, 2017.
Burnett, Elizabeth-Jane. *Of Sea*. London: Penned in the Margins, 2021.
Chen, Mel Y. *Animacies: Biopolitics, Racial Mattering, and Queer Affect*. Durham and London: Duke University Press, 2012.
Cohen, Jeffrey Jerome. 'Introduction: Ecostitial'. In *Inhuman Nature*, edited by Jeffrey Jerome Cohen, i–x. Washington, DC: Oliphaunt Books, 2014.
Coole, Diana H. and Samantha Frost. 'Introducing the New Materialisms'. In *New Materialisms: Ontology, Agency, and Politics*, edited by Diana H. Coole and Samantha Frost, 1–43. Durham and London: Duke University Press, 2010.
Doshi, Tishani. *A God at the Door*. Hexham: Bloodaxe, 2021.
Ghosh, Amitav. *The Great Derangement: Climate Change and the Unthinkable*. Chicago and London: University of Chicago Press, 2016.

Giraud, Eva Haifa. *What Comes after Entanglement? Activism, Anthropocentrism, and an Ethics of Exclusion*. Durham and London: Duke University Press, 2019.

Glotfelty, Cheryll. 'Introduction: Literary Studies in an Age of Environmental Crisis'. In *The Ecocriticism Reader: Landmarks in Literary Ecology*, edited by Cheryll Glotfelty and Harold Fromm, xv–xxxvii. Athens and London: University of Georgia Press, 1996.

Halberstam, Jack. *Wild Things: The Disorder of Desire*. Durham and London: Duke University Press, 2020.

Haraway, Donna J. *Staying with the Trouble: Making Kin in the Chthulucene*. Durham and London: Duke University Press, 2016.

Hewitt, Seán. *Tongues of Fire*. London: Jonathan Cape, 2020.

Hildyard, Daisy. *The Second Body*. London: Fitzcarraldo, 2017.

Hume, Angela. 'Introduction: Queering Ecopoetics'. *ISLE: Interdisciplinary Studies in Literature and Environment* 25, no. 1 (2018): 134–49.

Hume, Angela. 'Toward an Antiracist Ecopoetics: Waste and Wasting in the Poetry of Claudia Rankine'. *Contemporary Literature* 57, no. 1 (2016): 79–110.

Iovino, Serenella and Serpil Oppermann. 'Theorizing Material Ecocriticism: A Dipytch'. *ISLE: Interdisciplinary Studies in Literature and Environment* 19, no. 3 (2012): 448–75

Iovino, Serenella and Serpil Oppermann. 'Introduction: Stories Come to Matter'. In *Material Ecocriticism*, edited by Serenella Iovino and Serpil Oppermann, 1–17. Bloomington and Indianapolis: Indiana University Press, 2014.

Jones, Pattrice. 'Eros and the Mechanisms of Eco-Defense'. In *Ecofeminism: Feminist Intersections with Other Animals and the Earth*, edited by Carol J. Adams and Lori Gruen, 91–106. New York and London: Bloomsbury, 2014.

Keller, Catherine. *Cloud of the Impossible: Negative Theology and Planetary Entanglement*. New York: Columbia University Press, 2015.

Kimmerer, Robin Wall. *Braiding Sweetgrass: Indigenous Wisdom, Scientific Knowledge, and the Teachings of Plants*. Minneapolis: Milkweed Editions, 2013.

Mortimer-Sandilands, Catriona and Bruce Erickson. 'Introduction: A Genealogy of Queer Ecologies'. In *Queer Ecologies: Sex, Nature, Politics, Desire*, edited by Catriona Mortimer-Sandilands and Bruce Erickson, 1–47. Bloomington and Indianapolis: Indiana University Press, 2010.

Neimanis, Astrida. *Bodies of Water: Posthuman Feminist Phenomenology*. London: Bloomsbury Academic, 2019.

Nixon, Rob. *Slow Violence and the Environmentalism of the Poor.* Cambridge, MA, and London: Harvard University Press, 2011.

Parham, John. 'Sustenance from the Past: Precedents to Sustainability in Nineteenth-Century Literature and Culture'. In *Literature and Sustainability: Concept, Text and Culture,* edited by Adeline Johns-Putra, John Parham, and Louise Squire, 33–51. Manchester: Manchester University Press, 2017.

Pinkus, Karen. 'The Risks of Sustainability'. In *Criticism, Crisis, and Contemporary Narrative: Textual Horizons in an Age of Global Risk,* edited by Paul Crosthwaite, 62–77. New York: Routledge, 2011.

Rigby, Kate. *Dancing with Disaster: Environmental Histories, Narratives, and Ethics for Perilous Times.* Charlottesville and London: University of Virginia Press, 2015.

Seymour, Nicole. *Bad Environmentalism: Irony and Irreverence in the Ecological Age.* Minneapolis and London: University of Minnesota Press, 2018.

Sharpe, Christina. *In the Wake: On Blackness and Being.* Durham and London: Duke University Press, 2016.

Simpson, Leanne Betasamosake. *As We Have Always Done: Indigenous Freedom through Radical Resistance.* Minneapolis and London: University of Minnesota Press, 2017.

Smith, Zadie. *Grand Union.* London: Hamish Hamilton, 2019.

Tamás, Rebecca. *Strangers: Essays on the Human and Nonhuman.* London: Makina, 2020.

Todd, Zoe. 'An Indigenous Feminist's Take on the Ontological Turn: "Ontology" Is Just Another Word for Colonialism'. *Journal of Historical Sociology* 29, no. 1 (2016): 4–22.

Tsing, Anna Lowenhaupt. *The Mushroom at the End of the World: On the Possibility of Life in Capitalist Ruins.* Princeton and Oxford: Princeton University Press, 2015.

Vermeulen, Pieter. *Literature and the Anthropocene.* London and New York: Routledge, 2020.

Ward, Jesmyn. *Salvage the Bones.* 2011. London: Bloomsbury, 2017.

Ward, Jesmyn. *Men We Reaped: A Memoir.* 2013. London: Bloomsbury, 2018.

Yusoff, Kathryn. *A Billion Black Anthropocenes or None.* Minneapolis: University of Minnesota Press, 2018.

3

Medical Humanities

Marie Allitt

Life writing has a vital role in the field of medical humanities, centring the lived experiences of illness and giving voice to the unwell body. There has been a huge surge in writing first-person accounts of illness, or 'illness narratives', in the second half of the twentieth and early twenty-first centuries. This form has often sought to counter a perceived sense of objectification and depersonalization in biomedicine, and in particular the tendency for more attention given to disease rather than illness. The pathography – 'a form of autobiography or biography that describes personal experiences of illness, treatment, and sometimes death'[1] – has had a vital influence on the centring of the patient voice, which is regarded as the key identifier of the 'first wave' of medical humanities.[2] Access to such perspectives can enable patient-centred care, but more than that, it allows the patient to speak for themselves: 'Pathography restores the person ignored or canceled out in the medical enterprise ... it gives that ill person a voice.'[3] Illness narratives, especially those written by the ill person, are seen as acts of reclamation: reclaiming one's voice in the biomedical context, reclaiming one's own body, and reaching beyond the body.

We do not pay much attention to the body until it no longer does what we expect. In her essay collection *Constellations* (2019), which traces multiple experiences of illness and pain, including a total hip replacement and leukaemia, Sinéad Gleeson reminds us of the extent to which we take our bodies for granted and treat it as an 'afterthought':

> We don't stop to think of how the heart beats its steady rhythm; or watch our metatarsals fan out with every step. Unless it's involved in pleasure or pain, we pay this moving mass of vessel, blood and bone no mind. The lungs inflate, muscles contract, and there is no reason to assume they won't keep on doing so. Until one day, something changes: a corporeal blip. The body – its presence, its weight – is both an unignorable entity and routinely taken for granted.[4]

Like a device that stops working, we are not reminded of its fragility and complexity until it frustrates us. This is the general experience, but there are many who do not have the luxury of forgetting the vulnerabilities of their body and are forced to mask its flaws. Given that the body is at the centre of medicine, it is central to medical humanities scholarship. Patient narratives bring the subjectivity of the living body into the cultural and medical discourse; the unwell body can situate the location and intensity of pain, provide vital diagnostic elements through descriptions of sensations, articulate what might soothe and comfort, and crucially, speak back against the clinical systems which depersonalize and objectify bodies.

This chapter focuses on medical life writing, specifically illness narratives, highlighting some of the features in pathography from the late twentieth century up until today. Illness narratives encapsulate broader debates within the medical humanities about how to write about bodily experiences into language, how to give patients agency as narrators of their own pleasure and pain and how to find new forms for writing about the body that go beyond the limits of the medical case history. Illness narratives are an increasingly recognized genre of writing within contemporary literature, with recent examples particularly challenging preconceptions about life writing, and experimenting with fluidity and hybridity of form and genre, such as creative non-fiction, autofiction, essays and prose-poetry. Illness narratives, and medical life writing more broadly, are beginning to be taken more seriously and granted a deeper literary focus in recent years, a fact reinforced by Anne Boyer's cancer memoir, *The Undying*, winning the 2020 Pulitzer Prize for General Non-fiction. I centre the illness narrative as a significant example of contemporary literature and the body as both the foundational rock for the authority of the patient voice and its continual evolution as a reminder that we must continue to listen to the patient, to their voice, and put the body front and centre.

Early interventions in medical humanities aimed, as Anne Whitehead and Angela Woods explain, 'to produce a shift in clinical method towards attending to and interpreting patients' subjective experience as well as scientific knowledge and data'.[5] Medical humanities thus far has shown the importance of the patient's point of view, by demonstrating the entangled importance of how embodied and phenomenological knowledge must work with scientific and biological details.[6] Re-centring the voice and the body in pain serves to destabilize power binaries that set the clinical world against the person in need of care. While illness narratives have been integrated into medical education as a way to widen the viewpoint of future doctors, there has been wider cultural and critical response to such narratives that have shown the complexities of care, pain and suffering beyond the purely medical context: the patient voice shines a spotlight on difficult dynamics among families, shortcomings in social care, and the treatment of and preconceptions about illness and bodily dysfunction in society.

The pathography is also motivated by the need to tell one's story and orientate oneself in a world that has changed as a result. Anne Hunsaker Hawkins's *Reconstructing Illness* (1993) highlights the significance of telling one's story as a way to make sense of the sequence of events:

> Pathographies concern the attempts of individuals to orient themselves in the world of sickness ... to achieve a new balance between self and reality, to arrive at an objective relationship both to experience and to the experiencing self. The task of the author of a pathography is not only to describe this disordering process but also to restore to reality its lost coherence and to discover, or create, a meaning that can bind it together again.[7]

Hawkins describes a desire to write and create a narrative out of complex and chaotic experiences. However, the latter part of this statement does not feel as applicable to more recent conceptualizations of the pathography. I argue that we no longer see narratives as primarily attempting to recover coherence, order and chronology. Instead, recent pathographies consciously challenge representation, even disrupt coherence and chronology, and situate the body within histories and futures of experience. Recent illness narratives offer a sustained focus on chronic illnesses, exhibiting in turn, not illness as an interruption but as a reality of everyday life. This move on the one hand shows us how such illnesses and conditions are diagnostically on the rise and are receiving greater visibility but also demonstrates the extent to which lifelong illnesses and disabilities are poorly understood, accommodated or recognized by society.

The 1980s and 1990s saw a particular surge in personal narratives of illness, especially on the subject of cancer and mental illness, followed by influential scholarship, which has been vital to the expansion of the genre in contemporary works. Arthur Kleinman's *The Illness Narratives* (1988) offered early insight into the importance of story and creating narratives out of illness experiences, while the scholarship of Anne Hunsaker Hawkins and Arthur W. Frank's formative *The Wounded Storyteller* (1995) developed the wider framework of pathographical narrative theory. Hawkins and Frank provide typologies of pathographies, which have dominated many of the critical engagements with pathography to date. In situating the body more firmly in this discourse, G. Thomas Couser's *Recovering Bodies: Illness, Disability, and Life Writing* (1997) offers what he deems a more appropriate term, 'autopathography', which heightens 'awareness of one's mortality, threatening one's sense of identity, and disrupting the apparent plot of one's life'.[8] This anchors the pathography in the first person and the personal, highlighting the centrality of the body as fundamental to experience, and crucially provides more specific engagement with disability. However, in his 2011 *Memoir: An Introduction*, Couser recants his use of 'autopathography', recognizing that the 'path' was too narrowing a term and assumes the writers' life is defined by their illness or disability.[9] This might explain why 'pathography' has been used less; Couser later adopts the term 'autosomatography' which is more inclusive of different bodies and is perhaps more applicable to recent examples of illness and disability writing.

Further developments in this scholarship concern ways in which we read texts, what attention we give them, and how much we consider narrative as giving us access to experience. Ann Jurecic's *Illness as Narrative* (2012) offers key interventions for how literary scholars critique illness narratives. While Kleinman, Frank, Hawkins and Rita Charon have elucidated common narrative patterns that appear in illness narratives, there is the risk of overlooking representation and conflating the narrative with genuine access to the experience. Jurecic argues 'that one cannot fully understand writing about illness without recognizing the split in critical attitudes toward these works'.[10] Whether the work resists or challenges the hermeneutic impulse, it still requires an act of interpretation. Potentially the labels given to such works make a difference, whether they are categorized as biographies, autobiographies, memoirs, testimonies, pathographies or somatographies may affect our sense of the text's authority. However, given the inconsistencies in identifying the genre and its increased fluidity and hybridity, the critical framework brought to bear on the text becomes more important than ever. More recently Stella Bolaki's *Illness as Many Narratives* (2016) reminds us that we should keep the definition of narrative open and not stick rigidly to textual narratives, a point that is exemplified by the rise in graphic medicine and visual and embodied storytelling.

Recent illness narratives have deconstructed and rebuilt the genre, adapting forms and subject matter to express personal experiences of illness which cannot be divorced from how society sees such bodies. The topics of recent memoirs foreground chronic and lifelong conditions in particular, coinciding with the increased broader cultural visibility of endometriosis, fibromyalgia, chronic fatigue syndrome, irritable bowel syndrome and chronic pain. These developments in content and form have opened up opportunities for different bodies and bodily experiences to find space to speak: bodies and experiences shaped by race, disability, gender, sexuality, geography and politics. Such attempts seem to extend Frank's observation that 'the ill body's articulation in stories is a personal task, but the stories told by the ill are also *social*',[11] and further enact this social momentum. In this chapter, I offer readings of three pathographies which can be seen to challenge the idea of autobiography as an individual narrative, attempting to make space for communities of unwell voices; Audre Lorde's *The Cancer Journals* (1980), Patrick Anderson's *Autobiography of a Disease* (2017) and Molly McCully Brown's *Places I've Taken My Body* (2020). I suggest that the varying forms of the pathography enable writers to step outside of their bodies. Bodies are not eclipsed, but these narratives focus on how the world influences that bodily experience; how environment, society, politics, healthcare, employment and life events shape one's access to the world.

Finding selves and selfhood: Audre Lorde's *The Cancer Journals* (1980)

In the oft-discussed and foundational *The Cancer Journals*, Audre Lorde both draws on and departs from a conventional pathography structure. Lorde describes how she grapples with breast cancer and recovery in intensely physical terms. One of the late twentieth-century pathographies, and in many ways considered one of its kind for a long time, Lorde's text can also be seen to foreshadow and influence more recent illness narratives.

The nature of illness, in this case cancer, means the loss of bodily control and autonomy. After surgical intervention, Lorde feels that she has 'ceased being a person who is myself and become a thing upon a Guerney cart'.[12] This sense of loss and transformation to an object chimes with many patient experiences, especially, as Frank argues, due to the clinical gaze and the objectification that is often a result of modern biomedical practices.[13] Crucial to Lorde's narrative is her identity as a Black woman, as a lesbian, and as a breast cancer 'survivor'. She yearns for a community of women in the same position as her and is repulsed by the discourse of perfectibility and the expectation of covering up one's illness. Lorde frames this pathography as a much-needed outlet for her feelings but crucially desires usefulness: 'I had known the pain, and survived it. It only remained for me to give it voice, to share it for use, that the pain not be wasted.'[14] Lorde does not present a linear narrative from symptoms, diagnosis, treatment and recovery; instead her narrative moves between her perspective 18 months after her mastectomy and accounts of her experience during her treatment, recorded in diary entries. She offers a curated reflection that demonstrates contradictory viewpoints as well as feelings that are re-evaluated at a later point.

Her earlier words are woven alongside more recent reflections, layering her voice to provide insight into her evolving, changed and unchanged perspectives, as well as demonstrating changes within herself. Lorde must reconcile herself to an identity that is irrevocably changed because '[a]ny amputation is a physical and psychic reality that must be integrated into a new sense of self'.[15] But this *sense* of self is under threat from the pain and the memory of that pain; she finds in her diary a familiar urgency for release: 'I must let this pain flow through me and pass on. If I resist or try to stop it, it will detonate inside me, shatter me, splatter my pieces against every wall and person that I touch.'[16] What she needs in order to create a new self is a community of similar bodies from whom she can learn and share her experiences. But there is silence and an absence of bodies like hers: 'Where were the dykes who had had mastectomies? I wanted to talk to a lesbian, to sit down and start from a common language, no matter how diverse. I wanted to share dykeinsight, so to speak.'[17] Lorde foregrounds how her experience as a woman is tied to her sexuality and her breasts are fundamental to her place in the world. The invisibility of breast loss, Lorde shows, is harmful. For women in her position, the support offered contributes to a discourse of 'breast cancer as a cosmetic problem'[18] to be remedied with prostheses. Lorde sees this as a nostalgia and denial of what is an increasing reality for women. She refuses to wear a prosthesis or cover her body 'simply because it might make a woman-phobic world more comfortable',[19] arguing that what is needed is the visibility of cancer and all that comes with it: 'If we are to translate the silence surrounding breast cancer into language and action against this scourge, then the first step is that women with mastectomies become visible to each other.'[20] Lorde translates her pain and experience into a call for action and appeal to endure it all.

Lisa Diedrich argues that 1980 'mark[s] the emergence of a new figure – the politicized patient – and a new genre – the patient's counternarrative to medical discourse'[21] amidst the increasing activism, in the United States especially, with the respective women's health, AIDs and breast cancer movements. Lorde epitomizes the 'writer-activist'[22] position. However, as Diedrich continues, this 'emergent politicization', by the 1990s, 'gets covered over by a neoliberal mode of being ill and doing illness that emphasizes the discourses and practices of personal responsibility in matters of health'.[23] Despite the continuing focus on personal responsibility, the politicized patient has not gone away, and I argue, is re-emerging in contemporary pathographies and somatographies with the

increasing desire to share knowledge and insight in communities
of the unwell. There is a growing commitment in many modern
accounts of illness and disability to offering a range of perspectives
and to emphasizing the collective nature of these experiences; the
message that underpins Lorde's *The Cancer Journals*, as well as
many of the more modern pathographies that she inspired, is that
no one heals alone.

The pull of the I: Patrick Anderson's *Autobiography of a Disease* (2017)

How do you describe your illness experience when you were not
conscious or lucid during much of it? Patrick Anderson addresses
this question, among others, with his experimentation with point of
view. *Autobiography of a Disease* depicts his real-life experience with
life-threatening *Staphylococcus aureus* (MRSA) osteomyelitis and,
as the title suggests, is narrated from the point of view of bacteria.
This is a medical it-narrative, which is not only experimental in
style but also defamiliarizes and distorts bodily knowledge in order
to offer a new way of articulating the experience of illness.

In his Foreword Anderson tells us that 'I wanted to know and
understand what was happening – both for my own sake, and out
of anthropological curiosity – but I could not depend upon my
own capacity for knowing or understanding'.[24] How can we tell
our own experiences, Anderson asks, when so many actors play
a part? Especially in the context of severe illness, with lengthy
hospitalizations and surgeries, the personal perspective is inevitably
limited. Anderson's response is extensive and experimental: 'this
book takes something of a radical leap: it distributes agency of
narration – the power to describe – not just to the many human
actors involved in treatment and care-taking, but also to the
non-sentient beings involved in the practice of being-ill'.[25] Most
of the text is written in free indirect discourse, offering glimpses
of the inner feelings of not only Patrick but also those around him.
The text is split into six parts, with an 'Interlude' between each,
which are self-consciously from the perspective of the bacteria,
providing an opportunity for them to reflect on their role as part of
the broader story and relate their infectious history.

We slip in and out of the bacteria's point of view, from an omniscience in the free indirect discourse outside of the body, to the bacteria's omniscience inside the body, creating a narrative style that could be regarded as autofiction. For example, in the main text, one of the doctors describes the infected bone as 'mottled, like lace';[26] the Interlude that follows a few pages later responds to this analogy directly: *'They struck us as lovely, both the word and the object it described: Lace. What a perfect way to characterize the way we'd made room for ourselves, created space,'*[27] which suggests that the bacteria can hear, and understand to a degree, what is happening around the body. As a genre, autofiction is 'a form of autobiographical writing that permits a degree of experimentation with the definition and limits of the self, rather than the slavish recapitulation of known biographical facts'.[28] Anderson's adoption of the non-sentient focalization epitomizes this experimentation with the limits of the self. The narrative is framed 'not as a patient's monologue or biography, but as a profoundly social, richly durational, and multiply perspectival encounter'.[29] It is ultimately socially constructed, just as the body's experience in the world is always dependent on social, political and cultural factors. Examples of prolepsis demonstrate the extent to which Anderson could not access his own experiences: 'Later they [medical staff] told him that he would never remember it all, that what they called a side effect of his condition was to lose his grasp of what had happened, perhaps to recall certain details here and there, but never the story as a whole.'[30] Despite existing within the bounds of his body, the story of his body is out of his reach.

The world that Anderson builds relies heavily on the notes his mother kept throughout. Early on, his mother, Deirdre, is encouraged to '[w]rite it down. You have to write it down. All of it'[31] by the mother of another patient. This woman shares with Deirdre her book

> covered in what seemed an unknown language: numbers and graphs, long unpronounceable words, pictures of wounds … filled with hospital desiderata: temperature and blood pressure readings, quantities of pills and dosage times, the names of hypothesized conditions, medical license numbers, insurance contacts. She had chronicled weeks of her son's convalescence, a portrait in data of illness, but also an archive of not-knowing.[32]

She tells Deirdre that in keeping such records '[i]t keeps me from having to remember. And a few times, I've stopped them from killing him. One of them tried to give him a shot he'd already had';[33] the 'archive of not-knowing' could literally save his life. After this, Deirdre records all the details relating to Patrick's condition: this chronicle contributes to his records, though significantly, not wholly reliant on the doctors' viewpoint. The ways in which a patient's story is encoded in the official medical record is outside the control of the patient.

Anderson's story is ultimately one of mysterious infection. The story demonstrates a connection with the beginnings of AIDs decades earlier. Anderson is a gay man, and when at first the doctors are unsure of what is going on with his body, they broach the conversation of testing his HIV status, seeking his permission for a full viral DNA test. His status remains HIV negative, but it is a spectre that does not disappear from the text. Later, he is treated in one of the early AIDs centres; 'Its halls steeped in suffering, San Francisco General is one of the most important public places around. Ward 5B was made famous when HIV struck, the first clinical site dedicated to tracking and treating those who had been drawn into that viral flow.'[34] The spectre emerges yet again at this new hospital, where a conversation with his new nurse Delilah unearths the cold truth of his medical record:

> 'First sentence in your medical history includes the word homosexual. Why?' she asked the ceiling, 'why in the world would they put that here?' She shook her head again. 'Sorry. It's just, people like you and me haven't had the best of luck with that kind of record-keeping.'
>
> 'I had no idea that was in there.'
>
> 'Of course not. Another reason to be furious.' ... 'People aren't even involved in how they're recorded. Makes my blood boil.'[35]

It is hard not to see the prejudice and stigmatization in this depiction: while patients have little say in how their records depict them this detail speaks to wider prejudices within medicine and care. A label is imposed upon his body without his input. The medical record often runs counter to the patient's voice and yet is all about the patient's body. The pathography, or somatography, is the effort to push against this view, and Anderson's narrative is a creative example of how a co-constructed narrative that incorporates many different voices can disrupt the form of medical case histories.

Compilation and community: Molly McCully Brown's *Places I've Taken My Body* (2020)

One of the most rapidly growing areas of personal writings is that of the essay, interchangeably labelled personal essays, lyric essays, or more generally encapsulated under creative non-fiction. Molly McCully Brown's *Places I've Taken My Body* is just one example of this exciting and invigorating trend, offering insight into her experiences with cerebral palsy. Ann Jurecic argues that despite the continued influence of such important essays as Virginia Woolf's 'On Being Ill' (1926) and Susan Sontag's *Illness as Metaphor* (1979), there has been far less critical focus on the essay genre in illness writings and compels us 'to pay attention to the illness essay'.[36] Given the flourishing of creative non-fiction and the wider critical engagement with these emerging forms, the time has certainly come to engage more specifically with different styles and genres of illness writing and medical life writing.

What is it about the essay which creates fertile ground for the telling of personal stories? In a discussion on 'What Should an Essay Do?' Leslie Jamison explains that '[i]nstead of telling the straight story of memoir, they say: *This is the story of how my mind moves*'.[37] The essay proposes a new way of telling one's story – giving licence to exploration and making space for the complexities of representations of memory and truth. The essay form 'is by turns elusive, imagistic, ecstatic, discontinuous, and melodic, more often circling, symbolizing, and echoing life events than writing them out in causal, chronological ways',[38] resisting the expected structuring of autobiography. Existing and perhaps more traditional modes of memoir and life writing presume the writer already has the answers to their questions: in many cases that they know how a particular life event or situation ends. Creative non-fiction, however, allows the writer to explore what they do not yet know about their experience; because '[r]evelation, or discovery, emerges organically from the writing',[39] the essay can reveal the self, the body and the experience *to* the writer.

The relationship between individual essays and the wider collection is also important. Each essay can connect and overlap, building an overall narrative, or enabling contradiction and revision as a route to more fully working through and representing certain experiences. Vitally, it resists plot and resists the concept of the journey – already an uncomfortable concept in the discourse of chronic illness and disability. In discussing the essay collections of Nancy Mairs, Susannah B. Mintz suggests that 'the disjointed and open-ended structure of essay collections textually manifests Mairs's own disrupted corporeality, while at the same time working as a corrective to the closure of traditional autobiography and the stable subject narrated therein'.[40] The essay collection can be a productive form to explore one's own experience, while simultaneously critiquing the possibilities previously afforded by autobiography. Mintz further shows that '[e]ssay collections allow Mairs to create heterogeneous "bodies" of writing that range through memory, experience, and location in a way that simultaneously suspends the progress-narrative of classic autobiographical prose and evokes the open-ended corporeal reality of living with multiple sclerosis'.[41] The open-endedness is significant, enabling re-visitations of experiences, and suggests that autobiographical writings about disabled bodies are more like 'works-in-progress'[42] than an outright memoir or story of one's life: narratives born out of constant re-evaluations of one's body and relationship with the world.

The essay form gives McCully Brown, as it does for Mairs, opportunities to depict the inconsistencies of life: of the ups and downs in her relationship with her body, and the world's relationship with her disability, particularly in clinical contexts. Models of reading and understanding illness narratives can be greatly enriched by engaging more fully with disability studies, especially as we see so many contemporary illness narratives depicting chronic illnesses which may be read or interpreted as disabilities. Crucially, the ingredients of the lyric essay, or creative non-fiction more broadly, allow the narrative to go beyond one's own experiences and, as Mintz argues, avoid the narcissism which intense pain often generates.[43] Brenda Miller describes the use of 'peripheral-vision' in creative non-fiction: 'turning the gaze to focus on something that seems peripheral to the emotional center or ostensible topic. Instead of facing your "stuff" head on, you turn away from it, zero in on something that has fluttered up on the side, and see what angle it gives you'.[44] This strategy gives the essay form a unique perspective: a useful way in which to place the body off-centre but keep focused on one's place in the world.

One of the essays in McCully Brown's collection, 'The Virginia State Colony for Epileptics and Feebleminded', concerns the Central Virginia Training Center, a site near her school which she regularly passed by during her childhood but did not visit until she was eighteen. She 'knew vaguely that it was a residential facility for people with serious disabilities, and that it had a complicated history, tangled up with Appalachia, eugenics, and the Great Depression'.[45] It was 'a government-run residential hospital for people with serious mental and physical disabilities', and although there are few records of the men and women treated there, evidence indicates that involuntary sterilization practices, based on eugenicist philosophies, took place.[46] Those people who were released and went on to live independently often had no idea what had been done to them: no record of the bodily invasions. McCully Brown braids this historical detail with her personal accounts of her own bodily experience, recognizing that at least she has 'a record of every time a surgeon cut me open – the names of things that doctors declared wrong with me, the parts of me they've altered. I've lived my whole life with these catalogs'.[47] Legacies of the language used to categorize and describe her body have stayed with her just as much as the interventions themselves: even if the methods have evolved, it is hard to shake off the embedded structures of feeling: 'The more I learned, the less important and extraordinary my own individual pain seemed. Instead, the history from which my life extends came more sharply into focus: Much of the language I have for understanding my own body and brain is a permutation of vocabulary nurtured in the Colony.'[48] Even though it had played on her mind ever since she saw it first-hand, it was not until after college that McCully Brown could write about it: 'I turned toward trying to write about the Colony partly out of reflexive impulse to return to that landscape. But I was also casting around for something that mattered: a way to contribute, to understand and articulate the histories of brains and bodies like mine. A way to face myself as I truly was.'[49] In this essay, she pays tribute to those who could not speak for themselves, who never had the chance. Through her writing, she seeks to give voice to this silenced group of people who were treated at the Colony yet she is, at the same time, highly aware of the paradoxes and problems of this role as their interlocutor. If she could, she would dictate the words of those gone before, but there are no traces and no echoes. She cannot write their stories for them, but she creates a poetry collection in response, hoping 'that they might be an act of kinship'.[50] This 'act of kinship' is reminiscent of Lorde's need to 'pass [it] on', to counter the silence, share the knowledge and make bodies visible.

The braided essay technique that McCully Brown employs affords a way into such stories which can pay attention to those who have come before. The braiding technique weaves and alternates the strands of different stories and 'by multiplying pathways into a subject and allowing meaning to accrue across white space'[51] it builds towards understanding for how contrasting episodes relate to one another. This effect in particular allows for the history of bodies beyond the individual: 'a way for research and outside voices to intertwine with one's own voice and experience'.[52] Running through McCully Brown's collection is her account of her writing residency in Bologna, where she visits the anatomical theatre and engages with its history as one of the oldest anatomical schools. Here, she cannot help but feel its import and legacy in her own body, especially when her peripheral vision sees sculptures of splayed bodies on the walls: 'My own body feels skinless, rubbed raw. I imagine it, butterflied, on the marble table: brain and heart, liver and lungs, muscles and tendons all laid bare, all my brain's bad wiring in evidence, thickets of scar tissue every place a surgeon has reshaped me over the years.'[53] In the essay, 'The Skin I'm In', she acknowledges the bodies before her, that were abused, entrapped and experimented upon, which has led to the treatment that she has received: 'I owe the current shape of my body, almost every inch of mobility I've ever had, to scores of people taken apart without their consent, people no one cared enough to name or suture into any kind of remade whole once they had taken what they could.'[54] For McCully Brown, the most significant legacies of medical innovation are not told through the accounts of surgeons, but on and through the bodies that came before, which enabled knowledge to develop, but have no way to speak.

The body speaks

The significance of illness narratives, whether we label them a pathography or autosomatography, lies in their commitment to exploring the problems and possibilities of articulating the voices of patients. But, crucially, it is not a disembodied voice, and as we read such texts, we must also look to the body and allow it to speak for itself and for others. However, the person in pain often has to search for the words and answers themselves: they have to trawl the archives of suffering to find kinship – to scream out to be heard by others in the same position. In another essay collection, depicting the experiences of chronic pain, *Pain Woman Takes Your Keys and Other Essays from a Nervous System* (2017), Sonya Huber offers a profound insight into what this means by explaining that '[w]hen we name our symptoms accurately with words and confirm what the other is also feeling, we are doing research with our bodies as instruments'.[55] Huber shows that putting the illness experience into words is an act of communion. In some ways, the communication of such experiences, and the 'research', speaks to an ethnographic and autoethnographic urge to uncover answers and share knowledge with those who may not be able to access it. Giving voice to the bodily experience requires certain degrees of knowledge: knowledge which comprises the medical discourse of diagnosis as well as the non-clinical insight of experience. To gain this knowledge bodies are forced to undertake an autoethnography: to use their 'bodies as instruments'.

Anderson's *Autobiography of a Disease* also speaks to this ethnographic pull: 'I found myself deeply immersed in an accidental ethnography of what goes by the name of "care" in contemporary US medical practice.'[56] His 'anthropological curiosity' looks increasingly like a survival mechanism, to self-inform while also sharing and cautioning others who may find themselves in the same position. It is this pull towards ethnography that underpins some of the hybridity and fluidity of the genre in further recent works. Sarah Ramey's *The Lady's Handbook for Her Mysterious Illness* (2020), for example, draws together stories of others alongside her own fight for answers about their unknown or misunderstood conditions. Ann Cvetkovich's *Depression: A Public Feeling* (2012) and Jaipreet Virdi's *Hearing Happiness: Deafness Cures in History*

(2020) offer depictions of depression and deafness, respectively, in texts which hybridize the personal and the academic, underscoring the ethnographic drive that emerges from their lived experiences.

While personal narratives of illness and medicine are increasingly seen as important in medical contexts, the pathography, somatography or illness narrative compels a particular literary dimension to medical humanities. Literary medical humanities has distinct tools to critically engage with such foundational medical and health narratives and can situate patient counternarratives within a cultural and literary context. It is important that pathographies – especially the increasingly experimental forms – are not divorced from their literary contexts and that we continue to recognize that bodily sensations and somatic experiences are far from easy to put into words. As well as relating the clinical and illness experiences from the patient point of view, such texts expand our linguistic repertoire to articulate somatic sensations and push against the conventional images and language we use to describe, for example, pain, or dimensions of selfhood and identity, broadening not only our somatic vocabularies but re-framing preconceptions about bodies and experience. Bringing the medical humanities lens to literature more broadly can reveal the different ways that medicine and health are experienced and represented and expand articulations and understandings of the body.

There is no duty to share one's story, or to monetize one's pain, and speaking on behalf of others is not without its ethical challenges. Yet there is much to be gained by entering into dialogue with other bodies and other experiences of illness. In an increasingly neoliberal world, where we are constantly pushed to take personal responsibility for our own health, and access to healthcare often bankrupts the recipient of necessary care, the role of the illness narrative in creating and contributing to collective movements and sharing experiences is more important than ever. Many of the works that I have discussed in this chapter are concerned with creating communities and capturing multiple voices through experimentation with language and form, such as the 'braided' essays of McCully Brown and the autofiction of Anderson. The pathography has long held an activist edge, as I have argued in relation to Lorde's foundational *The Cancer Journals*, but now it must do the work of countering and undoing ingrained structures of medical paternalism which have run free of healthcare settings and permeated all aspects of society. The drive to make us take responsibility for our health is quickly becoming a drive to have us take responsibility for our care, and illness narratives have a vital role in countering the individualizing and isolating of bodily experiences.

Notes

1   Anne Hunsaker Hawkins, *Reconstructing Illness: Studies in Pathography* (1993; West Lafayette, Ind.: Purdue University Press, 1999), 1.
2   Anne Whitehead and Angela Woods, 'Introduction', in *The Edinburgh Companion to the Critical Medical Humanities* (Edinburgh: Edinburgh University Press, 2016), 1.
3   Hawkins, *Reconstructing Illness*, 12.
4   Sinéad Gleeson, *Constellations* (London: Picador, 2019), 1.
5   Whitehead and Woods, 'Introduction', 4.
6   Des Fitzgerald and Felicity Callard, 'Entangling the Medical Humanities', in *The Edinburgh Companion to the Critical Medical Humanities*, 36–47.
7   Hawkins, *Reconstructing Illness*, 2–3.
8   G. Thomas Couser, *Recovering Bodies: Illness, Disability, and Life Writing* (Madison: University of Wisconsin Press, 1997), 5.
9   Couser, *Memoir: An Introduction* (Oxford: Oxford University Press, 2011), 44.
10 Ann Jurecic, *Illness as Narrative* (Pittsburgh: University of Pittsburgh Press, 2012), 3.
11 Arthur Frank, *The Wounded Storyteller: Body, Illness, and Ethics* (1995; Chicago: The University of Chicago Press, 2013), 3.
12 Audre Lorde, *The Cancer Journals* (1980; New York: Penguin Books, 2020), 28.
13 Arthur Kleinman, *The Illness Narratives: Suffering, Healing and the Human Condition* (N.p: Basic Books, 1988), 5.
14 Lorde, *The Cancer Journals*, 9.
15 Ibid.
16 Ibid., 4.
17 Ibid., 42.
18 Ibid., 48.
19 Ibid., 53.
20 Ibid., 54.
21 Lisa Diedrich, *Treatments: Language, Politics, and the Culture of Illness* (Minneapolis: University of Minnesota Press, 2007), 26.
22 Ibid., 26.

23 Ibid., 27.
24 Patrick Anderson, *Autobiography of a Disease* (New York and London: Routledge, 2017), iix.
25 Ibid., ix.
26 Ibid., 69.
27 Ibid., 84. Italics in original.
28 Hywel Dix, 'Introduction', in *Autofiction in English* (Cham.: Springer International Publishing; Palgrave Macmillan, 2018), 3.
29 Anderson, *Autobiography of a Disease*, ix.
30 Ibid., 12.
31 Ibid., 13.
32 Ibid., 14.
33 Ibid.
34 Ibid., 106.
35 Ibid., 110.
36 Ann Jurecic, 'The Illness Essay', *Life Writing* 13, no. 1 (2016): 15–16.
37 Leslie Jamison, 'What Should an Essay Do?', *The New Republic*, 8 July 2013, n.p.
38 Susannah B. Mintz, 'On a Scale from 1 to 10: Life Writing and Lyrical Pain', *Journal of Literary & Cultural Studies* 5, no. 3 (2011): 245.
39 Brenda Miller, '"Lions and Tigers and Bears, Oh My!": Courage and Creative Nonfiction', in *Bending Genre: Essays on Creative Nonfiction*, ed. Margot Singer and Nicole Walker (New York: Bloomsbury, 2013), 104.
40 Mintz, *Unruly Bodies: Life Writing by Women with Disabilities* (Chapel Hill: University of North Carolina Press, 2007), 18.
41 Ibid., 27.
42 Ibid., 4.
43 Mintz, 'On a Scale from 1 to 10', 250.
44 Ibid., 107.
45 Molly McCully Brown, *Places I've Taken My Body* (2020; New York and London: Faber & Faber, 2021), 93.
46 Ibid., 80, 99.
47 Ibid., 98–9.
48 Ibid., 103.
49 Ibid., 102.
50 Ibid., 104.
51 Jennifer Sinor, 'Deserting the Narrative Line: Teaching the Braided Form', TETYC (2014), 189.
52 Brenda Miller and Suzanne Paola, *Tell It Slant: Creating, Refining, and Publishing Creative Nonfiction* (New York: McGraw Hill, 2019), 127.

53 McCully Brown, *Places I've Taken My Body*, 79.
54 Ibid., 80.
55 Sonya Huber, *Pain Woman Takes Your Keys and Other Essays from a Nervous System* (Lincoln & London: University of Nebraska Press, 2017), 34.
56 Anderson, *Autobiography of a Disease*, iix.

Bibliography

Anderson, Patrick. *Autobiography of a Disease*. New York and London: Routledge, 2017.

Bolaki, Stella. *Illness as Many Narratives: Arts, Medicine and Culture*. Edinburgh: Edinburgh University Press, 2016.

Cvetkovich, Ann. *Depression: A Public Feeling*. Durham, NC, and London: Duke University Press, 2012.

Couser, G. Thomas. *Memoir: An Introduction*. Oxford: Oxford University Press, 2011.

Couser, G. Thomas. *Recovering Bodies: Illness, Disability, and Life Writing*. Madison: University of Wisconsin Press, 1997.

Diedrich, Lisa. *Treatments: Language, Politics, and the Culture of Illness*. Minneapolis: University of Minnesota Press, 2007.

Dix, Hywel, ed. *Autofiction in English*. Cham: Springer International Publishing; Palgrave Macmillan, 2018.

Frank, Arthur W. *The Wounded Storyteller: Body, Illness, and Ethics*. 1995; Chicago: The University of Chicago Press, 2013.

Gleeson, Sinéad. *Constellations*. London: Picador, 2019.

Hawkins, Anne Hunsaker. *Reconstructing Illness: Studies in Pathography*. 1993; West Lafayette, IN: Purdue University Press, 1999.

Huber, Sonya. *Pain Woman Takes Your Keys and Other Essays from a Nervous System*. Lincoln and London: University of Nebraska Press, 2017.

Jamison, Leslie. 'What Should an Essay Do?'. *The New Republic*. 8 July 2013.

Jurecic, Ann. *Illness as Narrative*. Pittsburgh: University of Pittsburgh Press, 2012.

Jurecic, Ann. 'The Illness Essay'. *Life Writing* 13, no. 1 (2016): 13–26.

Kleinman, Arthur. *The Illness Narratives: Suffering, Healing and the Human Condition*. N.p: Basic Books, 1988.

Lorde, Audre. *The Cancer Journals*. New York: Penguin Books, 2020.

McCully Brown, Molly. *Places I've Taken My Body*. New York and London: Faber & Faber, 2021.

Miller, Brenda. '"Lions and Tigers and Bears, Oh My!": Courage
    and Creative Nonfiction'. In *Bending Genre: Essays on Creative
    Nonfiction*, edited by Margot Singer and Nicole Walker, 102–10.
    New York: Bloomsbury, 2013.
Miller, Brenda and Suzanne Paola. *Tell It Slant: Creating, Refining, and
    Publishing Creative Nonfiction*. New York: McGraw Hill, 2019.
Mintz, Susannah B. *Unruly Bodies: Life Writing by Women with
    Disabilities*. Chapel Hill: University of North Carolina Press, 2007.
Mintz, Susannah B. 'On a Scale from 1 to 10: Life Writing and Lyrical
    Pain'. *Journal of Literary & Cultural Studies* 5, no. 3 (2011): 243–60.
Ramey, Sarah. *The Lady's Handbook for Her Mysterious Illness*. London:
    Fleet, 2020.
Sinor, Jennifer. 'Deserting the Narrative Line: Teaching the Braided Form'.
    TETYC (2014): 188–96.
Virdi, Jaipreet. *Hearing Happiness: Deafness Cures in History*. Chicago:
    University of Chicago Press, 2020.
Whitehead, Anne, Angela Woods, Sarah Atkinson, Jane Macnaughton,
    and Jennifer Richards, eds. *The Edinburgh Companion to the Critical
    Medical Humanities*. Edinburgh: Edinburgh University Press, 2016.

4

Electronic Literature

Elizabeth Losh

For many decades, electronic literature was best known for producing works in emerging genres that were designed primarily for desktop computers. Text and images usually appeared on a monitor positioned in front of the user. Although the experience of reading might require input from a keyboard or mouse that disrupted conventions about how the text was delivered for consumption by the eye, the substitution of screen for page did not radically reconfigure the relationship between the reader's body and textual discourse, as the user progressed through her or his literary encounter with either a two-D hypertext page or a one-D output line of code.

This did not mean that the body was not a matter of concern for pioneering digital authors. It might even be a central topic in a work, as is the case in Shelley Jackson's *My Body – a Wunderkammer* (1997), in which the main navigation presents the reader with a choice of rectangles focused on different parts of a woman's body. In exploring the different anatomical segments represented by woodcut illustrations, the reader learns intimate details about the narrator's embodied experiences, such as what it feels like to have a nostril pierced or to be surprised by tender nipples during puberty.

With a similar interest in fragmented subjectivity, Juliet Davis's *Pieces of Herself* (2005) uses the trope of dressed-up paper dolls to structure a journey that interrogates the central figure's sex, gender and female identity by constructing a massive collage selected from hundreds of digital photographs and audio clips.

Using a drag-and-drop game interface, viewers scroll through conventional environments for gender play to collect 'pieces' of the self and arrange them inside an outline of a female body. As each piece enters the representation of feminine corporeality, it triggers audio derived from interviews with women, music loops or sound effects. Inspired by 'Elizabeth Grosz's theories about embodiment', the author describes *Pieces of Herself* as a comment upon the 'social inscription of the body'.[1]

Speaking from a position of masculine dominance, the narrator in Serge Bouchardon's *Opacity / Opacité* (2012) expresses his desire to make transparent all the mysteries 'hiding' from him inside his wife's interior life. By erasing pixels from an image of a woman with a naked torso, in coordinating action from the cursor to the screen, the reader participates in the husband's digital autopsy. As layers are removed, the organs in her circulatory, digestive, reproductive and nervous systems are gradually exposed as the husband's male gaze penetrates successive layers of her elaborate biology. Even as he delves deeper into this visible woman, her anatomy remains illegible and refuses meaning both to the narrator and to the reader.[2]

Although all these works reflect upon the nature of embodiment, particularly female experiences of embodiment from the position of 'this sex which is not one',[3] these compositions rely on technologies of representation that can reduce all the potential stimuli of the human sensorium to a lexicon of programming code. For example, an MP3 file can play sound, and a JPEG file can display an image, but both encode information as written text. According to Katherine Hayles, a leading scholar of electronic literature, the invention of computational media in the middle of the twentieth century caused information to 'lose its body' because the pattern of signifiers that encoded data did not depend on a particular medium. In *How We Became Posthuman* (1999), Hayles alerts her readers to the potential consequences of this new disembodied condition: 'Because information had lost its body, this construction implied that embodiment is not essential to human being. Embodiment has been systematically downplayed or erased in the cybernetic construction of the posthuman in ways that have not occurred in other critiques of the liberal humanist subject, especially in feminist and postcolonial theories.'[4]

In her later work, Hayles emphasized the importance of embodied cognition in our media-saturated experiences. For

Hayles this bodily awareness was typified by the work of telegraph operators who 'read' and 'write' without obvious mental engagement as they perform manual and auditory labour in specially trained somatic states.[5] Hayles critiques the relative superficiality of the 'epiphenomenon' of consciousness that falsely asserts its own superiority in an imagined mind/body hierarchy. The liberal human subject may exult in its abilities to decode text, transform it into mental sounds and pictures and indulge in fantasies of freedom from the embodied constraints of the material world. But the process of technogenesis has already entirely transformed how reading and writing operate, according to Hayles, given the plasticity of the human brain as a bodily organ, which rewires itself in response to the technologies it encounters. In its most banal form, this technological condition produces a moral panic about 'shallow reading' that is facilitated by the rhizomatic design for distraction enforced by internet platforms that compel constant peer-to-peer sharing on distributed social networks.[6]

In the cultural conversation about how technology shapes the body's experience of reading, there has also been a moral panic about the outsized role played by pornography in the literacy practices of digital culture. Scholars such as Susanna Paasonen,[7] Katrin Tiidenberg[8] and Patrick Keilty[9] have worked to remove the stigma associated with these common searches for sexual images and texts, but puritanical attitudes still suppress acknowledgement that this form of literature excites the body in significant ways. Linda Williams has argued that pornography is a 'body genre' – much like horror and melodrama – that can be categorized as a type of literature that produces a visible corporeal effect spurring emission of a bodily fluid.[10]

As electronic literature pursues greater respectability by anthologizing vetted works in the process of canon formation and by allying itself with elite professional organizations such as the Modern Language Association, the field may be even less likely to include online pornography as an object of legitimate study by its scholars. Nonetheless, several reputable works of electronic literature allude to the ubiquity of pornographic consumption as part of the everyday media diet of typical users. For example, Jonathan Harris's *Network Effect* (2015) is a compendium of video clips structured around action verbs describing common types of internet performance, such as 'craft', 'cook', 'dance' and 'protest'.

Significantly, Harris also includes 'strip', 'suck' and 'lick', although he avoids more vulgar terms for erotic activities. Furthermore, scholars of erotic fan fiction assert the importance of the literary activities of vibrant counterpublics who challenge norms about respectable patterns of cultural consumption and production. For example, critics have theorized about queer 'slash fiction' in which fans use the internet to publish and share stories featuring famous pop culture characters expressing their same-sex attractions in richly detailed online erotica.[11]

Religious ecstasy might also compel bodily engagement with a text, as physical rituals of connection dictate non-optical interactions with scripture. 'Medieval reading invokes emotive, bodily, and multisensory reading practices', Dorothy Kim points out, 'including touching, feeling, kissing, and licking manuscript parts and pages'. According to Kim, 'medieval manuscripts inscribe a history of the senses and the reader's/subject's/users' interaction with these fleshly interfaces. Medieval readers have deposited their breath, finger dirt, saliva, and probably bits of their dinners on the vellum page'.[12] Kim's essay wonders about the possibility that digital archives could evoke similar multisensory embodied experiences despite the seeming sterility of dematerialized electronic text and the distance between the body and the literary work that is imposed by the privileging of ocular perception that requires separation to keep the necessary semiotic pieces simultaneously in focus.

With the development of electronic literature written specifically for head-mounted displays, tablets, smart phones and – potentially – smart glasses and activity trackers as well, there are new human-computer relationships to be interrogated with digital works. Such reading devices can be equipped with 'eyes' (cameras), 'ears' (microphones) and 'skin' (touchscreens), as well as accelerometers and GPS tracking technologies that mimic proprioception. Because of medical, military and industrial uses for these technologies, they can also potentially 'smell' and 'taste'. Thus, an interface for reading can also 'read' the reader and the reading environment.

This chapter examines how the body of the computer interacts with the body of the reader in various ways, as experimental authors seek to expand the repertoire of digital reading practices. It analyses a number of recent works of electronic literature that complicate the earlier screen/page paradigm that posits reading as a state of objective detachment in which the body is largely a passive participant in knowledge transfer. Many of these works are also covered in 'Divergent Streams', the final chapter of Scott Rettberg's *Electronic Literature* (2019), a capacious account of the field that categorizes its major genres, such as 'hypertext fiction', 'interactive fiction', 'combinatory poetics' and 'kinetic poetry'.[13] According to Rettberg, this miscellany of recent works that reconfigure expectations about embodiment builds upon previous genres but also deploys new technologies to feature the body's engagement in the literary experience.

Reading the reader

By incorporating certain machine vision technologies, the body of the reader can actually shape the body of the text. For example, the falling letters of 'a poem about bodies and language' in *Text Rain* (1999) by Camille Utterback and Romy Achituv encourage its audience to use 'the familiar instrument of their bodies' to shape the contours of a projected digital concrete poem that is otherwise constantly in flux.[14] The reader's body serves as an obstacle upon which precipitating type can accumulate, particularly if arms or legs are outstretched into a horizontal surface.

Using a similar silhouette detection approach, *Still Standing* (2005) by Bruno Nadeau and Jason Edward Lewis encourages the reader to remain motionless, so that the outline of her or his body can be filled with lines of otherwise disorganized text. As Rettberg notes, there is something of an inverse relationship between *Text Rain* and *Still Standing*: in one case the text frames the reader's body, which cannot be penetrated by the words, and in the other case the reader's body serves as the container for the text. Both pieces reward bodily immobility with discursive legibility, and both treat the line between self and non-self as a barrier. In this way, both works recapitulate traditional tropes about reading that assume physical stillness and individual interiority.

In video documenting *Text Rain*, however, participants are encouraged to playfully deceive the detection system using 'any dark object' – such as an umbrella or a blanket – so these unnatural extensions of the body could also capture the falling text.[15] In contrast, the explanatory paper of Nadeau and Lewis shows readers dressed in short-sleeved T-shirts interacting with the system without any appendages or prostheses.[16] Although not naked, the model reader of *Still Standing* adopts a classical contrapposto position, and the text assumes the composure of the body's sinuously balanced sculptural posture as well.

These silhouette detection poems invite questions about self-recognition in their shadow play. The reader is expected to identify with the image that is mirrored back to them and to experience the familiar coherence of a personal profile and its proportions. Of course, the reader might also experience body dysphoria in the literary encounter with the animated text.[17] Who is that fat/skinny/short/tall person?

Looking at the boundedness of the human subject in literary works like *Text Rain* and *Still Standing* might raise philosophical issues about how the outlines of the body do or do not define the outlines of self. In imagining other ways to map the self to the body, Gregory Bateson's famous thought experiment might provide an alternative to using Cartesian dualism as its starting point:

> Consider a blind man with a stick. Where does the blind man's self begin? At the tip of the stick? At the handle of the stick? Or at some point halfway up the stick? These questions are nonsense, because the stick is a pathway along which differences are transmitted under transformation, so that to draw a delimiting line across this pathway is to cut off a part of the systemic circuit which determines the blind man's locomotion.[18]

In other words, for Bateson, the human subject is constituted by a cybernetic system of perception, reaction, interrelation and activity that is not confined to the outlines of the body in a figure/ground relation. The blind man is a reading subject whose self extends beyond his body into the apparatus with which he reads the world.

Cybernetic theories about the body's interpretive loops, which inspired Bateson and others in the Macy Group, have also influenced authors in electronic literature, albeit often through the more recent work of feminist science and technology critic Donna Haraway. For example, Diane Greco's *Cyborg: Engineering the Body Electric*, which was composed for Eastgate System's proprietary Storyspace platform, was published on CD-ROM five years after Haraway's seminal essay 'A Cyborg Manifesto' (1985) appeared. As in other works of posthuman electronic literature, the task of the reader to 'make sense of all these pieces' is complicated by the fragmentation of a body composed of '[s]pare parts, parts and wholes, prostheses, replacements, enhancements'.[19] Chapter titles include 'Your Body Is Meat', 'Machine Dreams', and 'Mind, Body, Anti-Body'. Notably, Greco stopped publishing electronic literature long before the rise of ubiquitous computing devices that could provide a more immersive or haptically enhanced reading experience than a CD-ROM work for a desktop machine. These technologies potentially allow readers to conduct their own thought experiments in real-time using prompts from the literary works with which they interact in more holistic ways.

A body of evidence

In addition to using silhouette detection, works of electronic literature can incorporate facial recognition technologies in order to interact with the reader's body. In the case of Serge Bouchardon's *StoryFace* (2018), a work of social satire that takes the form of fictional dating application, the reader is judged suspiciously by an algorithmic system that is constantly assessing her or his emotional authenticity in online social performance. Throughout the interactive narrative, *StoryFace* captures the reader's facial expressions in the device's camera and performs calculations based on the biometric data gathered, using commercially available machine vision software for labelling facial information. After the reader initially chooses between an experience in English and one in French, the system begins by guessing the reader's age and gender. Then it asks if the reader is seeking a male or female love interest. Before moving into the main activity of choosing and chatting with potential romantic partners of various stock types, the system translates the reader's facial expression into one of six emoji. Available affective states include anger, sorrow, happiness, nausea and two forms of surprise. As the reader seeks to choose chat responses to be attractive to the other party, the system continues to monitor the reader's emotions and will assign the reader's face-updated emoji if need be. If a response in flirtatious interplay is judged to be disingenuous, a loud buzzer sounds and the system threatens to tell the potential date that the reader is lying, chiding the reader with comments like 'Why do you pretend to be happy when you're actually sad?' Although it demands emotional authenticity, *StoryFace* compels the reader to communicate in what seems to be a debased language of emoji and text messages, although – as critics have pointed out – both emoji and text messages can be semiotically complex and ambiguous message units in highly compressed systems of digital signification.[20]

At the 2018 Electronic Literature Organization festival John Murray presented a prototype for *You're On: The Emotion Machine* in which the reading experience also begins with being read by facial recognition technologies. The machine translates the data into 'bars and percentages of the emotions it recognizes'. Although *You're On: The Emotion Machine* was only a work in progress at the time, Murray promised that eventually 'the user will be able to write their own text and read it back while monitoring the emotional responses on their face'.[21] Notably, Murray's PhD dissertation had gathered biometric facial data from six players of the game *The Wolf among Us* – along with data from their heart rates and skin conductivity – to try to see how emotion informs the paths chosen by an individual audience member as she or he explores diverging storylines in an interactive work.[22]

Of course, even traditional literature can be read in a nonlinear way. Different possible pathways for reading can be followed through the geometrical orientation of a page, as well as throughout the entire codex if a chapter is skipped or reread. For example, *The Wolf among Us* is based on an award-winning comic book series about fairy-tale characters. In consuming comic books, it is commonly accepted that the eye can travel in many possible directions – horizontally, vertically, diagonally and from periphery to centre or centre to periphery.[23] Although new assistive technologies for 'guided viewing' on e-readers may recommend a default path,[24] even a single frame might contain multiple points of attention without a clear order for a path of navigation. Additionally, a young child new to the reading process of a codex book covered with lines of text may also read in a non-standard sequence, as she or he attempts to follow the words on a printed page, as in the case in the original fairy-tale stories upon which *The Wolf among Us* is based. To decode the logic of a potential reading anomaly in the child, eye-tracking software can measure bodily engagement by extrapolating from the positions of the pupils.

Such eye-tracking software has been incorporated into works of electronic literature that read the reader. For example, *Focus* (2015) is an interactive textual installation that is based on Vito Acconci's 'READ THIS WORD THEN READ THIS WORD READ THIS WORD NEXT READ THIS WORD ...' The camera follows the reader's gaze, so the text appears at the same target location on the screen. According to one catalog description, *Focus* 'explores the physicality of the reading process'.[25] In Jiewen Wang's *The Singularity* (2020), a vortex of words typeset in an interactive font created by Santiago Ortiz follows the reader's head movements.[26] Against the black void, the white angular words – many of which are upside down – perform a three-D dance in a kind of responsive duet with the reader's movements. *The Singularity* is not – strictly speaking – an eye-tracking work because the text gyrates in response to the choreography of the head even if the reader's eyes are closed.

In addition to tracking eye movements, facial expressions or the presence of the human silhouette, hand motions or other gestures can be monitored by a digital reading apparatus. In its heyday, several works of electronic literature incorporated the Kinect motion-sensing input device, which was first released by Microsoft in 2010, primarily for use in video games. The Kinect was also used to adapt existing works of electronic literature, which had been originally written for the keyboard or mouse, to facilitate a wider range of bodily interaction. For example, it can be a challenge to navigate through Stephanie Strickland and Nick Montfort's expansive *Sea and Spar Between*, a generative code mash-up of Herman Melville and Emily Dickinson that generated about 225 trillion stanzas. Monika Górska-Olesińska and Mariusz Pisarski translated *Sea and Spar Between* into Polish and also adapted it for three-D interaction with the Kinect.[27]

In a work explicitly concerned with embodiment, the Kinect was used in Zuzana Husárová's *Enter:in' Wodies* (2012), an interactive exhibit in which the reader is supposed to 'imagine the person' whose interior 'you would desire to read'.[28] During the reading experience, the audience is able to 'choose from two models – man or woman'. According to the artist, the first text 'explains the initiation to enter other person'. Subsequently the reader interacts with the work 'by choosing the body parts by touching with your hands the imaginary being', which 'refer to seven organ systems'. Poems are connected with particular human biological systems, and the reader must make hand movements to uncover the words. The final text informs readers that they will now be leaving the other person's body.

In addition to all these algorithms of capture, it is also technically possible to use gait-tracking software to create literary art. According to data scientists, each human stride is apparently extremely distinctive and can be identified with computer vision and machine learning technologies.[29] Consequently the military and surveillance companies have developed pattern-recognition software that can identify specific motion signatures. Consequently, a digital writer could actually personalize texts for particular types of ambling pedestrians encountering exhibits of electronic literature in public spaces. So-called locative works in electronic literature already use GPS tracking or QR codes to track the reader's location and movement in order to reveal chapters in an interactive story situated in particular places or lines of poetry that are inspired by specific environments. Gait-tracking software or data from an activity tracker that measures steps could give readers of such locative media a different kind of embodied experience in their literary encounter with these site-specific works. After all, steps taken and paths followed have often been used as analogies to explain algorithmic processes. For example, in understanding how unit operations in computer code operate, Ian Bogost uses the metaphor of strolling through a city to understand the role of the *flâneur* as 'fundamentally a configurative one' in opening up new paths and closing others so that *flânerie* through the urban built environment performs a 'passage through space' that is similar to the 'configurative structure of procedural texts'.[30]

The interfaces of electronic literature can also read the skin on the body's surface as a kind of text. For example, writer Judd Morrissey collaborated with choreographer Mark Jeffery to stage *The Operature*, which combined live performance and augmented reality poetry. Dancers wore temporary tattoos that could be decoded by computer vision technologies that translated the images into text, much as a QR code can be translated into a hyperlink with a specific internet address. The tattooed images on the dancers' bodies included realistic cross sections of organs from medical illustrations and stylized depictions of hands and flowers from folk art. Dance movements in *The Operature* were punctuated with iPad interludes in which inscribed body parts were examined by the scanning technologies of the device. For instance, with the aid of the iPad in the hands of a skilled performer playing investigator, the audience could watch scenes from a Kenneth Anger film play, or coded 'stud files' cataloging sexual partners might appear. Conceivably, rather than respond to the artificial overlay on the skin of a tattoo or adhesive sticker, a literary work could be written that responds to organic distinguishing features, such as the moles, scars or birthmarks that distinguish a particular body.

Morrisey described *The Operature* as a 'provisional collective exploring forensics, anatomy, and 21st century embodiment through performance, language and emerging technologies'. The themes of the work highlighted anatomical science and the spectacle of discovery. Otherwise hidden content was revealed in the detective work of assaying a kind of crime scene in which the dancer's bodies were often presented as inert objects to be autopsied. The interaction between the reading machine and the computer-readable text generated both a homoerotic rendering of the bodily landscape and the digitally mediated output of technocratic knowledges.

Disciplining scores

In *My Mother Was a Computer* (2005), Hayles observes that 'as bodies enter more completely into the circuit, subjects cease to be circumscribed by these dynamics and are constructed through them'.[31] Using literary texts such as Henry James's *In the Cage* (1898) or *The Girl Who Was Plugged In* (1973) by James Tiptree, Jr. Hayles imagines a long history of subject formation by technologies that range from telegraphy to virtual reality. Of course, as these circuits are more likely to be determined by artificial intelligence rather than by human engineers and designers, the labyrinthine paths of algorithmic logic may cease to be decipherable in the embodied experience.

For example, Sascha Pohflepp's *Recursion* (2016) is a video artwork that presents a text that is generated by a neural network primed with a wide range of texts about humankind derived from philosophy, psychology and popular culture – including Wikipedia articles about the concepts of humanity, consciousness, the human body, emotion, economics, science, technology and human behaviour – as well as a select corpus of more idiosyncratic choices including Freud's *Civilization and Its Discontents* (1930); Hegel's *The Phenomenology of Spirit* (1807); Mary Douglas's *Purity and Danger* (1966); Joni Mitchell's 'California', The Beatles', 'Here Comes the Sun'; and Brian Eno's 'Spider and I'. After its initial supervised training, the AI was instructed to compose a text beginning with the word 'human', which was then read aloud in the video by performance artist Erika Ostrander.

According to Pohflepp, the work creates a feedback loop 'between us and the artificial other', using Benjamin Bratton's notion that 'the real uncanny valley [is] one in which we see ourselves through the eyes of an AI "other."'[32] In 'gazing back', he presents a structure in which 'human is modulated through machine', 'language is simulated by machine', and for the potential audience the 'human reflects herself in machine' that is simultaneously 'alien' while attempting to 'constitute the very self of us' through the 'de-specification of cognition'. Done with a sense of 'reversal' reflected back the 'mimetic other' in which the human mind performs the actual sense-making, Pohflepp assumes that the 'simulation always takes the mimic over the brink' by asking us to assume 'its vantage point'.[33]

When one watches Ostrander read aloud the sequence of words generated by Pohflepp's piece, it is striking to see how she struggles to articulate the stream of sometimes nonsensical syntax. The video presents a close-up of her face, in which the viewer can see her pupils move as she scans the text that she is reading. As she attempts to imbue the words with meaning, her embodied rendering of the AI language includes affective markers, such as raising her eyebrows, furrowing her brow, nodding her head and smiling.

In *Convergence* (2020), Alexander Schubert's version of a high-tech disciplining score, text, music, code and video are combined and remixed. The bodies of the musicians who participate in the piece respond to verbal orders such as 'vary your position', 'stroke up', 'stroke down', 'smile', 'pause', 'hold still', 'close your eyes', 'sing' and 'scream'. The synthesized robotic voice that directs the action might issue corrections, such as 'louder repeat', reflect on its alien positionality in noting 'how I see and hear you', and even imagine cosmic intercourse by commanding that someone 'fuck me so hard that I dissolve'. The quintet of performers can be altered with 'sliders' and 'values' so that the machine has the capacity to create alternative versions of the musicians. The moving images that represent their bodies undergo digital transformations, as they are morphed and composited by an authoring system, capable of changing the appearance of the musicians at will. Because the intelligence of the voice seems to have access to digital editing tools, the performers cannot refuse the dictates of this alien intelligence when it declares 'now I move your arm'.

According to Schubert, the performers 'demonstrate a world that is constructed and parametric. The friction between machine perception and human world perception is the starting point for questions that address the fluidity of the self and the restrictions of perception'.[34] Although the ballet of 'encoding and decoding' orchestrated by the voice in the video moves through its algorithmic loops relentlessly, as the musicians are partnered and mirrored by the system, they are ensured that it is an 'always loving' interaction with technology.

Both *Recursion* and *Convergence* posit a near future in which bodily human performance is constrained by a textual script that is dictated by an artificial intelligence. In both works there are also multiple acts of doubling and simulation, as the machine imitates the human, and the human imitates the machine. Although the performance of *Recursion* is more obviously literary, in offering its audience a dramatized reading, its reader struggles to maintain mastery over the torrent of computer-generated verbiage, and the reader's embodied performance dramatizes an attempt to normalize the asymmetrical power relationships in the situation by offering her reactions to lexical stimuli that appear to signal her interpretive labour and its challenges and rewards. *Convergence* also speaks to the procedural character of reading; however, in this case, the musicians that would normally read the scores to give voice to their instruments are instead read by an AI who treats them as the instruments to be scored.

A touching encounter

At the more intimate scale of a hand-held interface, creators of electronic literature have been exploring the ways that experiences of reading and writing could be enhanced. Without the distance enforced by a spectatorship in a screening, stage performance, or wall display, as is the case for the kind of electronic literature discussed in the previous section, which is often exhibited at international digital arts festivals, more personal and portable works can be in direct contact with an audience member's body in a bubble of perceived private space.[35] Tablets and other new devices also offer writers novel ways to reimagine the codex book, reconfigure the embodied experience of reading and conceptualize the activity of 'reading machines'. As Anastasia Salter observes, such touchscreen devices differ at the 'physical level', as well as 'represent a break from conventional eBook readers such as Amazon's Kindle, which in form, scale, and interface sought to reproduce the experience of a bound codex while augmenting only some elements of the text'.[36] Multi-touchscreen devices like the iPad that are optimized for many kinds of media consumption facilitate new multimodal practices and input methods. Of course, the price point of digital screens with computing power is not yet low enough to be like the cheap, ubiquitous and disposable electronic pads envisioned by Mark Weiser as an alternative to the Windows paradigm.[37] As in the case of the early modern literature of the codex, each digital tablet is still a relatively precious possession as a commodity. However, because these devices emanate less intense heat than those from an earlier generation of computing, these reading surfaces can also be present in the most private of domestic spaces like the bed.[38]

Pry (2013), by Samantha Gorman and Danny Cannizzaro, is a digital tablet novella designed primarily for the iPad that describes itself as 'a book to watch and a film to touch'. To navigate the activities of the protagonist's mind and body the reader is given two basic instructions for interacting with the screen: pinch open to see outside/memories; and pinch close to see inside/subconscious. Prying James's eyes open with the gesture of an expanded grasp often exposes a world constructed of cinematic representations, while to squeeze James's eyes shut often immerses the reader in the inner life of the 'troubled mind' that has been pried open, where mental activity often appears as text.

In addition to struggling with post-traumatic stress disorder, advancing blindness seems to contribute to James's general condition of deterioration and disability. An entire chapter of the book is devoted to braille reading and the degeneracies of sight. As the reader scans the braille dots with her or his fingers, words and scenes play over the screen.

In this chapter we also see signs of other time periods in home video footage from James's formative period with his family. But the footage lacks sharpness and is marred by interlace artefacts. Moving images from childhood are juxtaposed with more recent recovered memories from his time in military service and as a civilian demolitions expert. All of these elements suggest that the body is profoundly vulnerable and that consciousness must occupy a defensive position. In other words, the mind must maintain its separation from the body's precarity in order to maintain any agency.

As consumer platforms for media content delivery, commercial display devices like the iPad are currently designed to maximize affordances in two key but frequently separate areas: reading words on publications with remediated pages that may mimic the conventional features of a book with paper pages and viewing videos on the intimate scale of a personal screen as timeline-based media. The haptic interactions required for reading/viewing *Pry* and the resulting bodily fatigue from attempting to freeze one's hand in any one continuous modality causes the reader's general experience of the text to oscillate between written and cinematic forms of representation.

As Michele White points out in her book *Touch Screen Theory: Digital Devices and Feelings* (2022), the manual labour of using a touchscreen can be gendered and in some ways raced because women with long fingernails – a marker often associated with Black femininity – may find that they are not the imagined users of these technologies.[39] Much as some people might not be 'seen' properly by computer vision if the algorithm designed by white male engineers is not trained to recognize certain kinds of faces, the skin of the touchscreen requires a certain kind of touch.

In reading, the viewer's body is by necessity also part of the work. The user's hand that reveals content also conceals it because it must obstruct the screen in order to activate it. *Pry* (2014), technically speaking, approaches the body as a tool and input device. However, in addition to being a 'film to touch', *Pry* is a 'book to watch' and elicits the bodily engagement associated with spectatorship and imagined identification. Because so much of the narrative of *Pry* depends on first-person POV shots, it's worth considering both if the disembodied first-person representational strategy is inherently patriarchal and colonizing and what this perspectival viewpoint expresses about how to read digital text with cinematic conventions in mind. Moreover, the prominence of an award-winning work like *Pry* raises questions about what the potential cinematic turn in electronic literature might mean for the theoretical frameworks of the field that in the past has largely privileged written text as code?

In the case of *Pry*, how are we expected to interpret the many ways that shots are composed, framed, filtered and composited? For example, how do we understand how even seemingly minor conventional elements like lens flare do signifying work? Whether the spots on the image are intended to signal the camera optics of a traditional analogue image-capture device or post-production digital effects, the first-person point of view of the protagonist is denaturalized. Rather than be perceived as immediate, as action would be in a true virtual reality experience, it is hypermediated or remediated by interaction with the iPad and other technologies within the frame of *Pry*.[40]

First-person literature

At the same time that touchscreen apparatuses have become more readily available, less-expensive head-mounted displays have expanded what was once a very narrow media market for virtual reality. Many of these headsets are also more finely calibrated to avoid the problems of simulation sickness that were common in the cruder models of the past. In *Virtual Realism* (1998), philosopher Michael Heim discusses how early virtual reality technologies had a tendency to induce illness and bodily discomfort caused by the 'stress from the pressures on biological structures and rhythms' that disrupted the audience member's immersion in a digital fiction and sacrificed any feelings of transcendence from the experience.[41] Now VR delivery devices can also be made available as inexpensive mass-produced viewers, such as Google Cardboard, which is powered by the user's smart phone, thus enabling embodied viewing in the everyday life of a potential literary audience. For example, *Lincoln in the Bardo* is a virtual reality adaption of a 2017 experimental novel by American writer George Saunders that was directed by Graham Sack and produced by *The New York Times*. With the *Times* VR app and a Cardboard viewer, the audience member is placed in a circle of ghostly spectres. Although multiple characters present stories of their post-embodied existence, the central action is focused on the sixteenth president as he recovers the body of his dead son from a cemetery. As in the case of many successful VR stories in which the viewer is cast as a patient, prisoner, passenger or bystander, the perceived spatial constraints of the circle of the undead encourage immobility rather than exploration of the environment.

In *Gaming: Essays on Algorithmic Culture* (2006) Alexander Galloway observes that the first-person game genres are characterized by a distinctive merging of the point of view of camera and of character. As he points out, in traditional cinema the first-person POV usually signals intoxication, alienation or predatory interest (as is the case in *Rosemary's Baby*, *Psycho* or *Jaws*), but in videogames this first-person perspective is coded as phenomenologically normal and even socially appropriate. Galloway continues: 'In film, the subjective perspective is marginalized and used primarily to effect a sense of alienation, detachment, fear, or violence, while in games the subjective perspective is quite common and used to achieve an intuitive sense of motion and action in game-play.'[42]

In *Pry*, the first-person point of view is often very conventionally cinematically coded as pathological to emphasize James's disorientation, loss of control and sense of unreality. Through his failing eyes we see the fuzzy edges of the apertures of the ophthalmologist's machines or the blurry eye chart that goes out of focus. After a blast in the Middle East during his tour of duty, his thought text indicates that the 'world moves like a video game' as James is carried off by Luke who serves as both brother and rival in the story – doubling the narrative of Jacob and Esau in the braille Bible.

Galloway also emphasizes the importance of the relationship of the iconic weapon to a first-person visual framing as an extension of the player's agency and his ability to control action on the screen.

But perhaps equally essential to the FPS genre is the player's *weapon*, which generally appears in the right foreground of the frame. While a more detailed analysis would certainly include other elements such as the heads-up display, for simplicity's sake let me claim that these two elements alone – a subjective camera perspective, coupled with a weapon in the foreground – constitute the kernel of the image in the FPS genre.[43]

So where is James's weapon, according to Galloway's schema? Where is the instrument that allows him to exert any control over his environment and express any agency? Is it his clipboard that he uses on the demolition site? Is it the cards with the Iraq War's most wanted figures, which are used in an analogue rather than digital game play? Is it the beer bottle he hoists in his desolate apartment? Or is it the Gameboy that seems to serve as an object of comfort and distraction?

For a character who should have access to weapons and detonating equipment in his occupations as soldier and deconstruction worker, respectively, James is surprisingly disarmed. Even the transitional objects that are described in the story – a security blanket and a comforting stuffed animal – aren't accessible and easily available to hand. In 'Super 8' we see a rapid montage of tools, which presents a speedy succession of possible implements of power – shovel, pick, scissors, knife, etc. – but in Heideggerian terms they are not tools ready to hand. They exist in a disembodied inventory. By the end of the story the user's attention is directed away from James's hands and to his feet as he makes his way forward precariously both across the bridge before his disastrous fall into the water and nostalgically in the desert along the railroad tracks.

In her work on the 'assaultive gaze' in the necropolitics of video game mechanics Amanda Phillips argues that there are specific reasons that the virtual body of the player is effaced in first-person shooters in which the Cartesian head shot is highly prized and ragdoll deaths are mundane to the point of comedy. Of the visual presentation of first-person shooter targeting onscreen, Phillips writes that 'most of the complexities of the body' are 'left out of the simulation'; thus 'there is no incentive to perform the tasks normally associated with marksmanship: holding one's breath, propping the weapon on a stable surface, and so on'. 'Shooting a gun is a specific type of bodily experience', she writes.

> Muscles lift and hold the weapon, trembling with fatigue over time; eyes line up the sights, each fighting for dominance unless you hold one shut tight (a particularly bad habit in law enforcement); and breath and heartbeats interfere with a carefully drawn aim. If you don't remember to pull the trigger straight back with the tip of your finger, you'll pull the whole thing to the side. Some pistols will slice the hand open when held

incorrectly, and the kickback from a shotgun or rifle can leave a bruise if not braced properly.[44]

Of course, creating a work of electronic literature that involves picking up an actual weapon or similarly sized and weighted replica of one is certainly technically possible. In fact, Jesper Juul has written about the power and accessibility of stories written for so-called mimetic interfaces, such as the Nintendo Wii, in which the player can strum a guitar, swing a tennis racket or pull a trigger to move the narrative forward.[45] Despite their supposedly 'natural' or 'intuitive' interfaces, these play experiences can still be vexed by mismatches and misrecognitions with embodied cognition.

The legibility of the reader

In many ways, traditional e-readers such as the Amazon Kindle are the ultimate mimetic interface, in seeking to replicate ink on paper and the turning of a page. Yet some works of electronic literature draw attention to the dissimilarities of the screen and the book as interfaces for embodied interaction and the differences in the ways that they address the reader. Rather than collapse the categories of film and book into a single synesthetic experience, Amaranth Borsuk and Brad Bouse's *Between Page and Screen*, which was published in 2012, investigates 'the place of books as objects in an era of increasingly screen-based reading'. The actual pages of this artist's book contain no legible text; the reader is presented with only abstract geometric patterns and a URL leading to a website, where the book may be read by using any browser and a webcam.

Between Page and Screen is an epistolary work in which there is a series of letters written by two lovers 'struggling to map the boundaries of their relationship', contested territory that does not exist on either page or screen, 'but in the augmented space between them opened up by the reader'.[46] Borsuk claims to draw inspiration from the concept of 'projective mediumship' in the work of the poet H. D. The letters are full of homophones, puns, sight rhymes and linguistic play with the etymologies of the words 'page' and 'screen'. Sometimes the addressee is 'P' (for page), and sometimes it is 'S' (for screen), and there are also a number of interludes in which concrete poetry occupies the three-D space that the reader inhabits. Indeed, the reader cannot disappear from the text that he or she is engaged in reading because it is difficult to elude the gaze of the webcam while holding up one's copy of the book. Thus, the kinetic typography floating in three-D space between page and screen almost inevitably includes the human subject in the reading environment. Fans of the work can print out their own books with their own augmented reality texts using a DIY toolkit on the website. As Jessica Pressman points out, Borsuk and Bouse's work of electronic literature disrupts conventions around the scene 'of the silent, individual reader staring deep into an open book' as a 'symbol of interiority and selfhood'.⁴⁷ Instead of having the surface of the book be presented as a site of immersion, the webcam scans and reads its otherwise illegible contents and the reader's body intrudes into the space of their playful romantic dialogue.

The reader's body is not actually read by the textual machine of *Between Page and Screen*, as is the case in *StoryFace* and other works of electronic literature that integrate machine vision technologies. Nor does the reader's body serve as a complex input device, as is the case in *Pry*, which requires attention to the manual activity that reveals new content through multi-touch gestures. The reader is merely pointing the book at the screen or pointing the screen at the book. Nonetheless, the body's presence in the reading experience is unavoidable. When readers document their reading experiences with *Between Page and Screen* with screen capture software, inevitably they are also creating an individualized video selfie of their own reading experiences.

Like many other works of electronic literature in this survey, *Between Page and Screen* assumes a particular kind of body, one with hands that can manipulate objects and one with eyes that can see the animated shapes that the text assumes. Of course, there are works that do not assume that the reader is endowed with accurate vision and manual dexterity. For example, John Cayley's *The Listeners* (2015) uses a voice-controlled digital home assistant as an input device. Using Amazon's Alexa, speakers can move forward linearly in the linguistic performance by saying such things as 'Continue' or 'Go on', or they might respond to the performance by sharing an emotional state, such as 'I am filled with anger'. Cayley describes this kind of 'computationally engaged aural literature' as 'aurature'.⁴⁸

Given the ways that computational systems are enforcing what Ruha Benjamin has called 'new Jim Code' to police Black and brown bodies, I would hope that more works of electronic literature will appear in the near future that explicitly address questions about race, representation and interpretation.[49] For example, *AI, Ain't I A Woman?* (2018) by digital artist Joy Buolamwini is a video poem that pays homage to Sojourner Truth's famous extemporaneous speech. It is illustrated with examples of photos of famous Black women, which machine vision systems read as men. To assume that the reader's body is a generic entity that is not interpreted by intersecting systems of oppression is to merely transpose the existing literary discourse that privileges whiteness in digital culture without truly increasing the capacities of contemporary literature and the body.

Notes

1   Juliet Davis, *Pieces of Herself*, available online: https://collection.eliterature.org/2/works/davis_pieces_of_herself.html.

2   For more about the epistemology of the visible woman, see Paula A. Treichler, Lisa Cartwright, and Constance Penley, *The Visible Woman: Imaging Technologies, Gender, and Science* (New York: New York University Press, 1998).

3   Luce Irigaray, *This Sex Which Is Not One*, trans. Catherine Porter and Carolyn Burke (Ithaca, NY: Cornell University Press, 1985).

4   N. Katherine Hayles, *How We Became Posthuman: Virtual Bodies in Cybernetics, Literature and Informatics* (Chicago: University of Chicago Press, 2010), 4.

5   N. Katherine Hayles, *How We Think: Digital Media and Contemporary Technogenesis* (Chicago; London: The University of Chicago Press, 2012).

6   See Nicholas Carr, *The Shallows: What the Internet Is Doing to Our Brains*, 1st edn. (New York: W.W. Norton, 2010). Although she agrees with him about technogenesis, Hayles systematically dismantles Carr's argument in *How We Think*.

7   Susanna Paasonen, *Carnal Resonance: Affect and Online Pornography* (Cambridge, MA: MIT Press, 2011).

8   Katrin Tiidenberg and Emily Van Der Nagel, *Sex and Social Media* (Bingley: Emerald Publishing, 2020).

9   Patrick Keilty, 'Desire by Design: Pornography as Technology Industry', *Porn Studies* 5, no. 3 (3 July 2018): 338–42.

10 Linda Williams, *Hard Core: Power, Pleasure, and the 'Frenzy of the Visible'* (Berkeley: University of California Press, 1999).

11 Alexis Lothian, Kristina Busse, and Robin Anne Reid, '"Yearning Void and Infinite Potential": Online Slash Fandom as Queer Female Space', *English Language Notes* 45, no. 2 (1 September 2007): 103–11.

12 Dorothy Kim, 'Building Pleasure and the Digital Archive', in *Bodies of Information: Intersectional Feminism and the Digital Humanities*, ed. Elizabeth Losh and Jacqueline Wernimont (Minneapolis: University of Minnesota Press, 2018), 239.

13 Scott Rettberg, *Electronic Literature* (Cambridge: Polity Press, 2019).

14 'Text Rain | Camille Utterback', accessed 30 September 2021. Available online: http://camilleutterback.com/projects/text-rain/.

15 MediaArtTube, *Camille Utterback & Romy Achituv – Text Rain, 1999,* 2008. Available online: https://www.youtube.com/watch?v=f_u3sSffS78.

16 Jason Lewis and Bruno Nadeau, 'Inter-Inactivity', 1 January 2005.

17 Many scholars of electronic literature also study independent games about gender dysphoria such as Mattie Brice's *Mainichi* or Anna Anthropy's *Dys4ia*.

18 Gregory Bateson, *Steps to an Ecology of Mind: Collected Essays in Anthropology, Psychiatry, Evolution, and Epistemology* (Chicago: University of Chicago Press, 2000), 318.

19 'Cyborg: Engineering the Body Electric', available online: https://www.eastgate.com/catalog/Cyborg.html.

20 For example, see Crystal Abidin and Joel Gn, 'Between Art and Application: Special Issue on Emoji Epistemology', *First Monday*, 1 September 2018, https://doi.org/10.5210/fm.v23i9.9410 in which the editors of a special issue seek to investigate 'the uses and impacts of emoji within the domains of culture, race, language, and art and commerce'. Also note the analysis of how even an empty text message might have meaning in Jason Farman, *Delayed Response: The Art of Waiting from the Ancient to the Instant World* (New Haven: Yale University Press, 2018).

21 'ELO 2018: Database Collaboration, Facial Recognition, and Third Generation Electronic Literature', University of Bergen. Available online: https://www.uib.no/en/machinevision/120207/elo-2018-database-collaboration-facial-recognition-and-third-generation.

22 John Thomas Murray, 'Telltale Hearts: Encoding Cinematic Choice-Based Adventure Games' (UC Santa Cruz, 2018), available online: https://escholarship.org/uc/item/1n02n02z.

23 Scott McCloud, *Understanding Comics* (New York: Harper Perennial, 1994).

24 Adrienne Resha, 'The Blue Age of Comic Books', *Inks: The Journal of the Comics Studies Society* 4, no. 1 (2020): 66–81.

25 'Focus | ELMCIP', available online: https://elmcip.net/node/10846.

26 :: E-Trombone Jiewen.Wang ::, available online: https://jiewen.wang/
singularity/index.html.

27 DH 2016 Abstracts, available online: https://dh2016.adho.org/
abstracts/314.

28 Themelovin, 'Enter:In' Wodies', *Zuzana Husárová* (blog), 22 June
2012, available online: http://zuz.husarova.net/2012/06/22/our-
interactive-kinect-based-project-enter-in/.

29 Houman Hediyeh et al., 'Pedestrian Gait Analysis Using Automated
Computer Vision Techniques', *Transportmetrica A: Transport Science*
10, no. 3 (16 March 2014): 214–32.

30 Ian Bogost, *Unit Operations: An Approach to Videogame Criticism*
(Cambridge, MA; London: MIT Press, 2008), 75.

31 N. Katherine Hayles, *My Mother Was a Computer: Digital Subjects
and Literary Texts* (Chicago: University of Chicago Press, 2005), 9.

32 *Recursion | Transmediale*, available online: https://archive.
transmediale.de/content/recursion.

33 Sascha Pohflepp, 'Existence Proof – Elemental Machines Session,
Transmediale 2017', available online: https://www.academia.
edu/32383897/Existence_Proof_Elemental_Machines_session_
Transmediale_2017.

34 'Alexander Schubert – Convergence', available online: http://www.
alexanderschubert.net/works/Convergence.php.

35 For more about how Japan led the way in these new models of
content consumption, see Mizuko Itō, Misa Matsuda, and Daisuke
Okabe, *Personal, Portable, Pedestrian: Mobile Phones in Japanese
Life* (Cambridge: MIT Press, 2006).

36 Anastasia Salter, 'Convergent Devices, Dissonant Genres: Tracking
the "Future" of Electronic Literature on the IPad', *Electronic
Book Review*, 1 November 2012, available online: http://
electronicbookreview.com/essay/convergent-devices-dissonant-genres-
tracking-the-future-of-electronic-literature-on-the-ipad/.

37 Mark Weiser, 'The Computer for the 21st Century: Someday
Computers Will Be Ubiquitous and Largely Unnoticeable', *Scientific
American* 272, no. SPE (1995): 78–89.

38 In contrast, it is notable how the viewer perceives the incongruity
of the laptop in the bed of an exhausted worker on the cover of one
recent book on ubiquitous computing. See Melissa Gregg, *Work's
Intimacy* (Cambridge: Polity, 2011).

39 This book marks a significant update from her earlier work about
conventional computation with non-touchscreens in *The Body and
the Screen: Theories of Internet Spectatorship* (Cambridge, MA: The
MIT Press, 2006).

40 Jay David Bolter and Richard Grusin, *Remediation: Understanding
New Media* (Cambridge, MA: MIT Press, 2003).

41 Michael Heim, *Virtual Realism* (New York: Oxford University Press, 1998), 186.
42 Alexander R Galloway, *Gaming: Essays on Algorithmic Culture* (Minneapolis: University of Minnesota Press, 2010), 39.
43 Galloway, *Gaming*, 57.
44 Amanda Phillips, 'Shooting to Kill: Headshots, Twitch Reflexes, and the Mechropolitics of Video Games', *Games and Culture* 13, no. 2 (1 March 2018): 136–52.
45 Jesper Juul, *A Casual Revolution: Reinventing Video Games and Their Players* (Cambridge, MA; London: MIT Press, 2012).
46 Amaranth Borsuk, 'Between Page and Screen, a Digital Popup Book', Between Page and Screen. Available online: http://www.betweenpageandscreen.com/.
47 Jessica Pressmann, *Bookishness: Loving Books in a Digital Age* (New York: Columbia University Press, 2020), 71.
48 'The Listeners | Electronic Literature Directory', available online: https://directory.eliterature.org/individual-work/4819.
49 Ruha Benjamin, *Race after Technology: Abolitionist Tools for the New Jim Code* (Cambridge: Polity, 2020).

Bibliography

Abidin, Crystal, and Joel Gn. 'Between Art and Application: Special Issue on Emoji Epistemology'. *First Monday*. 1 September 2018. Available online: https://doi.org/10.5210/fm.v23i9.9410.

Ackermans, Hannah. 'Database Collaboration, Facial Recognition, and Third Generation Electronic Literature'. Available online: https://www.uib.no/en/machinevision/120207/elo-2018-database-collaboration-facial-recognition-and-third-generation.

Bateson, Gregory. *Steps to an Ecology of Mind: Collected Essays in Anthropology, Psychiatry, Evolution, and Epistemology*. Chicago: University of Chicago Press, 2000.

Benjamin, Ruha. *Race after Technology Abolitionist Tools for the New Jim Code*. Cambridge: Polity, 2019, 2020.

Bogost, Ian. *Unit Operations: An Approach to Videogame Criticism*. Cambridge, MA: MIT, 2008.

Bolter, Jay David, and Richard Grusin. *Remediation: Understanding New Media*. Cambridge, MA: MIT Press, 2003.

Cayley, John. 'The Listeners | Electronic Literature Directory'. Available online: https://directory.eliterature.org/individual-work/4819.

Davis, Juliet. *Pieces of Herself*. Available online: https://collection.eliterature.org/2/works/davis_pieces_of_herself.html.

Farman, Jason. *Delayed Response: The Art of Waiting from the Ancient to the Instant World*. New Haven: Yale University Press, 2018.

Galloway, Alexander R. *Gaming: Essays on Algorithmic Culture*. Minneapolis: University of Minnesota Press, 2010.

Gregg, Melissa. *Work's Intimacy*. Cambridge: Polity, 2011.

Hayles, N. Katherine. *My Mother Was a Computer: Digital Subjects and Literary Texts*. Chicago: University of Chicago Press, 2005.

Hayles, N. Katherine. *How We Became Posthuman: Virtual Bodies in Cybernetics, Literature and Informatics*. Chicago: University of Chicago Press, 2010.

Hayles, N. Katherine. *How We Think: Digital Media and Contemporary Technogenesis*. Chicago: The University of Chicago Press, 2012.

Hediyeh, Houman, Tarek Sayed, Mohamed H. Zaki, and Greg Mori. 'Pedestrian Gait Analysis Using Automated Computer Vision Techniques'. *Transportmetrica A: Transport Science* 10, no. 3 (16 March 2014): 214–32.

Heim, Michael. *Virtual Realism*. New York: Oxford University Press, 1998.

Irigaray, Luce. *This Sex Which Is Not One*. Translated by Catherine Porter and Carolyn Burke. Ithaca, NY: Cornell University Press, 1985.

Itō, Mizuko, Misa Matsuda, and Daisuke Okabe. *Personal, Portable, Pedestrian: Mobile Phones in Japanese Life*. Cambridge, MA: MIT Press, 2006.

Keilty, Patrick. 'Desire by Design: Pornography as Technology Industry'. *Porn Studies* 5, no. 3 (3 July 2018): 338–42.

Kim, Dorothy. 'Building Pleasure and the Digital Archive'. In *Bodies of Information Intersectional Feminism and the Digital Humanities*, edited by Elizabeth Losh and Jacqueline Wernimont, 230–60. Minneapolis: University of Minnesota Press, 2018.

Lewis, Jason, and Bruno Nadeau. 'Inter-Inactivity'. 1 January 2005. Available online: https://www.obxlabs.net/obx_docs/inter-inactivity.pdf.

Lothian, Alexis, Kristina Busse, and Robin Anne Reid. "Yearning Void and Infinite Potential': Online Slash Fandom as Queer Female Space'. *English Language Notes* 45, no. 2 (1 September 2007): 103–11.

McCloud, Scott. *Understanding Comics*. New York: HarperPerennial, 1994.

Murray, John Thomas. 'Telltale Hearts: Encoding Cinematic Choice-Based Adventure Games'. UC Santa Cruz, 2018. Available online: https://escholarship.org/uc/item/1n02n02z.

Paasonen, Susanna. *Carnal Resonance: Affect and Online Pornography*. Cambridge, MA: MIT Press, 2011.

Phillips, Amanda. 'Shooting to Kill: Headshots, Twitch Reflexes, and the Mechropolitics of Video Games'. *Games and Culture* 13, no. 2 (1 March 2018): 136–52.

Pohflepp, Sascha. 'Existence Proof – Elemental Machines Session, Transmediale 2017'. Available online: https://www.academia. edu/32383897/Existence_Proof_Elemental_Machines_session_ Transmediale_2017.

Pohflepp, Sascha. 'Recursion | Transmediale'. Available online: https:// archive.transmediale.de/content/recursion.

Pressmann, Jessica. *Bookishness: Loving Books in a Digital Age.* New Haven: Yale University Press, 2020.

Resha, Adrienne. 'The Blue Age of Comic Books'. *Inks: The Journal of the Comics Studies Society* 4, no. 1 (2020): 66–81.

Rettberg, Scott. *Electronic Literature.* Cambridge: Polity Press, 2019.

Salter, Anastasia. 'Convergent Devices, Dissonant Genres: Tracking the "Future" of Electronic Literature on the IPad'. *Electronic Book Review*, 1 November 2012. Available online: http:// electronicbookreview.com/essay/convergent-devices-dissonant-genres-tracking-the-future-of-electronic-literature-on-the-ipad/.

Themelovin. 'Enter:In' Wodies'. *Zuzana Husárová* (blog), 22 June 2012. Available online: http://zuz.husarova.net/2012/06/22/our-interactive-kinect-based-project-enter-in/.

Tiidenberg, Katrin, and Emily Van Der Nagel. *Sex and Social Media.* Bingley, UK: Emerald Publishing, 2020.

Treichler, Paula A, Lisa Cartwright, and Constance Penley. *The Visible Woman: Imaging Technologies, Gender, and Science.* New York: New York University Press, 1998.

Utterback, Camille. *Camille Utterback & Romy Achituv – Text Rain, 1999,* 2008. Available online: https://www.youtube.com/watch?v=f_u3sSffS78.

Weiser, Mark. 'The Computer for the 21st Century: Someday Computers Will Be Ubiquitous and Largely Unnoticeable'. *Scientific American –* 272, no. SPE (1995): 78–89.

White, Michele. *The Body and the Screen: Theories of Internet Spectatorship.* Cambridge, MA: MIT Press, 2006.

White, Michele. *Touch Screen Theory.* Cambridge, MA: MIT Press, 2022.

Williams, Linda. *Hard Core: Power, Pleasure, and the 'Frenzy of the Visible'.* Berkeley, CA: University of California Press, 1999.

5

Gender and Feminism

Boriana Alexandrova

In *Living a Feminist Life* (2017), Sara Ahmed conveys the relationship between feminism and the body very simply: a feminist consciousness *begins* with/in the body. 'Feminism can begin with a body', she writes, 'a body in touch with a world, a body that is not at ease in a world'.[1] This body awakening to feminism is the body that senses an injustice; the body that 'fidgets and moves around', unable to put their finger on what exactly has gone wrong, yet knowing, in their cells, that something has. Feminism, Ahmed tells us, 'often begins with intensity: you are aroused by what you come up against. You register something in the sharpness of an impression. Something can be sharp without it being clear what the point is … You sense an injustice'.[2] Our bodies, the sensations on our skin – goosebumps, pressures, irritations, heat, cold, itching, pain – speak to us of things they feel, things they know by feeling, while we don't yet have the words to explain or understand what it is we're feeling or its meanings. This basic premise of how our bodies know beyond, and sometimes in spite of, the languages available to us forms the foundations of feminist theory.

There are multiple and varied reasons for this practically automatic association of feminism with the body in the cultural and philosophical discourses of the 'West' and Global North. Indeed, self-identified feminist philosophers, activists and artists have debated and deconstructed this relationship for decades. Elizabeth Grosz, for example, one of the earliest and most influential Western feminist 'philosophers of the body', argued in her 1994 work, *Volatile Bodies*, that 'a feminist reconfiguration of the notion of the body' was, at that time, urgently needed because even feminist schools of thought, as she framed them, were falling prey to the logics of 'misogynist thought': one that pits mind against body, male versus female, privileges mind/male over body/female and relegates the 'female' to the realm of 'frail, imperfect, unruly, and unreliable' corporeality. 'Relying on essentialism, naturalism and biologism', she explained, 'misogynist thought confines women to the biological requirements of reproduction on the assumption that because of particular biological, physiological, and endocrinological transformations, women are somehow *more* biological, *more* corporeal, and *more* natural than men'.[3]

While Grosz was not actually suggesting that feminist theorists themselves were proponents of 'misogynist thought' as such, she raised concerns about certain feminist tendencies to either obliterate corporeality in favour of an equality achieved 'on intellectual and conceptual grounds or in terms of an abstract universalism or humanism'.[4] Alternatively, she cautioned that some feminist schools could become trapped in explicit or implicit biological essentialism – such as constructionist feminism, which Grosz suggests tends to uphold the problematic 'distinction between the "real" biological body and the body as object of representation'; or some second-wave anti-sex feminists, such as Catharine MacKinnon, Mary Daly, or Andrea Dworkin, whom she critiqued for, inadvertently and ironically, objectifying women's bodies as 'passive and reproductive but largely unproductive … capable of being acted on, coerced, or constrained by external forces'.[5]

Of course, Grosz herself has not remained immune to critique. In *Strange Encounters: Embodied Others in Post-Coloniality* (2000), Sara Ahmed points out the inadequate understanding of race, class, colonialism and *difference* (a highly charged philosophical term requiring its own deconstructive analysis) in much of the critical feminist scholarship on the body of the 1990s. In Grosz's *Volatile Bodies* in particular, Ahmed finds 'little mention of the racialised nature of the multiple and differentiated bodies [Grosz] dedicates her text to'[6] and suggests that, even in a study that explicitly urged philosophers to attend to 'the specificity of bodies' in all their racial, gender, class and physiological differences, a feminist 'philosophy of difference *can* involve a universalism; a speaking from the place of (for example) the white subject, who reincorporates difference as a sign of its own fractured and multiple coming-into-being'.[7]

Ahmed's critique pulls at several conceptual threads that we do not have the space to fully disentangle here, but these feminist debates on how we define, understand or creatively theorize 'the body' illuminate a reckoning of worlds: between the paradigms underpinning white, Western, Euro- and Anglo-centric academic praxis, and the voices of grassroots, intersectional, anti-racist and transnational feminist activists and artists. These distinct realms of feminist thought arrive at the encounter from vastly different methodologies of coming in/to and generating knowledge. One speaks from (and often to) the proverbial ivory tower of white, upper-class, Euro- and male-centric institutions (be they academic, medical, legal, religious or governmental), while the other speaks from the ground and the living experiences of communities that have historically been denied access to power within those institutions: women; migrants; communities violated by structural racism; ill, pathologized and variously environmentally disabled communities; colonized communities; queer communities; gender and sexual minorities; children. All of these feminist schools pursue specific social justice missions. However, one approaches these by seeking to locate, outline and define 'the body' as an object that can be fixed in place for scientific scrutiny (for example by using visual markers such as gender, race, class, sexuality or 'identity' to make the body legible, albeit also susceptible to external regulation). The feminist decolonial approach, by contrast, theorizes through 'the "lived" experience of critical thinking, of reflection and analysis', whereby 'our lived experience of theorizing is fundamentally linked to processes of self-recovery, of collective liberation'.[8] Thus, when Ahmed queries, 'is there something more at stake in the rendering of bodies as objects-in-themselves for feminist analysis?'[9] she is challenging the (intrinsically colonial) move of severing the body from the mind, as well as from the wider, interactive communal and environmental processes of living.

Queer and trans feminist theorists, including Judith Butler, Donna Haraway, Paul Preciado or Karen Barad, have widely interrogated the problems in delineating 'the body' as a fixed, objective and hard-bounded entity. Alongside Black and intersectional feminists, such as Patricia Hill Collins, Kimberlé Crenshaw and the artists and theorists explored later in this chapter, these thinkers problematize the very concept of theorizing embodiment through 'identity': that is, by determining a person's 'nature' or un/belonging in societal structures based on objective definitions of gender, race, disability or class. As Vietnamese-American writer and filmmaker Trinh T. Minh-ha puts it,

> Power has always arrogated the right to mark its others while going about unmarked itself. Within an economy of movement, the dominant self, the 'universal subject,' represents himself as flexible, explorative, 'uncolored' and unbounded in his moves, while those caught in the margin of non-movement are represented as 'colored,' authentic – that is, uncomplicatedly locatable and custom-bound. Always eager to demarcate the others' limits, We only set up frontiers *for ourselves* when Our interest is at stake.[10]

The act of 'marking' oneself or an-other 'arrogates' the power to determine and name a person's difference, their purported 'nature', from the outside. In *Gender Trouble* (1990), Butler critiques the act of determining sex and/or gender difference based on physiological markers – a process they identify as 'fragmentation': 'Not only is the gathering of attributes under the category of sex suspect, but so is the very discrimination of the "features" themselves. That penis, vagina, breasts, and so forth are *named* sexual parts is both a restriction of the erogenous body to those parts and a fragmentation of the body as a whole.'[11] This is to say that the act of naming body parts and giving them social meaning tears up the body – indeed, the person – into disparate pieces: a process which, in literal terms, can kill. Such naming acts, Butler argues, create only an illusion of unity, while actually 'serv[ing] the purposes of fragmentation, restriction, and domination'.[12] In Monique Wittig's terms, '[l]anguage casts sheaves of reality upon the social body, stamping it and violently shaping it'.[13]

These ideas resonate strongly in Barad's and Preciado's works, too, from the perspectives of theoretical physics and trans feminist psychoanalysis respectively. Barad, in agreement with Butler, asserts that 'theorizing must be understood as an embodied practice, rather than a spectator sport of matching linguistic representations to preexisting things'.[14] Preciado, meanwhile, proposes to think of 'the living body [not] as an anatomical object, but as what I call a "somatheque," a living political archive ... The somatheque is mutating. The monster [the trans somatheque] is one who lives in transition. One whose face, body and behaviours cannot yet be considered true in a predetermined regime of knowledge and power'.[15, 16]

When Ahmed argues that 'there is no body as such that is given in the world: bodies materialise in a complex set of temporal and spatial relations to other bodies, including bodies that are recognised as familiar, familial and friendly, and those that are considered strange' (Ahmed 2000, 40), she evolves the body-as-object into *embodiment*: a relational, moving, and contextually and situationally specific process of being. Oyèrónké Oyěwùmí explores this in the context of Yorùbá culture:

> From a Yorùbá stance, the body appears to have an exaggerated presence in Western thought and social practice, including feminist theories. In the Yorùbá world, particularly in pre-nineteenth-century Ọ̀yọ́ culture, society was conceived to be inhabited by people in relation to one another. ... Social hierarchy was determined by social relations. ... how persons were situated in relationships shifted depending on those involved in the particular situation.[17]

She gives several examples of this, such as the various de-gendered forms that *kùnlẹ̀* (kneeling) can take as a mode of respectful address towards an *ọba* (ruler) or Ẹlẹ̀dá (the Maker),[18] or in her description of 'the principle of seniority', which determines Yorùbá social hierarchies more so than (and even irrespective of) gender. Unlike gender, she explains, seniority is only comprehensible as part of relationships: 'A superior is a superior regardless of body-type.'[19] The challenge Oyěwùmí poses here specifically targets the 'Western' and 'European-derived' conceptual paradigms that treat gender and anatomic sex, as well as race and other visible bodily differences, as universal signifiers that can be read and categorized into a social hierarchy. She calls this 'assumption that biology determines social position' the 'bio-logic' and 'body-reasoning' of Western philosophical paradigms.[20] Moreover, she deconstructs the fundamental separation between 'Self' and 'Other' in Western conceptualizations of identity, arguing that this division between the 'I' (as a fixed and objective notion of self, possessive of a body,

'my body') and the world is a power-driven ideological construct –
one that a deeper exploration of relational cultures like the Yorùbá
can challenge.[21]

Bodies, spirits and space: History-making and communal embodiments

Oyěwùmí's anthropological analysis of Yorùbá 'world sense',
alongside the above-mentioned schools of queer theory, advances
the idea that feminist decolonial methods of knowledge-making
and knowledge-access take root in, but are not limited to, the
corporeal. Rather than viewing the body-as-object, they concern
themselves with embodied experience, as a moving and interactive
process, which is as much personal as it is communal (remember
the age-old feminist slogan: 'The personal is political'). In the
works and thought of Black, Indigenous, Latinx and Chicana
intersectional feminists explored here, knowledge develops through
one's own bodily senses as well as through ancestral and communal
world senses, which are moved not only by what we can see or
sense in the present moment – in the privacy of our own bodies and
imaginations – but also through a connection to our environments
(our physical surroundings as well as the in/animate beings they host)
and to a transtemporal, transgenerational and transdimensional
spiritual world: where '*spiritual and material* [as well as personal
and collective, present and historical] *are not dissociated*'.[22]

   In literature and art, these ideas take various material forms. For
example, *A Map to the Door of No Return* (2001), a semi-fictional,
book-length autobiographical prose poem by Trinidadian writer,
filmmaker and activist Dionne Brand, depicts Black, Caribbean and
Diasporic realities through a series of vignettes about the everyday
lives, cultural customs and personal, mythical and mundane stories
of Trinidad's inhabitants, past and present, including Brand's own
family. The indeterminate genre of the text itself embodies the
material and metaphorical realities of migration, displacement and
survival in the aftermath of colonial violence. Brand's narrator
journeys both physically and metaphorically, through the island
as through her own and others' histories in search of a 'door of
no return': the breaking point that triggered the mass murder,

displacement, enslavement and centuries-old abuse of her ancestors. We might imagine this door as the threshold of what Toni Morrison has conceptualized as 'the racial house'.[23] Humanity stepped through the Door of No Return into 'the racial house' with the advent of the transatlantic slave trade, triggering the birth of structural racism, the prison industrial complex and the global imperialist market we know today. Brand's metaphor of the Door of No Return, similar to Morrison's notion of Home, allows an imaginative journey to a *'spiritual location'*[24] where the trauma of slavery has not yet happened: an unmappable place, a spiritual memory and a life free of the racist house-cum-prison. Home is 'a-world-in-which-race-does-not-matter', which '[unmatters] race away from pathetic yearning and futile desire', and where safety and 'belonging' meaningfully materialize in Black Being.[25]

Both authors create a space for this spiritual journey of hopeful possibility while paradoxically holding still the knowledge that '[t]here is as it says no way in; no return'; no way back.[26] None of us have ever lived 'in a world in which race did not matter',[27] so isn't such a world not only historically immaterial from our vantage point but even unimaginable, unspeakable in the languages we know? Did the world, the Home, on the other side of this door ever even exist? All that is knowable of it now materializes in the embodied experiences and spiritual, ancestral and transgenerational memories of Black communities and bodies: bodies that carry an internal, trauma-laden psychic split that cannot be sutured. Yet the living wound of it compels the recognition that this violence is not past. The wound, like the search for the Door of No Return, illuminates 'a past that is not past, a past that is with us still; a past that cannot and should not be pacified in its presentation'.[28] In Saidiya Hartman's words, 'this history has engendered me',[29] and thus a threshold between past and present does not categorically exist in the material reality of the Black body. As Christina Elizabeth Sharpe frames it,

> Living in the wake [of slavery] means living the history and present of terror, from slavery to the present, as the ground of our everyday Black existence; living the historically and geographically dis/continuous but always present and endlessly reinvigorated brutality in, and on, our bodies while even as that terror is visited on our bodies the realities of that terror are erased. Put another way, living in the wake means living in and

with terror in that in much of what passes for public discourse *about* terror we, Black people, become the *carriers* of terror, terror's embodiment, and not the primary objects of terror's multiple enactments; the ground of terror's possibility globally.[30]

As a result, the Black body, this 'estranged body, the legislated body, the violated, rejected, deprived body' also becomes a 'consummate home' wherein 'race magnifies the matter that matters'.[31] Questions of history, questions of race and questions of home all culminate in the physical as well as untouchable, unlocatable, unnameable, yet viscerally palpable senses and sensibilities of Black bodies.

As so many Black authors, from Hartman to Marlene NourbeSe Philip, from Sharpe to Brand and Morrison, have demonstrated, the academic archive captures a painfully sparse and obfuscating history of slavery. The 'silence of the archive' emanates from '[t]he scarcity of African narratives of captivity and enslavement'. In Hartman's own search for Venus, 'an emblematic figure of the enslaved woman in the Atlantic world',

> [t]here is not one extant autobiographical narrative of a female captive who survived the Middle Passage. This silence in the archive in combination with the robustness of the fort or barracoon, not as a holding cell or space of confinement but as an episteme, has for the most part focused the historiography of the slave trade on quantitative matters and on issues of markets and trade relations.[32]

In other words, the gaping omissions in the history of slavery and racism are neither accidental nor merely empirical. They are ideological and deliberate: an 'episteme' of racist, gendered, sexual and colonial violation. The 'truth' of history, therefore, should be sought not only in what is visible on the surface but also in the archive's material fabric: what materials are present? What materials, voices, bodies are absent? What has led to these exclusions, inclusions and ruptures in the fabric of history? How are they distorting our understanding of it and shaping its legacy in the present?

NourbeSe Philip, in contextualizing the paradoxes and impossibilities of holding the history of the *Zong* massacre (preserved in the archive not as genocide or a murder trial, which it should have been, but as a court case over an insurance claim for 'loss of [slave] cargo' by the slave ship owners) in her epic anti-poem, *Zong!*, also testifies that even when presented with the '"complete" text of the [*Zong* court] case, the reader does not ever know it, since the complete story does not exist. All that remains are the legal texts and documents of those who were themselves intimately connected to, and involved in, a system that permitted the murder of the Africans on board the *Zong*'.[33] Neither the voices and testimonials, nor the names, of the people murdered on the ship remain. The historical record instead privileges the voices of colonizers and slave owners, whose language 'promulgated the non-being of African peoples'[34] and whose archive relegates the stories of racist brutality to 'the past'. 'In the face of such institutional neglect', Ann Cvetkovich argues, and '[i]n the absence of institutionalized documentation or in opposition to official histories, memory becomes a valuable historical resource, and ephemeral and personal collections of objects stand alongside the documents of the dominant culture in order to offer alternative modes of knowledge'.[35] The artworks explored here offer such 'alternative modes' of storytelling, remembering and archiving. In the absence of historical voices or names, the body and embodied experience become the archive – especially those aspects of it that evade verbal, visual or conventionally 'legible' representation.

Therefore, 'bodies' here are not understood as separate from their environments or relationships. 'The Black body is signed as physically and psychically open space, almost always in the Diaspora. A space not simply owned by those who embody it but constructed and occupied by other embodiments. Inhabiting it is a domestic, hemispheric pastime, a transatlantic pastime, an international pastime.'[36] In other words, the Black body, Black Being and embodiment, is moved and shaped by what Sharpe calls 'the weather': 'It is not the specifics of any one event or set of events that are endlessly repeatable and repeated, but the totality of the environments in which we struggle; the machines in which we live.'[37] Equally, it is not the singular identity or experience of any one individual body that holds the knowledge of the physical and psychic repercussions of racist and colonial violence. The history of slavery, which is not a linear timeline but a continuum of present, past and future, lives and breathes like an organic being through the bodies and environments (both material and spiritual) involved in its legacy. Just as there is no Map to the Door of No Return, there is no specific geographical location and no border demarcating the diaspora. How we demarcate one body from another in the weather in which we are all implicated becomes a political question of collective responsibility.

When Brand thinks of the Black body as an 'open space ... not simply owned by those who embody it but constructed and occupied by other embodiments', she holds two contradictory possibilities at once. On the one hand, she exposes 'the not unwilling commercial exploitation of the Black body', in which she claims both whites and Blacks engage.[38] On the other, the collective communion around the desire for survival, freedom and restoration of the wholeness of Black Being and Black history creates other possible futures. As Sharpe observes, Brand's text explores 'the paradoxes of blackness within and after the legacies of slavery's denial of Black humanity'.[39] It is the tension in these paradoxes – not the utopian, 'Edenesque' (as Morrison puts it) fantasies of a race-free world – that matters in the project of 'reclaim[ing] the Black body from that domesticated, captive, open space' which perpetuates the abuse of Black bodies.[40]

The metaphor of 'the Door of No Return', like 'the Black body', holds an untouchable, unmappable, unnameable, yet viscerally palpable (in Lorde's terms, 'erotic')[41] sense of Black Being through time and space, across bodily boundaries, which are as ethereal (and yet sensing and sensitive) as the door itself. 'This door is not mere physicality. It is a spiritual location. It is also perhaps a psychic destination. Since leaving was never voluntary, return was, and still may be, an intention, however deeply buried. There is as it says no way in; no return.'[42] As Brand evokes the simultaneous beingness and non-beingness of this door (this Map, this Return, this No),[43] she opens a space for communal connection and mutual validation of the unbearably contradictory and unspeakable effects of the transgenerational trauma of slavery. The door 'is not mere physicality' (my emphasis), yet the phrasing implies a physicality and palpability of some form: it is more than 'physicality', but the physical, the embodied, nonetheless pulsates within it. To this door, 'which is illuminated in the consciousness of Blacks in the Diaspora there are no maps', yet it does nonetheless make up 'a spiritual location', 'a psychic destination', a place – even if this place must mutate into 'dis/place'.[44]

As I have argued elsewhere, 'home for the exile is never fixed, defined, or definitional, but rather it exists in the very movement of material and psychic migration ... home is not simply a site of either blithe belonging or irrevocable loss: it moves in a spiralling, transformational, and transmaterialising dialectic of rupture and repair, pain and pleasure, longing and letting go'.[45] So within intersectional feminist politics, art and literature, 'the body' is not fixed. It is mobile, relational, held and creatively bursting with contradictions. It crosses temporal, intersubjective and interdimensional borders to no resolute end or destination.

Sensitive borders: Skin, touch, feelings and negotiating boundaries

In tracing the body's 'creative responses to exile',[46] Brand, Philip, Machado and other decolonial feminist writers compel us to question how and why the 'marking out [of] the boundaries of bodies' happens in our theories, politics and representations of embodiment.[47] Concepts of 'borders' and 'boundaries' perpetually recur in their artistic works, as in the critical theories and activist praxes entangled with/in them. In *Strange Encounters*, for example, Ahmed thinks about the skin as 'a border that feels'.[48] This idea builds and expands on the wider work of affect theorists and phenomenologists, such as Sue Cataldi, whose 1993 book *Emotion, Depth, and Flesh* influentially bridged feminist theory with Maurice Merleau-Ponty's ideas about relational embodiment and the extension of bodies into their environments. Ahmed and Jackie Stacey's edited collection, *Thinking Through the Skin* (2001), proliferated further scholarly and artistic perspectives on the skin as 'a border that feels', as a soft and permeable boundary between bodies and subjects, as a material as well as a psychic, sense-making surface: 'Skin opens our bodies to other bodies: through touch, the separation of self and other is undermined in the very intimacy or proximity of the encounter.'[49] Skin simultaneously demarcates and connects us; we read it in order to distinguish one self from an-other and we ascribe social meanings to what we deem 'legible' on the skin. Skin, Ahmed and Stacey argue, also allows us to think about the transformation of bodies through time: 'Skin is temporal in the sense that it is affected by the passing of time or, to put it differently, it materializes that passing in the accumulation of marks, of wrinkles, lines and creases, as well as in the literal disintegration of skin.'[50]

In her poetry collection, *She Tries Her Tongue, Her Silence Softly Breaks* (1989), NourbeSe Philip contemplates how in/sensitivity to the politics and embodied histories of our languages (mother tongues, father tongues, public discourses and poetic selves, or 'i-mages')[51] can make or break the bodies and 'erotic' knowledges implicated within them:

> What happens when you are excluded from the fullness and wholeness of language?
> What happens when only one aspect of a language is allowed you – as woman?
> – as Black? …
> What happens to a language that is withheld or only used in a particular way with its users – does it become dissociated?
> – one level business
> – one level orders, commands, abuses, brutality
> – one level education to a specific purpose and level
> What of celebration?
> What of love?
> What of trust between individuals?[52]

Similar to Lorde's theorization of the 'erotic',[53] Philip critiques the implicitly colonial move to disassociate language from feeling ('– one level business / – one level orders, commands, abuses, brutality'). To determine how, when and what about one should speak ('one level education to a specific purpose and level') is to exercise a disembodying move that ruptures the i-mages of woman, Black, human. An insensitivity to and in language, she argues, violates one's access to oneself and others ('What of love? / What of trust between individuals?'). As so many other feminist creators have argued, such access and intersubjective connectivity, whether that happens through mutual care, storytelling or physical and emotional intimacies, enables the liberation, healing and empowerment of the politically marginalized.

Through skin touch or skin ruptures, we may also explore how we navigate pleasure, pain, care, intimacy and our own senses of ourselves. Feminist disability theorists and phenomenologists Margrit Shildrick and Janet Price consider how the habitually internalized effects of 'normative separation' (that is, our senses of ourselves as distinct, detached and autonomous, resistant and even fearful of being touched or 'contaminated' by an-other's proximity) become radically challenged by relationships that require care. Price, who has a diagnosis of MS, writes of the 'qualitative difference' that she experiences in the physical assistance she receives from 'friends as opposed to care workers': the warmth and comfort of friends' emotional intimacy contrast the 'difference and discomfort [that] emerges in the touches that seem unfamiliar'. Shildrick, thereafter, reflects on how 'unsettled' she sometimes felt 'in the context of tactile interaction' because of her uncertainty of Price's 'overtly fluctuating sense of touch' (and therefore her boundaries) as a result of her MS: 'Lacking a clear sense of Janet's own corporeal boundaries, I found it difficult to know at any given moment whether a greeting hug was still experienced as a sign of affection, given and returned, an unfelt and therefore meaningless gesture or even a more or less painful assault.' The mutually constitutive experience of touch also meant that any uncertainty 'Margrit' felt about the tactile boundaries of 'Janet's' personhood spread to 'our understanding of our own bodies'. 'What does it mean to hold a hand that has temporarily lost sensation, that cannot press back in return? Why does your own hand suddenly feel so clumsy in its gestures?'[54]

The 'unsettlement' Shildrick contemplates, though clearly uncomfortable, holds the potential for such encounters to become sites of necessary disruption and reimagination of the normative order. As Minh-ha reflects in an essay on migration and cultural displacement, '[t]he more displacements one has gone through, the more music one can listen to. Appeal is a question of vibration ... Isn't it by the help of vibrations, often via the power of the word and the touch, that illnesses can be cured?'[55] In inadvertent yet palpable affinity with Oyěwùmí's notion of 'world-sense', Minh-ha entangles the concept of migrant unsettlement, of being refused entry and treated as societal 'refuse', with the ability to sense and internalize otherness in liberating, vibrant and visceral ways. The more 'unsettled' one feels in a relational encounter, the more acutely attuned one becomes to the other/otherness present (for better or for worse). Through such attunement, one lets an-other *in*, touches and is touched back, transforms and is reversibly transformed, *transmaterialized*.

The powerful potential of unsettlement, which always also connotes 'difference' and alienation, expresses itself potently in queer feminist readings and writings on/of horror, monstrosity and the uncanny. In the late 1980s and early 1990s, J. Halberstam and Eve Kosofsky Sedgwick introduced the idea of queer monstrosity through their respective studies of nineteenth-century Gothic literature and its resonances within modern queer politics, cinema and art. In *Skin Shows* (1995), Halberstam argues that 'the emergence of the monster within Gothic fiction marks a peculiarly modern emphasis upon the horror of particular kinds of bodies'.[56] They theorize how the representation of certain bodies as horrifying and uncanny materializes as subtle signalling of sexual and gender deviancy on the one hand, and racial and class difference transgressing the borders of colonial order on the other. The figure of the monster, they demonstrate, 'de-monstrates' the markings of deviance, which are exaggerated to such an extent as to make the deviant means and 'place of corruption' unmissable, even overwhelming: 'simply too much'.[57] Such exaggeration of monstrous visibility plays the function of moral performativity (here is how you identify the queer, the criminal, the foreigner, the corrupting element) while instilling in the reader the impulse to watch out for signs of monstrosity in the wider social and political world: to police and regulate deviant bodies on behalf of the powers that be, sustaining the normative order at all in/human costs.

Monsters, Halberstam suggests, also 'always combine the markings of a plurality of differences': a monster often embodies multiple signs of deviance simultaneously, e.g. sexual/gender fluidity, racialization, visually exaggerated disablement.[58] As such, monstrosity can unlock deeper understandings of how we navigate relationships with, responses to and fears of otherness. Among the most terrifying qualities of the monster is not simply their extravagant 'ugliness', their 'difference' from the normative subject, or the ways in which 'meaning itself runs riot' when we face the monster.[59] Monstrosity's greatest terror, Shildrick suggests elsewhere, is 'the risk of indifferentiation' from ourselves:

> Even the Monster of Cracow's gross violation of external order, its suturing together of surfaces that should remain apart, cannot disguise its claim on the human. It remains a figure of both horror and fascination. ... In collapsing the boundaries between self and other, monsters constitute an undecidable absent presence at the heart of the human being. Alongside their external manifestation, they leave also a trace embedded within, that, in Derridean terms,

operates as the signifier not of difference but of *différance*. What is at stake throughout is the risk of indifferentiation.[60]

However extravagant and otherworldly the monster's corporeality may be, they nonetheless always maintain a 'claim to the human': the monster typically suffers overt and covert inhumane treatment as moral punishment for embodying transgressive, albeit horrifyingly exaggerated, *human* traits. As such, they illuminate what limits and threatens the 'stable, autonomous and singular human subject', exposing the fragility of the 'modernist fantasy' of human orderliness and legibility.[61] The monster makes it impossible to take for granted or transcend the messy, painful, slimy, embarrassing, frightening, exposing, leaky, precarious and unpredictable realities of the body. They force us to confront and respond to our own fragility and terror of losing our senses of ourselves. Ultimately, the monster represents the rumbling chaos and unintelligibility within each of us: who or what might we become, and what might become of us, if we loosen our boundaries and let an-other in? Is monstrosity contagious? Am I intrinsically a monster without knowing it? If I show compassion, care and solidarity with the monster – if I allow them to emotionally touch me – will their monstrosity contaminate me? If we let the monster in, we might become part-monster too. And if we do, we also run the risk of becoming an enemy of the state: the abject we have loathed, feared and violated all along.

Queer and feminist cultures' fascination with horror, violence and monstrosity expresses itself in various modes, from drag and activism to fiction, theatre, performance art and television.[62] Queer horror, as a multimodal genre, acts as a reclamational response to the ideological 'monstering' and political as well as literal, physical brutalities that bodies on the margins of normative order have experienced and continue to experience in many contexts. In the same way that terms like 'queer' or 'witch' have been reclaimed to signify not shame and persecution but empowering political identities, artists and activists have turned the figure of the monster into a dazzling, camp and unapologetically disruptive political hero. Rather than fearing or reordering the monster, queer horror fully embraces them: the monster makes a space for us to confront our biggest fears about ourselves, turning them into camp comedy or magic, and permitting cathartic exaltation in gore, hysteria, mad laughter and chaos. The monster's threat of merging with us, or even lurking within us, becomes a provocation of radical acceptance and love of self and other – even if these selves prove incorrigibly ugly, disorderly, perverted or dangerous. As the final literary example I will explore here will show, queer horror can also turn the monstering mirror back on the fearful, normativizing eye that beholds it. If we fear to break the silence or challenge the oppressor, the queer monster will reflect that cowardice back to us. If we lack the drive or language to break historical silences, the monster will shed light on our complicity and challenge us to re-evaluate it.

Carmen Maria Machado's 2017 short story collection, *Her Body and Other Parties*, and specifically the opening story, 'The Husband Stitch', offer a potent example of this. While the entire collection features stories that teeter on the faintly detectable boundary between naturalist realism and magic, described by one of its early reviewers as 'a wild thing, this book, covered in sequins and scales, blazing with the influence of fabulists from Angela Carter to Kelly Link and Helen Oyeyemi, and borrowing from science fiction, queer theory and horror',[63] 'The Husband Stitch' stands out for the explicit ways in which it plays out the drama of intersubjectivity and bodily boundary-crossing, both in its narration and in the way it breaks the 'fourth wall' between text and reader. The story is narrated in the first person by a woman who leads a perfectly ordinary life: 'I am a good girl, from a good family.'[64] She meets her high school sweetheart at seventeen years old and eventually marries him; they have a son and their life together appears unremarkable – their marriage happy and sexually fulfilling. The characters remain unnamed throughout, knowable not by language markers but by their behaviours and textual 'vibrations', to invoke Minh-ha again. The narrator has only one identifying marker: a green ribbon tied around her neck.

Upon the characters' first meeting at a neighbour's party, she 'chooses' him with a kiss and thus their relationship begins with a rupture – in the fabric of the narrative as in the character's mouth and personal boundaries:

> He kisses her back, gently at first, but then harder, and even pushes open my mouth a little with his tongue, which surprises me and, I think, perhaps him as well. I have imagined a lot of things in the dark, in my bed, beneath the weight of that old quilt, but never this, and I moan. When he pulls away, he seems

startled. His eyes dart around for a moment before settling on my throat.

'What is that?' he asks.

'Oh, this?' I touch the ribbon at the back of my neck. 'It's just my ribbon.' I run my fingers halfway around its green and glossy length, and bring them to rest on the tight bow that sits in the front. He reaches out his hand, and I seize it and press it away.

'You shouldn't touch it,' I say. 'You can't touch it.'

Before we go inside, he asks if he can see me again. I tell him I would like that. That night, before I sleep, I imagine him again, his tongue pushing open my mouth, and my fingers slide over myself and I imagine him there, all muscle and desire to please, and I know that we are going to marry.[65]

The scene of their first kiss foreshadows a pattern that will carry on for the rest of their life together: she initiates contact, he reciprocates, 'gently at first, but then harder', testing the boundaries of how far he can go before he reaches her 'No', her absolute boundary: the ribbon. The narrator perpetually reminds him (and us) that 'You can't touch' the ribbon under any circumstances, though she never explains why that is.

As the story goes on and their perfectly 'sweet' courtship evolves into a passionate marriage, this episode repeats itself.[66] Yet every time it does, the boundary crossing gets a little more daring. Each time, she gets unsettled but she also wilfully participates, curious about her own desire, curious about what and how her body can do and feel, fascinated by 'the rhythm, the concrete sense of his need, the clarity of his release'.[67] The narrator recounts the events of what happened without naming her feelings, either to him or to the reader, but she conveys her emotional landscape by detouring into imaginary, at times fantastical fables:

'I need more,' he says, but he does not rise to do anything. He looks out the window, and so do I. *Anything could move out there in the darkness*, I think. A hook-handed man. A ghostly hitchhiker forever repeating the same journey. An old woman summoned from the repose of her mirror by the chants of her children. Everyone knows these stories – that is, everyone tells them, even if they don't know them – but no one ever believes them.[68]

The eerie sense of something ghostly, haunting, potentially lethal and eternal lurking in the dark, apparently outside rather than inside this intimate encounter, summons the murkiness and unspeakability of consent into our affective field. We soon discover that inside and outside, fable and truth, constitute the same reality (a monstrous reality made of a 'plurality of differences'). In Dorothy Allison's words, 'in a world of hard truth ... fiction can be a harder piece of truth'. Fantasy 'can become a curtain drawn shut, a piece of insulation, a disguise, a razor, a tool that changes every time it is used and sometimes becomes something other than we intended. The story becomes the thing needed'.[69]

In the narrator's fable, we sense a skin-bristling brush with violation, the precarity of being in a 'grey zone' where consent seems indeterminate. The imaginary shadows be/hold the knowledge of inexplicable but viscerally knowable wrongness: it

> begins with intensity: you are aroused by what you come up against. You register something in the sharpness of an impression. Something can be sharp without it being clear what the point is. ... You sense an injustice. You might not have used that word for it; you might not have the words for it; you might not be able to put your finger on it. ... Things don't seem right.[70]

Arousal can be pleasurable, exciting and frightening all at once; from the erotic springs vivid, vital and vicious knowledge.

As the characters marry and have a son, the pressure on her to explain her ribbon and allow him to touch it escalates. Not only does the husband perpetually find both direct and surreptitious ways to finger her ribbon, but as their son grows up, he starts asking about the ribbon, too. 'I tell him that we are all different, and sometimes you should not ask questions. I assure him that he'll understand when he is grown. I distract him with stories that have no ribbons: angels who desire to be human and ghosts who don't realize they're dead and children who turn to ash.'[71] Her use of fables to deter her son from tugging at her boundary parallels her similar attempts to 'draw the curtain shut' on her husband's transgressions. The fantastical horror stories of angels, monsters, ghosts and dead children externalize the living terror of unspeakable, unlocatable, yet palpably real sexual trauma.

The precarity of relational boundaries manifests further in one of the story's most distinctive structural features: the narrative breakage of the 'fourth wall'. Similar to the way Phoebe Waller-Bridge's Fleabag makes frequent eye contact with her viewer or David Slade's *Black Mirror: Bandersnatch* implicates the audience in brutalizing characters through its interactive, 'choose your own adventure' format,[72] in 'The Husband Stitch', the narrative is punctuated by occasional commands posed to the reader:

> (If you read this story out loud, please use the following voices:
> ME: as a child, high-pitched, forgettable; as a woman, the same.
> THE BOY WHO WILL GROW INTO A MAN, AND BE MY
>   SPOUSE: robust with serendipity.
> MY FATHER: kind, booming; like your father, or the man you
>   wish was your father.
> MY SON: as a small child, gentle, sounding with the faintest
>   lisps; as a man, like my husband.
> ALL OTHER WOMEN: interchangeable with my own.)
> (If you are reading this story out loud, make the sound of the
>   bed under the tension of train travel and lovemaking by
>   straining a metal folding chair against its hinges. When you
>   are exhausted with that, sing the half-remembered lyrics of
>   old songs to the person closest to you, thinking of lullabies
>   for children.)
> (If you are reading this story out loud, give a paring knife to the
>   listeners and ask them to cut the tender flap of skin between
>   your index finger and thumb. Afterward, thank them.)
> (If you are reading this story out loud, move aside the curtain
>   to illustrate this final point to your listeners. It'll be raining,
>   I promise.)[73]

These interjections (significantly demarcated by parentheses, visually representing boundaries) performatively embody the perpetual ruptures in the character's bodily and psychic boundaries throughout the story. The narrator does not ask whether the reader is able or willing to perform these tasks; the text simply demands that we do. Some of the commands are simple and unremarkable (make dramatic voices); some are eerie in their claim to clairvoyance ('It'll be raining, I promise'); some are silly, asking us to behave strangely but nonetheless harmlessly in public (make creaking sounds with a folding chair), while others demand that we urge fellow readers to self-harm (give the people around you a knife and ask them to cut themselves). The difficulty and injuriousness of the tasks escalate as the story progresses, just like the husband's assaults on the narrator's boundaries become increasingly persistent and violent. The text puts us in a position of querying our own limits: how far would I go, how much would I do to myself and/or others, in order to appease an authority? Without warning or consent, we enter into the power play of the story, compelling us to urgently interrogate our understanding and approach to boundaries (others' and our own). As hooks writes (echoing a widespread sentiment in social justice activism), 'All our silences in the face of racist assault are acts of complicity.'[74] Machado, therefore, leaves us with no option of remaining impartial.

The 'vivid or heightened language' of the fables, entangled with the abrupt breakage of the fourth wall, conveys what the narrator cannot speak: that everyone knows these stories of precarious violation; everyone tells them, even if they cannot put their finger on their knowledge that sexual violence in consensual relationships happens everywhere, every day. But even when 'everyone knows', even as the words are coming out of their mouths, somehow still 'no one ever believes' it. How can you expose a violation legitimated by laws of gendered ownership (marriage, motherhood) and paraded in plain sight? How do you identify the boundary distinguishing play and pleasure from violation? How far would we be willing – able – to push and stretch before our boundaries finally snap? To borrow Sedgwick's reading of Charlotte Brontë's Gothic novel *Villette*, 'The Husband Stitch' is 'piercing because so precarious, full of conviction yet somehow unreal'.[75] Here and throughout *Her Body*, Machado compels her readers to feel the vibrations of invisible, untraceable, unnameable violence – and then leaves it up to us to decide whether and how to break the spell of silent complicity; whether and how we will let the monster in, acknowledge the monster within, and in communion with it, change.

Conclusion

Feminist theory is, historically and intrinsically, 'theory in the flesh'.[76] It engenders the act of putting our embodied, often unnameable yet palpable knowledges into words, forging new languages to tell 'our stories in our own words' and 'bridge the contractions in our experience'.[77] As the artists and theorists explored in this essay have attested, there is infinite potential for liberation and transformation in thinking and feeling through 'the body', its sensitive borders and the organic, transdimensional ecosystems within which we relate and of which we are made. Tracing the significance of bodies and embodied knowledges, beyond fixed identity markers, across fields and genres has time and again offered rewarding and subversive methods of inquiry.

Yet as much as feminism and the body are inextricably linked – so much so that we can hardly think of one without the other – an inquiry into 'the body' as a feminist concern runs the risk of importing the very cultural and ideological biases that scholars like Oyěwùmí, Ahmed, Chandra Talpade Mohanty, Cleonora Hudson-Weems or Azza Basarudin, among many others, have critiqued. The concept of the body, like any theoretical framework, opens certain doors while simultaneously closing others; the inclusions it enables lead to parallel exclusions. A significant example is the conspicuous exclusion of Chinese women's literature from this essay. As scholars such as Tani Barlow, Grace Fong, Haiping Yan or Hui Wu have shown, searching for a universalized notion of either 'body' or 'woman' in Chinese women's literature skews the material, cultural and historical context in which those works were forged. In *The Question of Women in Chinese Feminism* (2004), Barlow shows that the very concept of 'woman', as understood in an Anglophone context, does not strictly exist in the Chinese language and cultural imaginary. Fong demonstrates, in her study of suicide writings by late-medieval Chinese women of the Ming-Qing period, how reading these texts through the framework of 'the body', though productive in its own right, could also obscure copious and crucial elements of the works because the relationship between gender, the body and women's experiences simply does not function in a parallel or culturally translatable way compared to the other artworks examined here.

I indicate these tangible problems of cross-contextual translation not to deter the genuinely valuable embodied methods and frameworks of engagement explored here, but I am rather suggesting that the questions they raise must remain integrated into our evolving understandings of the body's dis/place in our knowledges. What feels most needed at this moment for feminist and social justice art and theory is to 'loosen [our] attachment to the facts' and known frameworks and to embrace the 'continuous, fickle, evolving set of processes that eschews definition, or concreteness, or knowing'. Through 'a deep inhale', let us try and imagine otherwise.[78]

Notes

1   Sara Ahmed, *Living a Feminist Life* (Durham: Duke University Press, 2017), 22.
2   Ibid.
3   Elizabeth Grosz, *Volatile Bodies: Toward a Corporeal Feminism* (Bloomington: Indiana University Press, 1994), 13–14.
4   A charge mounted against Western feminism's so-called First Wave, including figures like Elizabeth Cady Stanton (1815–1902), Matilda Joslyn Gage (1826–1898) or Simone de Beauvoir (1908–1986). The 'generational waves' model of chronicling feminist history has been as popular and matter-of-fact in its applications as it has been criticized, not least for its Euro- and Anglo-centricity. For an introductory glance at the 'waves model', its history and problems, see Nancy Hewitt, ed., *No Permanent Waves: Recasting Histories of U.S. Feminism* (New Brunswick: Rutgers University Press, 2010).
5   Grosz, *Volatile Bodies*, 14, 17, 9.
6   Sara Ahmed, *Strange Encounters: Embodied Others in Post-Coloniality* (London and New York: Routledge, 2000), 41.
7   Ibid., 42.
8   bell hooks, *Teaching to Transgress: Education as the Practice of Freedom* (New York: Routledge, 1994), 61.
9   Ahmed, *Strange Encounters*, 41.
10   Trinh T. Minh-ha, *Elsewhere, within Here: Immigration, Refugeeism and the Boundary Event* (London: Routledge, 2011), 51.
11   Judith Butler, *Gender Trouble: Feminism and the Subversion of Identity* (New York: Routledge, 1990), 114.
12   Ibid., 115.
13   Monique Wittig, 'The Mark of Gender', *Feminist Issues* 5 (June 1985): 4.
14   Karen Barad, *Meeting the Universe Halfway: Quantum Physics and the Entanglement of Matter and Meaning* (Durham and London: Duke University Press, 2007), 54.
15   Paul Preciado, Paul, *Can the Monster Speak?*, trans. Frank Wynne (London: Fitzcarraldo Editions, 2021), 34–5.
16   Preciado is using the term 'monster' as a political reclamation, rather than derision, of transgender difference. These ideas will be developed further in my later discussion of queer monstrosity.

17 Oyèrónké Oyěwùmí, *The Invention of Women: Making an African Sense of Western Gender Discourses* (Minneapolis: University of Minnesota Press, 1997), 13.

18 Ibid., 36–7.

19 Ibid., 42, 38.

20 Ibid., 17.

21 Ibid., 15.

22 Ibid., 28.

23 Toni Morrison, 'Home', in *The House That Race Built: Original Essays by Toni Morrison, Angela Y. Davis, Cornel West, and Others on Black Americans and Politics in America Today*, ed. Wahneema Lubiano (New York: Vintage Books 1998).

24 Dionne Brand, *A Map to the Door of No Return: Notes to Belonging* (Toronto: Doubleday Canada, 2001), 1.

25 Morrison, 'Home', 3–5.

26 Brand, *A Map to the Door of No Return*, 1.

27 Morrison, 'Home', 3.

28 Christina Elizabeth Sharpe, *In the Wake: On Blackness and Being* (Durham: Duke University Press, 2016), 62.

29 Saidiya Hartman, 'Venus in Two Acts', *Small Axe* 26/12, no. 2 (2008): 4.

30 Sharpe, *In the Wake*, 15.

31 Morrison, 'Home', 5.

32 Hartman, 'Venus in Two Acts', 3–4.

33 Marlene NourbeSe Philip, *Bla_k: Essays & Interviews* (Toronto: BookThug, 2011), 196.

34 Ibid., 197.

35 Ann Cvetkovich, *An Archive of Feelings: Trauma, Sexuality, and Lesbian Public Cultures* (Durham, NC: Duke University Press, 2003), 8.

36 Brand, *A Map to the Door of No Return*, 38.

37 Sharpe, *In the Wake*, 111.

38 Brand, *A Map to the Door of No Return*, 38–9.

39 Sharpe, *In the Wake*, 14.

40 Brand, *A Map to the Door of No Return*, 43.

41 Audre Lorde, *Sister Outsider: Essays and Speeches by Audre Lorde* (Berkeley, CA: Crossing Press, 2007), 53–9.

42 Brand, *A Map to the Door of No Return*, 1.

43 Sharpe's writing on the meaning of 'living in the wake' of slavery resonates strongly here: 'To be in the wake is to live in the no's, to live in the no-space that the law is not bound to respect, to live in no citizenship, to live in the long time of Dred and Harriet Scott; and it is more than that' (Sharpe, *In the Wake*, 16).

44 Philip, *Bla_k: Essays & Interviews*, 254.

45 Boriana Alexandrova, *Joyce, Multilingualism, and the Ethics of Reading* (London: Palgrave Macmillan, 2020), 237–41.
46 Morrison, 'Home', 5.
47 Ahmed, *Strange Encounters,* 40.
48 Ibid., 45.
49 Sara Ahmed and Jackie Stacey, 'Introduction: Dermographies', in *Thinking through the Skin*, ed. Sara Ahmed and Jackie Stacey (New York: Routledge, 2001), 6.
50 Ibid., 2.
51 Marlene NourbeSe Philip, *She Tries Her Tongue, Her Silence Softly Breaks* (Charlottetown: University of Toronto Press, 1989), 12.
52 Philip, *She Tries Her Tongue,* 21–2.
53 Lorde's notion of 'the erotic' connotes a form of radical 'self-connection', 'firmly rooted in the power of our unexpressed or unrecognized feeling'; 'our deepest and nonrational knowledge', and one that, in spite of the conventionally sexual connotations of the term, does not confine itself 'to the bedroom alone' (Lorde, *Sister Outsider*, 56–7). Her ideas also resonate in bell hooks's *All about Love: New Visions* (New York: William Morrow, 2018) or in María Lugones's concept of 'loving perception' (Lugones, 'Playfulness, "World"-Travelling, and Loving Perception', *Hypatia* 2, no. 2: 3–19).
54 Janet Price and Margrit Shildrick, 'Bodies Together: Touch, Ethics and Disability', in *Disability/Postmodernity: Embodying Disability Theory*, ed. Marian Corker and Tom Shakespeare (London and New York: Continuum, 2002), 71–2.
55 Minh-Ha, *Elsewhere, within Here,* 55.
56 Judith Halberstam, *Skin Shows: Gothic Horror and the Technology of Monsters* (Durham: Duke University Press, 1995), 3.
57 Ibid., 2.
58 Ibid., 5–6.
59 Ibid., 2.
60 Shildrick Margrit, 'You Are There Like My Skin: Reconfiguring Relational Economies', in *Thinking through the Skin*, ed. Sara Ahmed and Jackie Stacey (New York and London: Routledge, 2001), 163.
61 Ibid., 160.
62 Notable art-activist examples include the works of US drag queen Sharon Needles, Korean-American performance artist, musician, writer, mystic and disability activist Johanna Hedva, queer punk riot grrrl and lesbian activist group Tribe 8, or the queer BDSM activists of the 1970s–1990s, such as Pat Califia, Gayle Rubin, Queen Cougar, or Amber Rae and Robin Sweeney. Cult films like John Waters's *Cry Baby* or *Pink Flamingos* (starring the legendary Divine) also play

with the camp and extravagant exaggerations of 'ugliness', disgust, perversion and criminality, compelling the audience to question what and why they/we fear and punish as deviant and transgressive.

63 Parul Sehgal, 'Fairy Tales about the Fears Within', in *The New York Times*, 4 October 2017, available online: https://www.nytimes.com/2017/10/04/books/review-her-body-and-other-parties-carmen-maria-machado.html.
64 Carmen Maria Machado, 'The Husband Stitch', in *Her Body & Other Parties* (London: Serpent's Tail, 2019), 3.
65 Ibid., 4.
66 Ibid., 7.
67 Ibid., 5.
68 Ibid., 5–6.
69 Dorothy Allison, *Two or Three Things I Know for Sure* (New York, NY: Plume Books, 1996), 3.
70 Ahmed, *Living a Feminist Life*, 22.
71 Machado, 'The Husband Stitch', 27.
72 Choose Your Own Adventure was a genre of interactive children's and Young Adult fiction that particularly grew in popularity in the 1980s–1990s. The form's characterizing feature was its involvement of the reader in 'choosing' the trajectory of the story, as each chapter would end on a dilemma, where the reader would be given a choice of several possible places in the book they could flip to, depending on which way they wished the character to go. Slade's *Bandersnatch*, produced and hosted by Netflix, is the first cinematic emulation of this narrative form, made possible by the interactive capabilities of smart digital technology. Fascinatingly, Machado's groundbreaking memoir on intimate partner violence within queer relationships, *In the Dream House*, features a 'choose your own adventure' chapter, performatively interrogating the fraught notion of 'choice' in abusive relationships. See Carmen Maria Machado, *In the Dream House* (Graywolf Press: Minneapolis, 2019), 189–203.
73 Machado, 'The Husband Stitch', 3, 12, 16.
74 bell hooks, *Killing Rage: Ending Racism* (New York: Holt, 1996).
75 Eve Kosofsky Sedgwick, *The Coherence of Gothic Conventions* (New York: Methuen, 1986), 133.
76 Cherrie Moraga and Gloria Anzaldúa, eds, 'Entering the Lives of Others: Theory in the Flesh', in *This Bridge Called My Back: Writings by Radical Women of Color*, ed. Cherrie Moraga and Gloria Anzaldúa (Albany: State University of New York Press, 2015), 19.
77 Ibid.
78 Lola Olufemi, *Imagining Otherwise* (London: Hajar Press, 2021), 19.

Bibliography

Ahmed, Sara. *Strange Encounters: Embodied Others in Post-Coloniality*. London and New York: Routledge, 2000.

Ahmed, Sara. *Living a Feminist Life*. Durham: Duke University Press, 2017.

Ahmed, Sara, and Jackie Stacey. 'Introduction: Dermographies'. In *Thinking through the Skin*, edited by Sara Ahmed and Jackie Stacey, 1–17. New York: Routledge, 2001.

Alexandrova, Boriana. *Joyce, Multilingualism, and the Ethics of Reading*. London: Palgrave Macmillan, 2020.

Allison, Dorothy. *Two or Three Things I Know for Sure*. New York: Plume Books, 1996.

Barad, Karen. *Meeting the Universe Halfway: Quantum Physics and the Entanglement of Matter and Meaning*. Durham and London: Duke University Press, 2007.

Barlow, Tani E. *The Question of Women in Chinese Feminism*. Durham and London: Duke University Press, 2004.

Basarudin, Azza. *Humanizing the Sacred: Sisters in Islam and the Struggle for Gender Justice in Malaysia*. Seattle: University of Washington Press, 2016.

Brand, Dionne. *A Map to the Door of No Return: Notes to Belonging*. Toronto: Doubleday Canada, 2001.

brown, adrienne maree. *Pleasure Activism: The Politics of Feeling Good*. Chico: AK Press, 2019.

Butler, Judith. *Gender Trouble: Feminism and the Subversion of Identity*. New York: Routledge, 1990.

Cvetkovich, Ann. *An Archive of Feelings: Trauma, Sexuality, and Lesbian Public Cultures*. Durham, NC: Duke University Press, 2003.

Fong, Grace. 'Signifying Bodies: The Cultural Significance of Suicide Writings by Women in Ming-Qing China'. *NAN NÜ* 3, no. 1 (2001): 105–42.

Grosz, Elizabeth. *Volatile Bodies: Toward a Corporeal Feminism*. Bloomington: Indiana University Press, 1994.

Halberstam, Judith. *Skin Shows: Gothic Horror and the Technology of Monsters*. Durham: Duke University Press, 1995.

Hartman, Saidiya. 'Venus in Two Acts'. *Small Axe* 26/12, no. 2 (2008): 1–14.

Hewitt, Nancy A., ed. *No Permanent Waves: Recasting Histories of U.S. Feminism*. New Brunswick: Rutgers University Press, 2010.

hooks, bell. *Teaching to Transgress: Education as the Practice of Freedom*. New York: Routledge, 1994.

hooks, bell. *Killing Rage: Ending Racism*. New York: Holt, 1996.

hooks, bell. *All about Love: New Visions*. New York: William Morrow, 2018.

Hudson-Weems, Clenora. *Africana Womanism: Reclaiming Ourselves*. London and New York: Routledge, 2020.

Lorde, Audre. *Sister Outsider: Essays and Speeches by Audre Lorde*. Berkeley: Crossing Press, 2007.

Lugones, María. 'Playfulness, "World"-Travelling, and Loving Perception'. *Hypatia* 2, no. 2 (1987): 3–19.

Machado, Carmen Maria. 'The Husband Stitch'. In *Her Body & Other Parties*, 3–31. London: Serpent's Tail, 2017.

Machado, Carmen Maria. *In the Dream House*. Minneapolis: Graywolf Press, 2019.

Minh-Ha, Trinh T. *Elsewhere, within Here: Immigration, Refugeeism and the Boundary Event*. London: Routledge, 2011.

Mohanty, Chandra Talpade. 'Under Western Eyes: Feminist Scholarship and Colonial Discourses'. *Boundary* 12/13, no. 3 (1984): 333–58.

Moraga, Cherríe, and Gloria Anzaldúa, eds. 'Entering the Lives of Others: Theory in the Flesh'. In *This Bridge Called My Back: Writings by Radical Women of Color*. Albany: State University of New York Press, 2015.

Morrison, Toni. 'Home'. In *The House That Race Built: Original Essays by Toni Morrison, Angela Y. Davis, Cornel West, and Others on Black Americans and Politics in America Today*, edited by Wahneema Lubiano, 3–12. New York: Vintage Books, 1998.

Olufemi, Lola. *Experiments in Imagining Otherwise*. London: Hajar Press, 2021.

Oyěwùmí, Oyèrónkẹ́. *The Invention of Women: Making an African Sense of Western Gender Discourses*. Minneapolis: University of Minnesota Press, 1997.

Philip, Marlene NourbeSe. *She Tries Her Tongue, Her Silence Softly Breaks*. Charlottetown: University of Toronto Press, 1989.

Philip, Marlene NourbeSe. *Zong!* Middletown: Wesleyan University Press, 2011.

Philip, Marlene NourbeSe. *Bla_k: Essays & Interviews*. Toronto, Ontario, Canada: BookThug, 2017.

Preciado, Paul. *Can the Monster Speak?* Translated by Frank Wynne. London: Fitzcarraldo Editions, 2021.

Price, Janet, and Margrit Shildrick. 'Bodies Together: Touch, Ethics and Disability'. In *Disability/Postmodernity: Embodying Disability Theory*, edited by Marian Corker and Tom Shakespeare, 62–75. London and New York: Continuum, 2002.

Sedgwick, Eve Kosofsky. *The Coherence of Gothic Conventions*. New York: Methuen, 1986.

Sehgal, Parul. 'Fairy Tales about the Fears Within'. In *The New York Times*, 4 October 2017. Available online: https://www.nytimes.com/2017/10/04/books/review-her-body-and-other-parties-carmen-maria-machado.html.

Sharpe, Christina Elizabeth. *In the Wake: On Blackness and Being*. Durham: Duke University Press, 2016.

Shildrick, Margrit. 'You Are There Like My Skin: Reconfiguring Relational Economies'. In *Thinking through the Skin*, edited by Sara Ahmed and Jackie Stacey, 160–74. New York and London: Routledge, 2001.

Wittig, Monique. 'The Mark of Gender'. *Feminist Issues* 5 (1985): 3–12.

Wu, Hui. 'Post-Mao Chinese Literary Women's Rhetoric Revisited: A Case for an Enlightened Feminist Rhetorical Theory'. *College English* 72, no. 4 (2010): 406–23.

Wu, Hui, ed. *Once Iron Girls: Essays on Gender by Post-Mao Chinese Literary Women*. Translated by Hui Wu. Lanham: Lexington Books, 2011.

Yan, Haiping. *Chinese Women Writers and the Feminist Imagination, 1905–1948*. London and New York: Routledge, 2006.

6

Race and Post-colonialism

Rebekah Cumpsty

The body in contemporary literature is a receptor to and cipher for ongoing and reactivated forms of colonialism.[1] In Tsitsi Dangarembga's trilogy, which includes *Nervous Conditions* (1988), *The Book of Not* (2006) and *This Mournable Body* (2018), it is the body that makes legible the interrelated regimes of misogyny, racism, coloniality and capitalist imperialism.[2] The books begin in 1960s Rhodesia, covering the Second *Chimurenga* (Zimbabwe Liberation War 1966–1979), and conclude in post-independence Zimbabwe. Through Tambudzai (Tambu) Sigauke's perspective, the novels expose the compounding systems of patriarchy and colonial education, and the ways in which a post-independence neoliberal agenda extends the conditions of coloniality and colonialism, as well as the psychological effects of this material and epistemological violence.

Working through theorizations of race and the racialized body from Frantz Fanon, Anibal Quijano, Walter Mignolo and Anne McClintock, this chapter uses Dangarembga's trilogy as a case study to demonstrate how the body in literature indexes the interrelation of racism, coloniality/modernity and neoliberal capital. The material, epistemological and psychological control of the colonized body is made possible through racialized discourse. This discourse both fabricates the racialized body and maintains the hegemonic regimes of Eurocentric power and knowledge. While Dangarembga's trilogy understands the body to be on the frontline of colonial brutality, it also presents decolonial alternatives. These arise, firstly, through the implicit anti-colonial critique of the largely retrospective narrative, and secondly, through Nyasha's women's group at the close of the series. Moreover, Dangarembga's appropriation of the bildungsroman genre can be read as a decolonial gesture that centres the development of a Black, female character grappling with the material conditions of coloniality/modernity. The chapter begins with theorizations of racialized/colonial difference. Then, following Frantz Fanon and David Marriott, racialization in the novels is read as a process of epidermalization, petrification/fragmentation and sociogenesis.[3] Fanon's work on Blackness and the construction of race is seminal to post-colonial studies broadly, and Marriott's contemporary writing of the body, in particular.

Coloniality, colonialism and the racialized body

Given that, as David Marriott[4] notes, it is 'racism that produces the racialized body', then it is colonialism and coloniality that, respectively, create and maintain these regimes of power and knowledge. Colonialism and coloniality are distinct, but related terms, as Nelson Maldonado-Torres makes clear:

> Colonialism denotes a political and economic relation in which the sovereignty of a nation or a people rests on the power of another nation, which makes such nation an empire. Coloniality, instead, refers to long-standing patterns of power that emerged as a result of colonialism, but that define culture, labor, intersubjective relations, and knowledge production well beyond the strict limits of colonial administrations. Thus, coloniality survives colonialism.[5]

Colonialism in its historical and reactived forms is undergirded by the logic and epistemic frame of coloniality. Race and capital are the two primary axes of coloniality.[6] Race codifies difference along the lines of 'a supposedly different biological structure that placed some in a natural situation of inferiority to the others'.[7] Capital leads to 'the constitution of a new structure of control of labor and its resources and slavery, serfdom, small independent commodity production and reciprocity, together around and upon the basis of capital and the world market'.[8] The coloniality of power refers to the 'interrelation' of 'modern forms of exploitation and domination'; the coloniality of knowledge is concerned with the 'impact of colonization on the different areas of knowledge production' and the universalization of a Eurocentric epistemic framework; the coloniality of being makes 'reference to the lived experience of colonization and its impact on language'.[9] These related forms of coloniality denote the ways in which knowledge production, power/domination and modes of being have been and continue to be informed by core European ontologies.

Scientific discourse is instrumental in fabricating notions of race and the racialized body. Mignolo explains the imbrication of these concepts:

> Science (knowledge and wisdom) cannot be detached from language; languages are not just 'cultural' phenomena in which people find their 'identity'; they are also the location where knowledge is inscribed. And, since languages are not something human beings have but rather something of what humans beings are, coloniality of power and of knowledge engendered the coloniality of being.[10]

Science and history under the matrix of the coloniality of knowledge conceived of 'human' as white, male and European. This figure was the developmental goal of a teleology of progress beginning with 'primitive man' and concluding with the civilized and cultured male as demonstrably 'human'. History, Quijano writes, 'was conceived as an evolutionary continuum from the primitive to the civilized; from the traditional to the modern; from the savage to the rational; from pro-capitalism to capitalism'.[11] Under coloniality 'non-Europe belonged to the past, and so it was possible to think about relations between them in an evolutionary perspective ... the "inferior" "races" are inferior because they are "objects" of study or of domination/exploitation/discrimination, they are not "subjects," and, most of all, they are not "rational subjects"'.[12] Anne McClintock traces a similar genealogy of European racism.[13] Prior to 1850s, she identifies two primary explanations for the origins of racial difference. Monogenesis saw Adam as the single creative source from which successively uneven and imperfect incarnations were fashioned, depending on their climate. Polygenesis described different races emerging spontaneously in different places, with those in European climes understood as superior to the inherent degeneration of more southern regions. After the publication of Darwin's theory of evolution in 1859, the rationale of creationism waned, while the discourse of racialized difference expanded with 'the allure of numbers, the amassing of measurements and the science of statistics, giving birth to "scientific" racism, the most authoritative attempt to place social ranking and social disability on a biological and "scientific" footing'.[14] Anatomical differences were categorized in order to establish and universalize European subjecthood, what McClintock calls the 'Family of Man' on the one hand, and colonized others construed as inferior objects, on the other.[15]

This racist evolutionary perspective underpins what Sylvia Wynter calls the coloniality of being. Wynter identifies the 'overrepresentation of the "ethnoclass (i.e., Western bourgeois) conception of the human, Man," which has come to signify the "human itself"'.[16] Under this reading, conceptions of human are informed exclusively by an ethnoclass ontology that supposes only Western males of a certain class to be the source of human, against which all others are unfavourably compared. The coloniality of knowledge/being universalized this ethnoclass 'Man'. Following Wynter, Rebecca Duncan asserts the need to decolonize the 'human', in order to 'address how this category has been implemented over the history of "coloniality/modernity" … to suppress alternative forms of being and knowing in the interest of identifying exploitable and expendable lives and environments on a planetary scale'.[17] To begin to decolonize the category of the human is to, first, understand its colonial genealogy and, second, to recentre the material and subjective experiences of lives construed as expendable. Applied in a different context, Duncan identifies an aesthetic of objectification which designates the space of colonial difference. Taken from Mignolo, colonial difference is the consequence of the conjunction between capital and epistemology[18] and describes 'a subject position situated within coloniality's invented matrix of race, gender and nature, which thus bears the brunt both of its epistemic impositions and of the material degradations these legitimate'.[19] In Dangarembga's fiction, the subject position of colonial difference is occupied by Tambudzai. While this is a site characterized by material and ontological violence, it is also a 'loc[us] of enunciation' for potential decolonial gestures, such as the critique of colonial education and neoliberal imperialism voiced by Tambudzai.

Racialized alterity, a facet of colonial difference, is the focus of Frantz Fanon's work. The construction of Blackness condemns the 'Black man' to a 'zone of nonbeing, an extraordinarily sterile and arid region ... a veritable hell'.[20] Coloniality/colonialism is a 'total project' that leaves no part of the body, subject, society or reality untouched.[21] Racism specifically, a function of this totalizing project, acts on and through language, as well as the body and the psyche.

> In the white world, the man of colour encounters difficulties in elaborating his bodily schema. The image of one's body is solely negating activity. It's an image in the third person ... A slow construction of my self as a body in a spatial and temporal world – such seems to be the schema. It is not imposed on me; it is rather a definitive structuring of my self and the world – definitive because it creates a genuine dialectic between my body and the world.[22]

The decolonial effort begins, for Fanon, with the 'disalienation of the black man', which 'implies a brutal awareness of social and economic realities'.[23] This is augmented by an awareness of the two-part 'inferiority complex' imposed through coloniality/modernity: '[f]irst, economic. Second, internalization or epidermalization of this inferiority'.[24] Constructions of Blackness are tied to economic underdevelopment in the colony and to the ways in which this ontology and material reality register and act on the schema of the Black body. Fanon describes this epidermalization as a burden that disrupts the coherence between body and self/world. This inferiority is registered by and inscribed at the 'bodily level'.[25]

Simply put, race is not an essential category; instead racism creates and maintains the racialized body. David Marriott explains this construction through Fanon's 'stages of racialization – epidermalization, petrification, sociogeny'.[26] Epidermalization describes 'the imposition of a second historical racial schema on the corporeal schema proper', which 'is realized as an imaginary veiling of the body (as fetish, phobia, stereotype, scopophilia) and represents, finally, a racialized disfigurement or 'corporeal malediction'.[27] In other words, there is a somatic model, upon which a secondary Eurocentric/racialized mode is imposed, which shrouds and, therefore, disfigures the Black body for self and society. In *The Wretched of the Earth* (1961), '"petrified" and "petrification" describe the psychosocial effects of colonialism on the bodies and culture of the colonized'.[28] Colonial difference 'produces a certain *style* of embodiment (petrified, rigidified, inanimate, ankylotic)', forcing the 'colonial body' to perform the discourse of 'subjugation'.[29] Race is 'sociogenic' or socially produced, rather than inherent or essential.[30] Fanon writes: 'it is the colonist who *fabricated* and *continues to fabricate* the colonized subject'.[31] In turn, Marriott writes: 'the racialized body ... is formed through racist doctrine and belief, and is the channel and point of transmission through which a racist notion of humanity is inherited and passed down'.[32] The racialized body is often the cipher through which racism becomes legible and natural.

Patriarchal control and colonial education in *Nervous Conditions*

In *Nervous Conditions* Dangarembga artfully exposes how the 'articulated categories' of race, gender and class 'come into existence *in and through* relation to each other – if in contradictory and conflictual ways'.[33] Tambudzai's body is the figure which makes these discourses evident. As McClintock describes, European colonialism met pre-existing organizations of power, which were undermined, reinforced or repurposed for imperial ends. Colonized women, for instance, endured formal colonialism differently than their male counterparts, as they were marginalized by compounding regimes of patriarchal and colonial power.[34] As Ann Laura Stoler explains 'changes in household organization, the sexual division of labor, and the gender-specific control of resources ... have modified and shaped how colonial appropriations of land, labor, and resources were obtained'.[35] Although Dangarembga read Fanon after completing the manuscript, the novel speaks back to Fanon's male subject,[36] as is evident in the title and epigraph, taken from Jean-Paul Sartre's preface to *The Wretched of the Earth*: 'The condition of the native is a nervous condition.'[37] Instead, the novel describes the double colonization of women, subordinated by 'colonialism and patriarchy as co-conspirators'.[38] The colonized/

racialized/gendered body 'cannot exist for itself', Jennifer Williams explains, because coloniality 'literally steals the ontological freedom of native people'.[39] 'The existence of the colonized subject ends up fragmented, split between her/his own subjectivity and the colonizer's objectivity.'[40] Thus, when reading gender and race in Dangarembga's writing, it is necessary to add fragmentation to Fanon's and Marriott's stages of racialization.

The novel, a post-colonial bildungsroman,[41] is focused on Tambudzai's 'escape' and her cousin, Nyasha's 'rebellion', from the 'entrapment' of capitalism, patriarchy and colonialism.[42] Their 'nervous conditions' expose the 'inherent paradox' of these collaborative regimes, all of which depend on the productive and reproductive labour of women.[43] As Cindy Courville explains, 'under both traditional and colonial law, they [African women] were denied ownership and control of the land and the goods they produced. It was the unpaid labour of women and children which subsidized the colonial wage'.[44] Tambudzai identifies education as her escape from misogyny and rural poverty, but her elder brother, Nhamo, and her father, Jeremiah, undermine her effort to raise money for her fees. Nhamo steals the maize she has grown from seed to sell and, with cruel irony, gives it to his friends at school. When her teacher takes her into town, Tambudzai is able to raise £10 for her maize, but her father asserts his rights to her productivity: 'Tambudzai is my daughter, is she not? So isn't it my money?'[45] Tambudzai feels the 'injustice of [her] situation'.[46] Prior to his death, Nhamo was doted on as the only male child, his education was prioritized, and their uncle chose Nhamo to attend the mission school, at which he is principal. Nhamo parrots the patriarchal/colonial perspective, reducing people to bodies as labour and waste, when he explains that he does not like taking the bus home from the mission because 'the women smelt of unhealthy reproductive odours, the children were inclined to relieve their upset bowels on the floor, and the men gave off strong aromas of productive labour'.[47]

The opening chapters blister with Tambudzai's rage towards patriarchal control and colonial underdevelopment. Told retrospectively, this first-person narrative addresses an anonymous 'you'. 'I was not sorry when my brother died. Nor am I apologising for my callousness, as you may define it, my lack of feeling.'[48] This 'you', Kwame Anthony Appiah notes, is distanced from the narrator but not 'an Other from Elsewhere'.[49] Despite this remove, the narrative address assumes a shared and intimate concern with 'how the postcolonial Western-educated woman and her sisters, daughters, mothers and aunts, peasants or workers, wage-earners or wives, shall together find ways to create meaningful lives, escaping the burden of their oppression as women, but also as black people'.[50] Tambudzai is well aware of the burden of womanhood and Blackness at the outset of the novel: 'with the poverty of blackness on one side and the weight of womanhood on the other ... My mother said being black was a burden because it made you poor ... My mother said being a woman was a burden because you had to bear children and look after them and the husband'.[51] However, it is when Tambudzai's teacher, Mr Matimba, takes her to Umtali to sell her maize that her body is overtly racialized. She is called 'munt', 'plucky piccannin' and 'Kaffir'.[52] As a subject of Rhodesian colonial authority, Tambudzai's bodily difference is thus systemically racialized. Mr Matimba becomes obsequious to placate the white people, speaking 'in the softest, slipperiest voice I had ever heard him use'.[53] But here too, Tambudzai's resistance is voiced in her description of the white people: 'I did not like the way they looked, with their skin hanging in papery folds from their bones, malignant-looking brown spots on their hands, a musty, dusty, sweetish odour clinging around the woman like a haze.'[54] While the white body is meant to signify colonial superiority, it is withered and malignant under Tambudzai's gaze.

The disruption of Tambudzai's bodily schema and the effects of colonial difference can be traced to her uncle's mission education. Mbuya, Tambudzai's grandmother, provides a history of colonial settlement and education. She explains that '[w]izards well versed in treachery and black magic came from the south and forced the people from the land ... At last the people came upon the grey, sandy soil of the homestead'.[55] The history of settler colonialism in Zimbabwe is an account of what Donald S. Moore calls 'racialized dispossession', whereby '[r]ace became discursively deployed to legitimate the expropriation of African lands in the name of imperial and later national improvement'.[56] The impoverishment of the family's homestead is a direct result of this racialized dispossession and the reason they are financially dependent on Babamukuru. Mbuya's history links colonial occupation to mission education when she describes 'holy' 'wizards' who establish a mission school. Babamukuru is the first in the family to attend this school. The missionaries 'thought he was a good boy, cultivatable, in the way that land is, to yield harvests that sustain the cultivator'.[57] The metaphor of agricultural and human labour further demonstrates the legacies of land dispossession. However, the mission education 'indicated that life could be lived with a modicum of dignity in any circumstance if you worked hard enough and obeyed the rules ... endure and obey, for there is no other way'.[58] Mbuya connects the racialized dispossession of land with the cultivation and regulation of her son as a colonized subject. Babamukuru, however, had 'defied' the spell of poverty 'through hard work and dedication' and was able to gain '[p]lenty of power. Plenty of money. A lot of education. Plenty of everything'.[59, 60] It is due to Babamukuru's influence that Tambudzai identifies education as a way out of colonial difference and impoverishment, but Nyasha exposes the paradox of this sentiment.

Nyasha's body is the site on which the contradictions of patriarchal Shona[61] culture and colonial education clash and are thereby made evident. When she returns with her parents from their years in England, it was 'obvious' she had been away. Her dress and mannerisms have changed, and she struggles to speak Shona:

> She did not talk beyond a quick stuttered greeting ... I missed the ebullient companion I had had who had gone to England but not returned from there. Yet, each time she came I could see that she had grown a little duller and dimmer, the expression in her eyes a little more complex, as though she were directing more and more of her energy inwards to commune with herself about issues she alone had seen.[62]

Jennifer Williams describes Nyasha's body as 'a dialectic space',[63] which necessarily mediates between subjective/internal and objective/external realities. When she withdraws, she 'switched herself off',[64] a precursor, perhaps, to her disordered eating. Nyasha's 'rejection of food bears witness to the Nausea of a Being subjected to a corporeal schema not of her own design'.[65] Nyasha occupies the space of colonial difference: her anorexia and bulimia signify the subjective and material violence of this position. Deepika Bahri notes that '[r]ural poverty, female disempowerment, and continuing colonialism in educational and economic institutions' imperil the state;[66] similarly, Nyasha's and Tambudzai's colonial difference is made evident through a bodily grammar of anorexia, bulimia, depression and paralyses. Nyasha's relationship to her body is necessarily altered by epidermalization: a colonial and patriarchal frame veils her body, even from herself, as she internalizes the logic of coloniality that construes her body as Black and female, valued for its productive and reproductive labour.

Nyasha explains that her rebellion/disorder is about 'more than just food. That's how it comes out, but really it's all the things about boys and men and being decent and indecent and good and bad'.[67] Nyasha directs her rebellion at her father, a colonized intellectual, who represents these conspiratorial systems and wants her educated, chaste and fed. Through Nyasha, and then through Tambudzai, the novel depicts the fabrication of a racialized body. However, the novel complicates the process of epidermalization, petrification and sociogeny because it is focalized through characters who are both Black and female. In order to depict the distorting effects of these co-implicated regimes the novel depicts petrified and fragmented modes of embodiment.

In *Nervous Conditions*, *The Book of Not* and *This Mournable Body* petrification and the descriptive fragmentation of bodies register the material violence and psychophysical instability of colonial difference. The coloniality of being 'produces a certain *style* of embodiment (petrified, rigidified, inanimate, ankylotic) ... the colonial body mimes or act outs various rigidities as the continuous message of its own subjugation'.[68] Nyasha's anorexia and bulimia do not correspond to a petrified style of embodiment; instead bodily fragmentation is not only a form of embodiment but also a textual encoding of her ambivalence and resistance. She at once acknowledges the material and epistemological regimes that act upon her and seeks to expel them.

When Babamukuru insists that Tambudzai's parents have a Christian wedding, thereby entirely invalidating their already existing marital relationship and children, Tambudzai cannot voice her dissent and so her body petrifies.

[T]he morning of the wedding, I found I could not get out of bed. I tried several times but my muscles simply refused to obey the half-hearted commands I was issuing to them. Nyasha was worried. She thought I was ill, but I knew better. I knew I could not get out of bed because I did not want to.[69]

Tambudzai's paralysis is her response to the rigidity of the colonial system that Babamukuru enacts. When he enters the room, Tambudzai describes how '[t]he body on the bed didn't even twitch.

Meanwhile the mobile, alert me ... smiled smugly, thinking that I had gone somewhere where he could not reach me'.[70] A body petrified under the burden of congealing regimes of power/knowledge, the text precisely describes both petrification and fragmentation, the disarticulation of 'the body' and self, 'I'.

At the close of *Nervous Conditions*, Tambudzai learns that she has earned a highly coveted place at the Young Ladies College of the Sacred Heart. When she arrives at Sacred Heart she is disappointed to find 'not ... a single black face' that did not belong to her party, she is then led to the 'African' dormitory, a room designed for four but made to hold six. Tambudzai's muted disappointment finds clearer expression in Nyasha, who grows weaker and thinner. In ambiguous and conflating repetitions of 'they', Nyasha identifies the totalizing system of coloniality (sociogeny) and her parents as the cause of her bodily disarticulation. She says:

'They've done it to me ... It's not their fault. They did it to them too ... but especially to him. They put him through it all. But it's not his fault, he's good.' Her voice took on a Rhodesian accent. 'He's a good boy, a good munt. A bloody good kaffir ... They've taken us away ... They've deprived you of you, him of him, ourselves of each other.'[71]

Nyasha's diagnosis of their condition, their racialization through colonial difference, is passed down through colonial education into the family, from parents to children. Nyasha makes Tambudzai aware of this, but it is only once she is at Sacred Heart that Tambudzai reconciles this with her own experience.

The Book of Not: Colonial difference, educational institutions and the racialized body

In *Nervous Conditions* the Second *Chimurenga* is referred to only in passing, but in *The Book of Not* the brutality and related trauma of the war are a central concern. This is evident in the contrast between the two primary spaces of the novel: the homestead and Sacred Heart. In both places, the novel's repeated attention to the body encodes the material and subjective effects of colonialism and capitalism. At the homestead the degradations of racialized deterritorialization and underdevelopment reach a violent climax; at the convent, which instantiates the colonial difference as it espouses and structures the coloniality of knowledge/being, Tambudzai describes the fragmentation of her body and self.

The novel begins with Tambudzai, now sixteen, at the homestead. It is May in her second year at Sacred Heart and she, her aunt and uncle have been called to the homestead. Babamukuru is accused of being Mutengesi (a betrayer), 'one whose soul hankered to be one with the occupying Rhodesian forces'.[72] A *Morari* (night-time political gathering) has been called, where Tambudzai is to 'witness the pulverising of a person, the mincing of a man'.[73] The novel's somatic register is set from the opening lines: 'Up, up, up, the leg spun. A piece of a person, up there in the sky. Earth and acrid vapours coated my tongue.'[74] The disembodied leg belongs to Netsai, Tambudzai's younger sister, who has stepped on a landmine. Unlike Babamukuru and Tambudzai, Netsai is a respected combatant, 'the young woman of war'.[75] The sometimes-abstracted violence of national politics is viscerally embodied by the uncanny horror of the severed leg and Tambudzai's reaction:

> In the darkness, Netsai's leg arced up ... How miserable I was, for nothing lay in my power ... and in my quiet misery my chest quaked, bones vibrated in and out as though the strings of my heart strained and tore, and I felt as though I jumped on to the spinning limb and rode it as it rotated.[76]

Tambudzai's fear and helplessness are described through somatic sensations that mirror the fragmentation of her sister's body. While the preceding novel plots as a bildungsroman, describing Nyasha's and Tambudzai's development into adolescence, it also traces how these young women are gendered and racialized. Their petrified and fragmented forms of their embodiment at the close of *Nervous Conditions* are shown to be only a facet of the sociogenic violence of Rhodesian colonialism. The explosion that mutilates Netsai further demonstrates the physical brutality of this system. The title, *The Book of Not*, seems to describe the site of colonial difference where the subject is negated.

Tambudzai is traumatized by the attack on Netsai and its implications for her and the country. She describes her second year at Sacred Heart as a 'deterioration of hope' as she is unable to concentrate on her lessons, her mind constantly drawn back to the explosion. While she still sees education as her escape from patriarchal control and poverty, Tambudzai is repeatedly confronted by the paradox of colonial education. This is evident, first, as a spatial and then an institutional reality. From her classroom window at Sacred Heart Tambudzai can 'see the mountains' where her 'sister still talks about walking ... that perseverating path towards that exploding off of a leg'.[77] The convent is at once isolated from the war and provides Tambudzai a view of its devastation. The majority of its students are white and wealthy and it is located in an affluent, white suburb of Umtali on the opposite side of town from the mission. The residents of the houses on the approach to the school 'served aces down the centres of their tennis courts, or dived splash bombs into their swimming pools, and gardeners clad in orange overalls looked over at us, the intermediates'.[78] The imbrications of colonialism, class and race are clearly registered in this tableau, with Tambudzai describing her intermediate, even contradictory position. Sacred Heart is a microcosm of the rot of colonial Rhodesia.

The school is a colonial institution and clearly encodes the dominant racist exploitative logic; it establishes and maintains the space of colonial difference Tambudzai and her classmates inhabit. The novel's descriptive focus on the body makes legible the co-implication of epistemological and capitalist degradation evinced both by the quota for 'African' students and their segregation to a single dormitory. The room chosen for the 'African' dormitory is isolated at the end of the corridor and has its own ablution facilities, and the human waste produced in the dormitory drains straight outside.

> That final dormitory was allocated its end position in order to allow a drain to run outside, down beside the fire escape, from the small bathroom and laundry which opened off the bedroom. This dormitory, which was the only one to have its own ablution section, was called the African dormitory because we six young women slept there.[79]

Here the management of human waste demonstrates the material and social organization of the school. Rather than have the Black pupils and their waste defile white bodies and infrastructure, Tambudzai and her peers are segregated. In *Purity and Danger*,[80] Mary Douglas explains that societies are organized around a fear of dirt or pollution, which is understood as anything that is out of place. The bodies of these Black students are construed as a polluting presence whose danger to the racialized colonial order needs to be managed and mitigated. When Tambudzai's tampon clogs the bathroom in her dormitory, she and the other 'African' students are publicly shamed and their humiliation is somatically described: they 'all dropped and contracted and cringed'.[81] From her perspective, Tambudzai explains:

> The situation was this: I was in two aspects a biologically blasphemous person ... My corporeal crime indicted me on two counts. First there were the secretions that dripped crimson in the toilet bowl, or, stopped with cotton wool, clogged the school's waste system. Then there was the other type of gene that made me look different from the majority of pupils.[82]

Tambudzai understands her crime to be corporeal, related first to her menstruating body and second to her racialized body. Tambudzai is made to inhabit the colonial difference, her body descriptively fragmented. She has epidermalized this racialized schema such that she sees her 'bodily aberrations' as her downfall.[83] The colonial logic of the school establishes and maintains this disjointed reality. When she urgently needs to 'open [her] bowels' and uses the junior (white) hostel bathrooms, Tambudzai is taken to the principal, and given a black mark, she is also excoriated in her report card and then additionally punished by Babamukuru. For daring to defecate in the white girls' bathroom Tambudzai is punished at each level of the colonial/patriarchal hierarchy. In this way she is made to learn and to internalize the regimes of power and knowledge that define colonial Rhodesia. The text foregrounds her humiliation by removing any discretion from the description: 'I opened the door without sufficient care of my nether regions, which felt messily moist and sticky.'[84] This shame is amplified by Babamukuru's punishment which requires Tambudzai to write a letter of apology. To steady her, Nyasha explains that this is the inescapable reality of coloniality/colonialism: 'You'll have to deal with it ... I always told you about England.'[85] Once again, Tambudzai's denigration is echoed in Nyasha's petrified embodiment. Following this exchange, Nyasha becomes motionless, 'abject and corpselike, seemingly without a pulse'.[86] Colonial difference creates and requires the annihilation of the colonized subject. This logic is made legible through the fragmented and petrified descriptions of Nyasha's and Tambudzai's. Indeed, Nyasha helps Tambudzai to make her 'phrases of self-deprecation yet more annihilating' in the letter.[87]

The process of internalization/epidermalization and fragmentation further manifests as a terror of being in proximity to a white person, of soiling them: 'I was appalled at having let my skin and this white person's touch ... it was taboo: this person and that one could not touch.'[88] The institution is a microcosm; the behaviours of the white students and teachers index the racism of the broader society. Tambudzai describes this racism as a bodily revulsion, 'a pulling back of their very aura from contact with you ... looks of such horror flooded their faces at this accidental contact that you often looked around to see what horrendous monster caused the expression, before you realised it was your person'.[89] Tambudzai and her peers spend 'a lot of time consumed by this kind of terror'. But '[w]e didn't speak of it amongst ourselves. It was all too humiliating, but the horror of it gnawed within us'.[90] The students are silenced and petrified by this terror. Nevertheless, Tambudzai is desperate to 'excel'.[91] She is driven to achieve through competition with her peers, in a system of grades and punitive demerits that refigure the neoliberal labour economy she is soon to enter. When Tracey Stevenson is given the academic award that should rightfully have been hers, Tambudzai is confronted, once again, with the realization that her present and future possibilities are limited by her racialized and gendered body.

Bhakti Shringarpure asserts that the 'boarding school in *The Book of Not* and the psychiatric institution in *This Mournable Body* are productive critical spaces to situate decolonial critiques'.[92] Both institutions present on a smaller scale, the 'intimate geopolitics' of a decolonizing nation. Thus, the convent transforms Tambudzai 'into an example of the failure that is wrought upon the individual and society due to these structurally and morally bankrupt colonial institutions'.[93] Despite this failure, the novel explores another avenue of potential decolonial resistance when Tambudzai contrasts the perpetuation of 'reprehensible' colonial systems with '*Unhu*, that profound knowledge of being, quietly and not flamboyantly ... what others now call ubuntu, demanded ... that I be well so that others could be well also'.[94] Tambudzai's resistance is incomplete; nevertheless, the novel explores a framework of knowledge and social organization other than racialized colonialism. The final novel in the trilogy extends this theme of decolonial critique, first in the psychiatric unit where the 'nervous condition' that has plagued Tambudzai since adolescence culminates. The patriarchal and colonial regimes that give rise to Tambudzai's nervous pathology are merely echoed in the 'problematic nature of therapy methods and the openly racist co-inhabitants'.[95] Like colonial education, colonial hospitals are epistemically and materially harmful, necessarily impeding subjective and bodily coherence. The decolonial alternative posed by *The Mournable Body* is Nyasha's programme for female war veterans, which seems to enact the *uhnu* of the previous novel. Here, women's education, stories and well-being are centred and celebrated, and Tambudzai finds some healing and coherence. However, as Minna Johanna Niemi cautions, even this seemingly utopian community 'creates a romanticised version of female patriotism, which becomes a counterpoint to the patriarchal society and overarching white capitalist power; however, while so doing, it fails to see that *ubuntu/unhu* capitalism also often becomes exploited by neoliberal forces'.[96]

Forms of fragmentation: Coloniality and neoliberal capitalism in *This Mournable Body*

In the final instalment of Dangarembga's trilogy, Tambudzai's victimization by and complicity to patriarchal, colonial and capitalist regimes come to a close. The muted individualist and competitive neoliberal ideology of the preceding novels takes centre stage in a contemporary Zimbabwe 'cultivating ultra-neoliberal policies'.[97] Neoliberal conditions are evident in *This Mournable Body*, Minna Johanna Niemi explains, in that first, 'neoliberal political changes have created a major economic crisis in the country, and Tambudzai's drastic disappointments and unlucky decisions need to be interpreted in these poverty-stricken circumstances'.[98]

Second, the novel depicts 'neoliberal promises of success, which mislead people struggling in poverty'.[99] Third, narcissistic codes of neoliberal behaviour are connected to the novel's 'criticism of Tambudzai's sell-out mentality, which becomes evident through her neglect of the well-being of others: she is a sell-out because she deliberately turns against other members of the black community in order to find a way to succeed in the white capitalist world'.[100] Neoliberal ideology and state organization do not redress the material and epistemic inequalities of colonialism; rather, they reactivate and compound these structures as is evident in the eco-tourism company Tracey Stephenson now runs. Repression by Rhodesian white minority rule is replaced by economic neglect and community members turned 'citizen-consumers' forced to compete for economic survival.[101] The colonial boarding school is replaced by 'white capitalist companies'.[102] Like the colonial and patriarchal regimes of the previous novels, the capitalist logic of uneven development is addressed thematically, formally and somatically. The title of the novel is inspired by Teju Cole's essay on bodies that remain unmournable in Euro-American public discourse.[103] While *Nervous Conditions* and *The Book of Not* are told in past tense first-person, *This Mournable Body* is told in the present tense, second-person. Across these narratives of escape and disillusionment the 'I' establishes the intimacy, reflection and impeded development of a post-colonial bildungsroman; the 'you' distances and refers to the reader, making them complicit. The 'challenge of integrating the self across the divides of a bifurcated, fragmented national space with competing memories of the war' seems to find expression in the sometimes disjointed narrative that mimics Tambudzai's rage, anxiety and eventual breakdown.[104] Read in concert with the preceding novels, it is difficult to overlook the shift from past to present tense and the negation of the subject 'I' for the object 'you', which might be read as Tambudzai's objectification within the site of colonial difference. The disappointment of her ambitions and the fragmentation of her self are described somatically, encoding and making legible neoliberal, colonial and patriarchal regimes.

At the close of *The Book of Not* and the outset of *This Mournable Body*, Tambudzai has left her relatively well-paying and stable job as a copywriter at an advertising agency because her work is repeatedly stolen by a white male colleague. She finds it almost impossible to find another job and is destitute. The violence of the liberation war and ongoing coloniality are compounded by neoliberal capitalism, poverty and 'gendered distribution of opportunity'.[105] This is clearly depicted when Tambudzai, along with a group of bus travellers, assaults her attractive and well-dressed hostelmate Gertrude. Echoing her jealous attack on Ntombi in the previous novel – 'I felt her skin bunching under my fingernails'[106] – the violent, disjointed bodily register persists as Tambudzai, now in the second person, describes:

> The sight of your beautiful hostelmate fills you with an emptiness that hurts. You do not shrink back as one mind in your head wishes. Instead you obey the other, push forward. You want to see the shape of pain, to trace out its arteries and veins, to rip out to the pattern of its capillaries from the body. The mass of people moves forward. You reach for a stone. It is in your hand. Your arm rises in slow motion.[107]

The corporeal register of this passage gives tangible shape to the 'durable presence' of these regimes,[108] where violence is directed, not at those in power but at other Black women. Wendy Brown calls this 'the triumph of the weak as weak'.[109] Enraged by the contradictions of uneven development, Gertrude is the mob's scapegoat and Tambudzai gives voice to the desire to see this fury enacted and embodied. Her disorientating psychological impulses are matched by the staccato, freeze-frame depiction of her almost disembodied arm rising, as if of its own accord. The aesthetics of embodiment foreground the epidermalization of neoliberal capitalist and racialized schemas and the consequent fragmentation of Tambudzai's emotional and psychological coherence. 'You are an ill-made person. You are being unmade', Tambudzai explains when, following a violent breakdown at school, she wakes in a psychiatric hospital.[110, 111] This aesthetic of fragmented and objectified embodiment persists across the novel, and Tambudzai links her breakdown to 'the hurts of adulthood [that] have not assailed you as violently as those of childhood. Nevertheless this lesser assault is too much and again you cannot speak of Tracey Stevenson'.[112] Tracey was the white student at Sacred Heart who received the award for best O-level results that, outside of a racialized institution, would have been Tambudzai's.

Tracey reappears as the owner of Green Jacaranda, an eco-tourism business, run on her brother's farm until it is occupied by 'ex-combatants'.[113] She then turns to her Black Zimbabwean employees, Pedzi and Tambudzai, to develop tourist initiatives that make urban and rural poverty marketable as a 'Ghetto Getaway' and an 'authentic' village experience. Evidently, it is not only the body that is racialized; Shona culture is reduced to a pre-colonial stasis. Penny Cartwright identifies the novel's critique of such 'cultural enclosure projects', noting recurrent images of containment juxtaposed with a metonymic and fragmented narrative gaze.[114] Cultural enclosure exposes the ways in which the neoliberal economy is built on and reactivates colonial racial hierarchies in a language of marketability. This venture fails, in part due to Tambudzai's insensitivity to and alienation from her community, and in part because her mother, coerced into baring her breasts in 'authentic African' fashion, attacks a German tourist trying to take her photograph. The limits of cultural/racial enclosure are depicted in textual and bodily fragments as Tambudzai describes how 'grief … wraps around your heart and constricts to stop it … You have no strength to lift her [Mai], because your tears are falling onto your mother's skin. Your heart bursts. You burst with it'.[115] The return to skin, not racialized, but asserting filial connection, foreshadows Tambudzai's return to Nyasha and her employment at a security company owned and run by female war veterans. Here her Aunt Lucia 'lecturers' her 'concerning the unhu, the quality of being human, expected of a Zimbabwean woman'.[116] Returning to and perhaps redressing the epistemological and material violence of coloniality and colonial difference, Tambudzai is reminded at the novel's close that 'your education is not only in your head anymore … your knowledge is now also in your body, every bit of it, including your heart'.[117]

The hopeful conclusion of the trilogy rests on a reassertion of bodily coherence that refuses, if only partially, the imposition of a colonial and neoliberal bodily schema. Working for a company owned by and employing other Black women, *This Mournable Body* presents 'self-ruled Afri-capitalism' as an *uhnu*-inspired alternative to neoliberal capitalism.[118] The split-tongue voice that at once narrates and criticizes Tambudzai's development across the trilogy shows her culpability within and rejection of colonial education and neoliberal capitalism. The novels trace the process of racialization that physically and ontologically fabricates the racialized body: epidermalization, petrification, fragmentation, sociogeny. The female body and related somatic aesthetics make legible the interrelated and reactivated regimes of misogyny, racism, coloniality and capitalist imperialism, as well as Tambudzai's and Nyasha's embodied resistance.

Notes

1   I have made a similar argument elsewhere. See Duncan, Rebecca, and Rebekah Cumpsty. 'The Body in Postcolonial Fiction after the Millennium'. *Interventions* 22, no. 5 (2020): 587–605. Rebekah Cumpsty 'Tracing the Transnational: Scaling (Neo)Imperial Realities through the Body in Chris Abani's Fiction', *Interventions* 22, no. 5 (2020): 1–17.

2   I am grateful to Rebecca Duncan and Lobke Minter for comments on this chapter.

3   David Marriott, 'The Racialized Body', in *The Cambridge Companion to the Body in Literature*, ed. David Hillman and Ulrika Maude (Cambridge: Cambridge University Press, 2015), 163–76.

4   Marriott, 'The Racialized Body', 163.

5   Nelson Maldonado-Torres, 'On the Coloniality of Being', *Cultural Studies* 21, nos. 2–3 (1 March 2007): 243.

6   Aníbal Quijano, 'Coloniality of Power and Eurocentrism in Latin America', *International Sociology* 15, no. 2 (2000): 215–32.

7   Anibal Quijano and Michael Ennis, 'Coloniality of Power, Eurocentrism, and Latin America', *Nepantla: Views from South* 1, no. 3 (2000): 533.

8   Quijano and Ennis, 'Coloniality of Power', 533.

9   Maldonado-Torres, 'On the Coloniality of Being', 242.

10 Ibid.

11 Aníbal Quijano, 'Coloniality and Modernity/Rationality', *Cultural Studies* 21, nos. 2–3 (1 March 2007): 176.

12 Quijano, 'Eurocentrism', 221.

13 While the focus here is the racialized body and the construction of colonized others, it is important to note the necessarily related construction of whiteness.

14 Anne McClintock, *Imperial Leather: Race, Gender and Sexuality in the Colonial Contest* (London and New York: Routledge, 1995), 49.

15 McClintock, *Imperial Leather*, 50.

16 Sylvia Wynter, 'Unsettling the Coloniality of Being/Power/Truth/Freedom: Towards the Human, After Man, Its Overrepresentation—an Argument', *CR (East Lansing, Mich.)* 3, no. 3 (2003): 260.

17   Rebecca Duncan, 'De/Zombification as Decolonial Critique: Beyond
     Man, Nature and the Posthuman in Folklore and Fiction from South
     Africa', in *An 'Other' Zombie Project: Decolonising the Undead*
     (Bloomsbury, 2022), 1.
18   Walter Mignolo, 'The Geopolitics of Knowledge and the Colonial
     Difference', *The South Atlantic Quarterly* 101, no. 1 (2002): 57–96.
19   Duncan, 'De/Zombification'.
20   Frantz Fanon, *Black Skin, White Masks*, trans. Richard Philcox,
     Revised edition (New York : Berkeley, CA: Grove Press, 2008), xii.
21   John Drabinski, 'Frantz Fanon', in *The Stanford Encyclopedia of
     Philosophy*, ed. Edward N. Zalta (Redwood: Stanford University
     Press, 2019), available online: https://plato.stanford.edu/archives/
     spr2019/entries/frantz-fanon/.
22   Fanon, *Black Skin, White Masks*, 90.
23   Ibid., xiv.
24   Ibid., xiv–xv.
25   Jennifer Williams, 'Performing Trauma: The Body as Site of (De)
     Colonization in Tsitsi Dangarembga's Nervous Conditions', in
     Africanizing Knowledge (London: Routledge, 2017), 273.
26   Marriott, 'The Racialized Body', 163.
27   Ibid., 164.
28   Ibid., 166–7.
29   Ibid., 167.
30   Ibid., 169.
31   Frantz Fanon, *The Wretched of the Earth*, Reprint edition
     (New York: Grove Press, 2005), 2.
32   Marriott, 'The Racialized Body', 163.
33   McClintock, *Imperial Leather*, 5.
34   For an extended discussion of gender and colonialism see Ann
     Laura Stoler, *Carnal Knowledge and Imperial Power: Race and
     the Intimate in Colonial Rule* (Berkeley; Los Angeles: University of
     California Press, 2010); Elleke Boehmer, *Stories of Women: Gender
     and Narrative in the Postcolonial Nation* (Manchester: Manchester
     University Press, 2005).
35   Ann Laura Stoler, 'Carnal Knowledge and Imperial Power: Race and
     the Intimate in Colonial Rule', in *The New Imperial Histories Reader*
     (London: Routledge, 2020), 177.
36   Hershini Bhana, 'The Condition of the Native': Autodestruction in
     Dangarembga's Nervous Conditions', *Alternation* 6, no. 1 (1999):
     117–37.
37   Fanon, *The Wretched of the Earth*, liv.
38   Williams, 'Performing Trauma', 274.
39   Ibid.
40   Ibid, 273.

41   For more on *Nervous Conditions* as a post-colonial bildungsroman
     see Hay, Simon, 'Nervous Conditions, Lukács, and the Postcolonial
     Bildungsroman', *Genre: Forms of Discourse and Culture* 46, no. 3
     (2013): 317–44.

42   Tsitsi Dangarembga, *Nervous Conditions* (Minneapolis: Graywolf
     Press, 2021), 11.

43   Williams, 'Performing Trauma', 275; Deepika Bahri, 'Disembodying
     the Corpus: Postcolonial Pathology in Tsitsi Dangarembga's
     "Nervous Conditions"', *Postmodern Culture* 5, no. 1 (1994),
     available online: https://doi.org/10.1353/pmc.1994.0046.

44   Bahri, 'Disembodying the Corpus'.

45   Ibid., 52.

46   Ibid., 27.

47   Ibid., 12.

48   Ibid., 11.

49   Ibid., 7.

50   Ibid.

51   Ibid., 33.

52   Ibid., 49, 50.

53   Ibid., 48.

54   Ibid., 48–9.

55   Ibid., 35.

56   Donald S. Moore, *Suffering for Territory* (Durham, NC: Duke
     University Press, 2005), 4.

57   Dangarembga, *Nervous*, 37.

58   Ibid.

59   Ibid., 79.

60   The threads of neoliberal logic are present in this first book and
     extended in the rest of the trilogy.

61   In a recent seminar at Stellenbosch Institute for Advanced Study
     (STIAS), Dangarembga problematized 'Shona', as a colonial
     imposition that occluded 'the Wamaungwe, Wabudsha and Waeru,
     etc., depending on locality'. Michelle Galloway, 'Unravelling the Full
     History of the Shona Subject: Who, How, If and, Where to, after All
     That – STIAS Webinar by Tsitsi Dangarembga', *Stellenbosch Institute
     for Advanced Study* (blog), 21 April 2021. Available online: https://
     stias.ac.za/2021/04/unravelling-the-full-history-of-the-shona-subject-
     who-how-if-and-where-to-after-all-that/. I use it here advisedly.

62   Dangarembga, *Nervous*, 81–2.

63   Williams, 'Performing Trauma', 278.

64   Dangarembga, *Nervous*, 70.

65   Williams, 'Performing Trauma', 280.

66   Bahri, 'Disembodying the Corpus'.

67   Dangarembga, *Nervous*, 278.

68 Marriott, 'The Racialized Body', 176.
69 Dangarembga, *Nervous*, 244.
70 Ibid.
71 Ibid., 293.
72 Tsitsi Dangarembga, *The Book of Not*, Main edition (London: Faber & Faber, 2021), 9.
73 Dangarembga, *Not*, 9.
74 Ibid., 5.
75 Ibid., 20.
76 Ibid., 5.
77 Ibid., 26.
78 Ibid., 29.
79 Ibid., 63.
80 *Purity and Danger* (London: Routledge, 2002).
81 Dangarembga, *Not*, 77.
82 Ibid., 79.
83 Ibid.
84 Ibid., 82.
85 Ibid., 111.
86 Ibid., 112.
87 Ibid.
88 Ibid., 39.
89 Ibid., 72.
90 Ibid.
91 Dangarembga, *Not*, 33.
92 Bhakti Shringarpure, 'The Decolonial Gesture in Tsitsi Dangarembga's Trilogy', *Journal of African Cultural Studies* 32, no. 4 (2020): 454.
93 Shringarpure, 'Decolonial Gesture', 457.
94 Dangarembga, *Not*, 124.
95 Shringarpure, 'Decolonial Gesture', 457.
96 Minna Johanna Niemi, 'Critical Representation of Neoliberal Capitalism and Uneven Development in Tsitsi Dangarembga's This Mournable Body', *Journal of Southern African Studies* 47, no. 5 (2021): 871.
97 Niemi, 'Critical Representation', 870.
98 Ibid., 874.
99 Ibid.
100 Ibid.
101 Ibid.
102 Ibid.
103 Teju Cole, 'Unmournable Bodies', *The New Yorker*, 9 January 2015, available online: http://www.newyorker.com/culture/cultural-comment/unmournable-bodies.

104 Eleni Coundouriotis, 'Narration in the Second Person: Destabilizing the Real in This Mournable Body', *Journal of African Cultural Studies* (February 2020): 448.
105 Duncan and Cumpsty, 'The Body in Postcolonial Fiction after the Millennium', 600.
106 Dangarembga, *Not*, 131.
107 Tsitsi Dangarembga, *This Mournable Body* (Minneapolis, Minnesota: Graywolf, 2018), 21.
108 Ann Laura Stoler, *Duress: Imperial Durabilities in Our Times* (Durham: Duke University Press Books, 2016), 9.
109 Wendy Brown, *States of Injury* (Princeton, N.J: Princeton University Press, 1995), 67; Niemi, 'Critical Representation', 878.
110 Dangarembga, *Mournable*, 101.
111 For more on depression in *This Mournable Body* see Amy Rushton, 'On the Back of a Hyena: Depression and the (Post-) Colonial Context in Tsitsi Dangarembga's This Mournable Body', *Moving Worlds* 19, no. 2 (2019): 21–36.
112 Dangarembga, *Mournable*, 107.
113 Ibid., 264.
114 Penny Cartwright, 'Cultural Enclosure, World Making and the Novel Form'.
115 Dangarembga, *Mournable*, 280.
116 Ibid., 283.
117 Ibid., 284.
118 Niemi, 'Critical Representation', 887.

Bibliography

Bahri, Deepika. 'Disembodying the Corpus: Postcolonial Pathology in Tsitsi Dangarembga's "Nervous Conditions"'. *Postmodern Culture* 5, no. 1 (1994). Available online: https://doi.org/10.1353/pmc.1994.0046.
Bhana, Hershini. 'The Condition of the Native: Autodestruction in Dangarembga's Nervous Conditions'. *Alternation* 6, no. 1 (1999): 117–37.
Brown, Wendy. *States of Injury*. Princeton, NJ: Princeton University Press, 1995.
Cartwright, Penny. 'Cultural Enclosure, World Making and the Novel Form'. University of Oxford Postcolonial Theory and Writing Seminar. 8 March 2022.
Cole, Teju. 'Unmournable Bodies'. *The New Yorker*, 9 January 2015. Available online: http://www.newyorker.com/culture/cultural-comment/unmournable-bodies.

Coundouriotis, Eleni. 'Narration in the Second Person: Destabilizing the Real in This Mournable Body'. *Journal of African Cultural Studies* (February 2020). Available online: https://www.tandfonline.com/doi/abs/10.1080/13696815.2019.1704695.

Dangarembga, Tsitsi. *This Mournable Body*. Minneapolis, Minnesota: Graywolf, 2018.

Dangarembga, Tsitsi. *Nervous Conditions*. Minneapolis: Graywolf Press, 2021.

Dangarembga, Tsitsi. *The Book of Not*. Main edition. London: Faber & Faber, 2021.

Douglas, Mary. *Purity and Danger*. London: Routledge, 2002.

Drabinski, John. 'Frantz Fanon'. In *The Stanford Encyclopedia of Philosophy*, edited by Edward N. Zalta. Redwood: Stanford University Press, 2019. Available online: https://plato.stanford.edu/archives/spr2019/entries/frantz-fanon/.

Duncan, Rebecca. 'De/Zombification as Decolonial Critique: Beyond Man, Nature and the Posthuman in Folklore and Fiction from South Africa'. In *Decolonising the Undead: Rethinking Zombies in World Literature, Film and Media*, edited by Giulia Champion, Roxanne Douglas and Stephen Shapiro, 141–58. London: Bloomsbury, 2022.

Duncan, Rebecca, and Rebekah Cumpsty. 'The Body in Postcolonial Fiction after the Millennium'. *Interventions* 22, no. 5 (2020): 587–605.

Fanon, Frantz. *The Wretched of the Earth*. Reprint edition. New York: Grove Press, 2005.

Fanon, Frantz. *Black Skin, White Masks*. Translated by Richard Philcox. Revised edition. New York: Grove Press, 2008.

Maldonado-Torres, Nelson. 'On the Coloniality of Being'. *Cultural Studies* 21, nos. 2–3 (2007): 240–70.

Marriott, David. 'The Racialized Body'. In *The Cambridge Companion to the Body in Literature*, edited by David Hillman and Ulrika Maude, 163–76. Cambridge: Cambridge University Press, 2015. Available online: https://doi.org/10.1017/CCO9781107256668.012.

McClintock, Anne. *Imperial Leather: Race, Gender and Sexuality in the Colonial Contest*. Routledge, 1995.

Michelle Galloway. 'Unravelling the Full History of the Shona Subject: Who, How, If and, Where to, after All That – STIAS Webinar by Tsitsi Dangarembga'. *Stellenbosch Institute for Advanced Study* (blog), 21 April 2021. Available online: https://stias.ac.za/2021/04/unravelling-the-full-history-of-the-shona-subject-who-how-if-and-where-to-after-all-that/.

Mignolo, Walter. 'The Geopolitics of Knowledge and the Colonial Difference'. *The South Atlantic Quarterly* 101, no. 1 (2002): 57–96.

Moore, Donald S. *Suffering for Territory*. Durham, NC: Duke University Press, 2005.

Niemi, Minna Johanna. 'Critical Representation of Neoliberal Capitalism and Uneven Development in Tsitsi Dangarembga's This Mournable Body'. *Journal of Southern African Studies* 47, no. 5 (2021): 869–88.

Quijano, Aníbal. 'Coloniality and Modernity/Rationality'. *Cultural Studies* 21, nos. 2–3 (1 March 2007): 168–78.

Quijano, Aníbal. 'Coloniality of Power and Eurocentrism in Latin America'. *International Sociology* 15, no. 2 (2000): 215–32.

Quijano, Anibal, and Michael Ennis. 'Coloniality of Power, Eurocentrism, and Latin America'. *Nepantla: Views from South* 1, no. 3 (2000): 533–80.

Shringarpure, Bhakti. 'The Decolonial Gesture in Tsitsi Dangarembga's Trilogy'. *Journal of African Cultural Studies* 32, no. 4 (2020): 455–59.

Stoler, Ann Laura. 'Carnal Knowledge and Imperial Power: Race and the Intimate in Colonial Rule'. In *The New Imperial Histories Reader*. London: Routledge, 2020.

Stoler, Ann Laura. *Duress: Imperial Durabilities in Our Times*. Durham: Duke University Press Books, 2016.

Williams, Jennifer. 'Performing Trauma: The Body as Site of (De) Colonization in Tsitsi Dangarembga's Nervous Conditions'. In *Africanizing Knowledge*, 273–88. London and New York: Routledge, 2017.

Wynter, Sylvia. 'Unsettling the Coloniality of Being/Power/Truth/Freedom: Towards the Human, After Man, Its Overrepresentation – An Argument'. *CR (East Lansing, Mich.)* 3, no. 3 (2003): 257–337.

7

Disability

Susannah B. Mintz

In 2014, when I embarked on a study of disabled detectives, I was surprised (as were many people to whom I described this endeavour) to learn just how many novels, TV series and films featured sleuths with some form of physical or cognitive impairment. I had a similar experience a few years later when, with co-editor G. Thomas Couser, we began compiling titles for a two-volume encyclopaedia called *Disability Experiences* (2019), in which the final two hundred 'memoirs, autobiographies, and other personal narratives' were but a sampling of the rich international archive of contemporary life writing about disability and illness.[1] A quick survey of past issues of the *Journal of Literary and Cultural Disability Studies* reveals an impressive array of topics, from graphic novels to dwarfism to Young Adult fiction to Indigenous art to the 1960s counterculture movement. The essays in the 2018 *Cambridge Companion to Literature and Disability* range similarly from medieval lit to modernity, from genre fiction to question of race, gender and crip-queer intersectionality, and this wider scope of inquiry has been accompanied by several recent period-specific studies of disability history.[2] I cite here too the eclecticism of final projects I've received in disability classes when students are invited to turn their newfound understanding to whatever sort of media or social phenomenon intrigues them; recent topics have included the animated series *Avatar*, Broadway musicals, disability camps, afterschool programmes in China, 'special ed' interests in Ghana, the 'inspiration porn' of *America's Got Talent*, one season of *American Horror Story* and the homilies of John Paul II. This is all to suggest a vibrant and ever-replenishing field of possibilities for bringing disability awareness to bear on bodies and minds in the service of particular artistic and/or sociopolitical goals. And it indicates the exciting breadth of what David Bolt has called 'the focused phase' of disability studies, in which we target our investigations in the application, refinement and complication of disability studies scholarship's foundational propositions.

Literature, Petra Kuppers declares in her Afterword to the *Cambridge Companion*,[3] 'has been an invaluable tool in creating and maintaining disability culture's thin and constrained archive', a ready venue for 'defiance' and 'talking back'[4] to ableist construals of disability as cause for charity, mourning or fear. Kuppers describes teaching a poetry workshop in which attendees are invited to 'un-cable from the stereotypes of disability', and her account emphasizes not the acknowledged difficulty of such unburdening but the 'fun we are having', in writing 'toward pleasure, hope, [and] unknown futures'.[5] The Afterword calls our attention to the *site* of literary production, too – the material conditions of where literature is created, in a complex interplay of bodies, topographies, climates and the myriad social attitudes that prescribe things like access to a park where a writer might wish to sit and muse awhile. The structural pathways of a park that '[does] not take wheeled use into account' become a condition of creating as much as a vista that might be commented on in a poem or essay, and in this sense Kuppers returns the embodied author to our understanding of how disability literature comes into being and the type of reading practices that best suit it. Activist and essayist Eli Clare similarly links body and landscape in *Brilliant Imperfection* (2017) in his refutation of 'arbitrary cultural value[s]'[6] that privilege non-disabled forms of being and that obscure the forms of knowing the world that pertain specifically to impairment. Describing himself on 'steep stretches' of mountain trails, Clare writes that he 'drop[s] down onto [his] butt and slide[s] along using both [his] hands and feet'. 'Only then', he tells us, 'do I see the swirl marks that glaciers left in the granite, tiny orange newts climbing among the tree roots, otherworldly fungi growing on rotten logs'.[7] Like Kuppers, Clare makes disability the condition of an embodied lyricism, of ways to imagine oneself in the environment, of *what else* can be discovered and known about the world. It is precisely 'shaky balance' that affords Clare this 'intimacy with the mountain', and in turn produces the pages of *Brilliant Imperfection* that we read.

Clare's assertion of disability not just as a feature of embodiment and/or mentality but as a modality, a kind of epistemological method, characterizes a great deal of recent creative and scholarly treatments of disability. 'Reading and writing disability differently', Tanya Titchkosky argues, 'resists the illusion that disability is a limit without possibility' or a 'worrisome problem' to be eradicated from view.[8] So artist Riva Lehrer, born with spina bifida, declares herself in the prologue to her 2020 memoir *Golem Girl* '*monstrare*: one who unveils'.[9] Deemed a 'vegetable'[10] and subjected to substantial medical intervention in the name of 'normalcy', Lehrer turns the putative 'monstrosity' of her impairments into the creative basis of her identity as a writer and painter. Lehrer describes at length the integration of disability in every aspect of her process of making. She decries the common workshop practice of standing at an easel for hours at a time as impossible for her to sustain, for example, and explains her selection of subjects – other disabled artists, writers, scholars, activists and performers – as a deliberate provocation of 'beauty' in the refusal of traditional standards of artistic content. No painting simply adorns our walls, Lehrer claims; it explicitly informs our ideas about human form, longevity, proportionality and the object world. In this way, Lehrer's art (and the memoir that recounts its creation) unveils the monster and *is* the monster, as the artist reshapes the dynamics of how she is 'framed' and asks us to consider whose assessment is determining what is worthy, possible or real.[11]

Writing about disability both constitutes and commemorates the humanity of a denigrated self, and it offers what Rosemarie Garland-Thomson calls 'subjugated knowledges':[12] *new* knowledge generated by a perspective that undermines the rote reiteration of myths and stereotypes about disability and manifests creative gain.[13] The poet Laurie Clements Lambeth, who has multiple sclerosis, says that the disease 'brought [her] to poetry', '[her] new physical life giving birth to [her] life in words'.[14] Describing the increasing numbness of MS and alluding to its so-called exacerbations (unpredictable flare-ups), Lambeth cites the 'chaotic quality' of 'a disability that shifts and interrupts, leaves and reenters one's life in new, surprising ways' and explains that MS 'entered [her] poetry'[15] as a form of experience that encouraged her investigation of contact between body and world. Once a hopeful cartoonist, Lambeth becomes a poet of outlines, of numbness and the fear – as well as the appeal, often eroticized – of what happens when we cannot distinguish between things. Claiming the agency of shaping language, she arrives organically at a crip poetics that exemplifies the idea of disability gain: in 'alter[ing her] perception' of herself, MS (which Lambeth declares she would not want to be rid of) invests the writer with the 'power' and 'beauty' of verse, which might in turn inspire 'empathy'.[16]

Lambeth's poem 'Dysaesthesia' (defined as 'wrong feeling') makes – and breaks – a body of words. It is comprised of two columns, one upright against the left margin, the other jutting raggedly towards the right across a gap that curves down the centre of the page like a spine. On the left, the speaker acts, seeming to conduct her life, but uses a series of dependent clauses that suspend her in a limbo of irresolution: 'when I tell', 'when I lift', 'when I pour', 'when I hear'. On the right, objects, adjectives, sensations, pile up as disconnected elements of a scene whose narrative coherence we cannot be assured: 'my palms', 'the hands', 'the milk bottle', '*spark* or *burn*', 'flameless, sourceless'.[17] It is possible to read each column independently, to make a kind of sense of these discontinuous parts, just as we also read across the blank space between them: we carry meaning from one site to the other, we supply information that may be missing, we fill in to impose order on indefinable, 'chaotic' corporeal experience – or perhaps we choose to investigate the confusion, to get curious about differences we might be able to name (*dis/abled*, *other*, *wounded*) but not precisely to *feel*. The poem accords with what Lambeth has described of her body's sensations and its interactions with surfaces: her inability to 'detect the difference'[18] between finger and fabric, for example, or the pain that flares and 'smolder[s]' from within, 'without cause'.[19] Thresholds blur, trigger and reactions do not perfectly correspond. The poem inscribes another kind of discontinuity, between the speaker's physical reality and a world characterized by assumptions, expectations of wholeness, and normative codes of syntactical progression.

The poem installs '*real pain*' at its core[20] in the figure of James Dean from *Rebel without a Cause*, a movie the speaker invokes for the scene 'in the police department', where Dean, his character 'so angry / he pummels a desk', actually breaks his hand. '*[T]hat's real pain*', says Lambeth's speaker, 'and I read my hand like his'. But in what way are they alike? Varying degrees of authenticity are at work here – perhaps even intentionality, a question about what we do 'to' ourselves, and how much control we have, or allow ourselves to *want* to have, over corporeal sensation. The author reads herself through a male actor who displays a feeling at once scripted and actually but inadvertently demanded by his body, seeking an analogue on screen for 'this mistake' between 'spine and skin' that makes her own hands hurt in a way that seems almost disconnected from self because her nerves are misfiring. *Realness* is what breaks through Dean's performance (*'wait for it: / he broke his hand there'*): if a viewer knows what happened, the illusion of acting is disrupted; and 'realness' seems to appeal to Lambeth's speaker in the causal sequence of banging a hand, breaking it, and feeling pain that is recognizable, explicable, because her own pain, defying a desire to know and stabilize the origins of things, also defies the attempt to match sensation with words. At the same time, what fascinates may be less the apparent accessing of the realness of pain than the momentary rupture of its performance. Can we locate the *precise* instant of Dean's unscripted suffering? Would that be the 'right' kind of feeling? And what does it mean for the speaker of this poem to seek identification in the person of the wounded white male?

'Dysaesthesia' does not finally adjudicate between right and wrong sensation, authentic or performed pain, biological and social articulations of what embodiment means. The expression that results from a body that does not reliably know itself, its edges or points of contact, evidences both a desire to make sense ('When I tell Ian my hands are on fire', 'and Ian asks me if I mean …'[21]) and a willingness to reside in a state of uncertainty. The poem ends not definitively but with inquiry: 'How to discern' what is what? And 'who operates' this body? The spine down the page (Lambeth calls it a 'gutter') is blankness, numbness, an eerie absence where neural continuity should be. At the same time it is the very core of the poem, making its meaning, making the poem *work* and making us work as readers along with the text's unconventional shape. This is poetry and MS '[helping] each other along',[22] as the author tells us, and no attempt is made to discount or distract from disability, to recuperate or transcend the body's illogical connections. Openness towards the unknown is tinged with mournfulness, it must be said – even a hint of desperation about not knowing 'how else to say it', what pain is *like*, how to bridge that distance – and so there is loneliness, too, in those final queries. Still, the poem has invited us to watch, in the way its characters watch a film, with curiosity about how bodies become what they are to us, and with a kind of delight about being in company with those who can bear witness to (*wait for it*), even if they cannot share, our experience.

Michael Davidson writes in *Concerto for the Left Hand* (2008) that because disability 'lays bare the body as an unstable, uncontainable site', we can export modernism's 'aesthetic defamiliarization' to understand the art that results from it.[23] Announcing itself as a record of somehow 'improper' feeling, Lambeth's 'Dysaesthesia' is also a narrative poem that refuses to abide by its own organizing structural premise. Lines appear stabilized along a left-hand margin but culminate in disconnected fragments of image; units of meaning emerge from grammatical rules only to collide in ways that threaten incoherence. The scenes, the poem's various occasions, move left to right, but also down (and even back up) separate columns. The speaker relates all of this – her experience of her body as an interior as well as in relation to surfaces, others, even James Dean on screen – as if she is in charge (at least, trying and hoping to be), but the poem keeps defying her role as organizer of the story of her body. Neither poem nor body in this instance conforms to a normative illusion of 'static integration', in Margrit Shildrick's words. To the contrary, both are 'in bits and pieces', displaying a constitutive 'disarticulation' that, Shildrick argues, most embodied beings both understand of themselves and thoroughly repress.[24] Lambeth's work evinces the fear that comes from not being able to distinguish the self's own borders – how to know ourselves if we can't tell where we *are*? – and so the poem simply 'reshap[es] the outline':[25] crafting a new body, an unfamiliar but nonetheless arresting and provocative textual body that in turn invites (or demands) alternative habits of reading, even a willingness to read emptiness as substance.

Where Lambeth's work plumbs both creative and ontological possibilities of misalignment and disconnect between body and feeling, self and surface, Petra Kuppers writes embodiment as an ever-fluctuating network of connections. Her most recent collection of verse, *Gut Botany* (2021),[26] describes the way all things are implicated in each other, as bodies encounter other bodies, environments, and creative marketplaces that are all too frequently mediated by corporate interest. Kuppers's work has long been inflected by an ethical commitment to eco-corporeality, to acknowledging and respecting the coexistence of bodies and spaces.[27] Described as a 'queer ecosomatic investigation', *Gut Botany* charts an elaborate interpenetration of matter, from the innermost sites of the body (uterus, oesophagus, endocrine system) to the settings in which bodies confront one another and become meaningful (courthouse, waiting room, theatre, lovers' bed, outer space, hiking trail). What we think we know of these entities and locations is contested – they become unfamiliar – by the encounter of disability. 'This is the inside. / This outside', begins the section called 'Contours',[28] the repeated pronoun referring to nothing we can identify beyond some distinction indicated by that gap – another emptiness that, as in Lambeth's poem, thrums with purpose. For something is always happening, we might say from a cripistemological perspective, in the space beyond norms and conventions, even if it isn't spelled out.

In the section called 'Moon Botany', Kuppers dramatizes her assertion elsewhere that our readings of disability literature must take into account the circumstances of their production. This series of seven poems was created in tandem with artist Sharon Siskin, who (as explained in the Notes) 'went on wheelchair-inaccessible nature hikes and brought back found objects' from the 'Oregonian outback'.[29] The poems happen because the author exists in relation to somewhere specific; that locatedness – in which landscape has been altered by human behaviours – brings these texts into being. A garden path might as well be the surface of the moon, the series slyly says to us, if it is not made accessible to a range of mobility types. In this way, the objects described in the poems take on an otherworldly effect, their strangeness acting as a kind of invitation to 'transformation'.[30] Puff balls, cattails, ink cap mushrooms, mice bones: these become the material of an 'armchair botany'[31] that revels in the interconnectedness of living things. It also strongly critiques ableism, environmental destruction and the tendency of human encroachment to disregard the very notion of habitat, where things are 'supposed' to be.

Boundary transgressions go in more than one direction, in other words; they may refuse dominant paradigms in a revolutionary and liberatory sense, or they may represent the insidious creep of humanity. The speaker of 'Found on the Pond Deck' can 'pour [her] liquid body', for instance, extending the limits of physicality in both an erotic and a nurturing way; she can displace herself across distance through her artistic collaboration and the imaginative act of visualizing the origin of the artefacts she poetically handles. One speaker 'remember[s] [her] watery nature',[32] another 'deliquesce[s]',[33] a third 'might be a horsetail fern'.[34] But when the planks she's sitting on 'expectorate their innards', it's because they *used* to be whole, part of a forest.[35] The poet waiting in a wheelchair on a redwood deck thus exemplifies at once the rigidity of ableism, its refusal to make space for alternative modes of locomotion or cognition, and dilations of greed, the ever-expanding capacity of corporations to justify damaging a landscape. In this tension of power and possibility, disability is written as fulcrum: awaiting the return of her non-disabled collaborator so that artwork can happen, the poet becomes the locus of a series of distensions and contractions that remap terrain and challenge the conception of personhood as solitary and contained. In the collaborative interplay of the series, power dynamics are disrupted, the privileging of a singular artist resisted; in the generative and hybrid relationship of poet/wheelchair/collaborator, what a 'body' is also comes under revision. *Gut Botany*'s title reminds us that we have whole landscapes within us, that we are always already composite entities made up of multitudinous other beings, while its various sections demonstrate that what we might prefer to think of as 'outside' of self – the vast (maybe unfathomable) expanses of environment, the political sphere, the operations of economy and social structure – will have felt consequences deep within.

To craft a poetic persona through *botany* does not simply suggest organic continuity in paradigm-busting free play, however, since botany is by definition a science devoted to classification, with important distinctions made between plants that are edible, medicinal and poisonous. Is Kuppers therefore courting the very strategies of identification that have historically been dangerous for disabled people, people of colour and women? 'A system of identification that seeks to fix individual bodily identity', as Ellen Samuels has shown, relies on the notion of 'fixed and legible bodily truths'[36] – including (particularly in the nineteenth century) an unchanging yet largely symbolic conception of disability 'defined in opposition' to the categories of 'normal' and 'natural'.[37] Kuppers's botany, then, can also be read as a pointedly ironic rebuke of ontological hierarchies that are both cause and effect of the kind of '*moral* certainty' about biological identity difference that is so often mobilized in the service of oppression.[38] Locating the clues to identity in the *gut* as opposed to more visible markers of the body, Kuppers clearly indicts what Samuels calls 'the sciences of the surface, which purported to read a person's character from its external signs'.[39] Invoking *science* as a methodology for shattering the discourse of ableism becomes Kuppers's shrewd way of revising what is knowable, of suggesting alternative means to as-yet-unknown ends. Who is the 'gut botanist', after all, toiling in writing workshops and theatres?

Kuppers's work reminds us that 'normalcy' is *produced* – or as Titchkosky puts it, 'enforced, imitated, enacted; taught and bought; sold and recycled; enhanced, longed for and resisted'.[40] Terese Marie Mailhot responds eloquently to the enormous inscriptive force of institutional systems in her lyrical memoir *Heart Berries* (2018), a revised origin myth speaking to and for Indian women.[41] A First Nation Canadian Mailhot writes depression and mental illness as part of an 'Indian condition'[42] that seems both inherited – it is the grief of 'ancestors'[43] – and socially constructed, a function of 'conditio*ning*' at the hands of white clergy who 'contaminated generations of our people'.[44] The chapter called 'Indian Sick' begins with a pile-up of self-accusations: 'I was weak minded. I was dramatic and unhinged', 'I wasn't stable', 'I didn't perform'.[45] But when Mailhot writes that 'illness carried [her] into white buildings, into the doctor's office and the therapist's' – spaces where 'the wrong [eyes] make [her] feel like a monster'[46] – 'craziness'[47] becomes linked as much to the subjugation of colonialism as to biology or genes.[48] Here Mailhot precisely dramatizes the power of diagnosis as a knowledge system that far from neutrally categorizes embodied realities, one that defines certain feelings or behaviours as not only disorderly but morally defective. This is the social model of disability, the positioning of the impaired person as a social 'misfit' – what Garland-Thomson has described as 'slamming against an unsustaining environment'.[49] Writing in this sense of misfit allows Mailhot to pry self and environment apart again, to delineate encounters in which apparently pathological symptomology may seem an entirely appropriate response to the teachings of a culture in which 'being Indian' is 'a crime'.[50] Illness in this context then becomes a kind of 'basic agency'[51] – illness as decriminalized self – that propels the retelling of one's story. It is not that subjectivity must be disentangled from disease or diagnosis before it can narrate its truths, but that dominant epistemological presumptions can be shown up for their inadequacy, their coercive or oppressive consequences for variant bodyminds.[52]

Much of *Heart Berries* reads as an homage to 'traditional [Salish] storytelling', which Mailhot describes as 'sparse and interested in blank space'.[53] A memoir told in fragmented essays, it has the halting feel of a repeatedly interrupted story (as if by authority figures, uninterested in the tale), or one whose author doubts and restricts herself. Individual 'chapters', and the book as a whole, proceed in an associative fashion that can, particularly in terms of chronology, be challenging to track. The use of the second person can disorient a reader's sense of audience; 'you' refers to specific individuals (such as Mailhot's husband, author Casey Grey, or her mother, Wahzinak) but implicitly to an audience, especially white readers, to whom the speaker might also say, 'I don't understand … why you would look at me the way you did.'[54] An allusive, elliptical quality draws us close to the events being narrated even as we may feel deliberately held away from their import, their details, their pain. In these prosodic ways, *Heart Berries* encodes resistance to normative paradigms of both ethnicity and cognition within which Mailhot is called upon to say who she is. Like its author, the text has 'knowledge of what a normal person might do'[55] but cannot always – or, more properly, often refuses to – abide by conventional expectations or patterns. Thus, the text offers and withholds, wields itself as a weapon 'against erasure'[56] even as its refusal to clarify 'things [Mailhot] can't forget or explain'[57] measures the silencing effects of trauma.

Hilary N. Weaver argues that for Indigenous peoples 'it is important to understand mental health issues within the context of historical wounding'.[58] The refracting style of *Heart Berries* suggests that the effort to know and heal oneself happens within a relay of competing psychological assaults: here, the symbolics of 'Indianness' perpetuated by white culture and the violence of being made to believe oneself 'too ugly for this world';[59] a diagnostic system that both validates symptoms (bipolar disorder, PTSD, alcoholism) and leverages terminology against bodies of colour;

the white women who make Mailhot feel 'inferior'[60] and the white men who crave her exoticism, her language, and her pain. Mailhot invokes the very stereotypes – 'dirty', 'squaw',[61] 'drunk Indian'[62] – that she also rejects as inciting self-harm; she invokes 'ancestors',[63] 'ancestors',[64] 'ancestors',[65] too, in a kind of plea, as if the text itself acts as a reminder of the collective suffering, solidarity and wisdom that precede any local moment of choice (when Mailhot decides not to terminate a pregnancy, she 'thought of the bones from [her] lineage'[66]). Her abusive father's 'ghost' haunts her as mirror and cautionary tale, but so too does her 'mother's looming spirit' who 'guid[es] [her] some days',[67] acting as a conduit inwards towards memory and outwards towards the healing that happens only in community. As Weaver explains, Indigenous conceptions of disability have more to do with being out of balance with the collective than with some moralized accusation of deficit, so that 'health' becomes an inclusive process of recovering 'harmony' rather than being cured.[68] For Mailhot, the memoir that emerges from complex vectors of knowing evidences an incomplete repair, comprised as it is of absences, allusions and the glancing obliqueness of metaphor. At the same time it reads as the fullest expression of a self who will not stay put within any one version of ethnic, gendered, emotional or writerly wellness.

Given that *Heart Berries* is ultimately a testament to the challenge, maybe the impossibility, of claiming 'authenticity',[69] it makes sense that blood functions both figuratively and physiologically to complicate a familiar suspicion in literary disability scholarship of the deployment of bodily metaphors to ableist ends. Blood is at once the site of illness – Mailhot reports that several of her female relatives died from blood-related conditions – and a signifier of connections of body, identity and community, as Mailhot wonders if she has the 'blood memory' of her ancestors,[70] writing that she has 'sacred blood' just as she also 'inherited black eyes and a grand, regal grief'.[71] Aspects of embodiment are figured in such moments in the common sense of kinship identity, and it is precisely that prior familial connotation that disrupts a conflation between illness and metaphorical damage while also signalling that we apprehend ourselves as bodyminds within the meaningful narratives of heritage. 'In my culture', Mailhot explains, 'I believe we carry pain until we can reconcile with it through ceremony. Pain is not framed like a problem with a solution'.[72] Such attitudes towards corporeality directly challenge Western medicine's tendency to singularize body 'problems' and ableist inducements towards cure and correction.[73] Weaver explains that in Native societies, valuing relational interdependence over mainstream scripts that privilege autonomy and overcoming, disability may be viewed as 'only one element of [an] individual's existence, not the defining element'.[74] Mailhot's admission that she 'didn't know if what [she] felt was authenticity, or a disease that would overtake [her]',[75] actually blurs the dichotomy between health and illness because feeling 'ill' as a validation of identity both legitimates illness as 'real' and suggests that genuine selfhood resides naturally in states of being that do not conform to some definition of symptom-free healthiness. 'Blood', therefore, as a complex marker of susceptibility, heredity and resilience, returns us to a sense of inward-most identity – but one that is neither autonomous nor isolated and cannot be understood outside of its connection to others, particularly female kin.

Mailhot's slim volume potently condemns a system that simultaneously mobilizes mental illness as a justification for the oppression of Indigenous people and denies resources for the treatment of impairment and disease. Conditions that cannot be verified – whether by casual sight or medical scan – give the lie to expectations of proof that can be especially damaging to people with disabilities who may already face serious challenges in their effort to access care. Anand Prahlad's 2017 memoir *The Secret Life of a Black Aspie* comes at this conundrum from a different direction, recounting decades of trying to hide his impairment from a neurotypical world. Complicating matters for Prahlad is the stigma of cognitive impairment within Black community, which threatens to thwart the very disclosure the memoir is invested in making. 'Blackness [at times] exacerbates the presence of ableism', as Therí Alyce Pickens contends,[76] and in Prahlad's words, 'the biggest thing about being an older black man with Asperger's is that ... [m]any white people simply can't see black people at all ... And many black people can't believe in disabilities'.[77] *Black Aspie* thus references the problematic of not being 'seen' in more than one way, since Blackness is itself consistently erased from the historical record no less than from physical, social and public locations – 'removed from space', as Pickens writes, 'to make room for the more recognizable subject: the white able body'.[78] In divulging the particularities of his consciousness to readers, Prahlad's memoir acknowledges fears

that disability makes 'our "race" seem vulnerable'[79] – his parents
worried that he 'was the sign of their sins'[80] – and thus evokes an
American history of Blackness and of mental illness in which, to
quote Michelle Jarman, 'cultural meanings of race and madness
have been intricately entwined'.[81]

As Jarman and many others have shown, Black identity in the
United States was shaped in part through the systematic deployment
of stereotypes of disability, particularly mental illness, used to justify
first the abuses of slavery and later the supposed 'obviousness' of
racial hierarchies. The memoir is haunted by the legacy of racist
pseudo-science whereby the attempt to escape from bondage was
'proof' of psychiatric disorder and oppression was naturalized as
a function of 'deterministic medical constructions of moral and
mental (in)capacities'.[82] These freighted meanings of 'crazy' collide
in *Black Aspie* with passages that recount its author's struggle to
pass as 'normal' and to understand if the disjunct he feels in social
situations is 'because of Asperger's or because of race'.[83] At the same
time, the historical past blurs into an ever-present traumatic past,
whereby slavery 'was just yesterday': Prahlad writes that he 'heard
stories all the time about slavery',[84] and his perceptual experience
is populated by the spirits of slave children with whom he forms
profound relationships. Prahlad declares too that his female
forebears 'acted like they were "crazy"' to elude predatory slave
'bosses' who were 'afraid of "crazy" slave women'.[85] In this sense
'madness' as a family inheritance is directly tied to the formation
of Black identity within a legacy of shared trauma that is itself
something of a trickster matriarchy enduring on 'waves of ironic
laughter'.[86] Here the narrator's disability, explicitly situated in
terms of genealogy, refutes what Orlando Patterson calls the 'natal
alienation' of enslaved people, who, Patterson argues, 'were not
allowed freely to integrate the experience of their ancestors into
their lives'.[87]

Fashioning a story of self as a function of these mutually informing
yet resistant identities – through the fraught reverberations of
slavery and out of the shame of cognitive impairment – becomes an
audacious exercise in manifesting what Prahlad says people 'can't
imagine'.[88] He declares in the introduction that he 'want[s] to put
[his] mind on display', to share it with readers because 'sharing
is more the point than the stories'.[89] The memoir thus opens as
an exercise in making *knowing* known. *Black Aspie* repeatedly

collapses both time and space, as various homes and even sensations become 'dimensions', 'vortex[es]', 'portals' and 'tunnel[s]'[90] that explode a white, Western concept of linearity and firmly establish a community of 'strange Black minds' – the phrase is Pickens's[91] – as the very mechanism of the memoir's epistemology.

Prahlad announces at the start that '[his] mind works differently'[92] and that his memories 'have no time line' – in fact, they very likely come 'from some other life before this one'.[93] How might a memoir that defies memory be composed? What, *who*, will be the consciousness guiding the narrative? How will continuity – of life line, of self – be established? But also why are these the determining features of a self, a life or a story? *Black Aspie* dispenses with certain conventional notions of self-representation. Most notably, while the memoir gives us the basic chronology and major events of Prahlad's life, it seems more accurate to say that it is organized by colour – such as the 'white castle'[94] of school, the variegated 'redness'[95] of an ashram where Dennis Folly becomes Swami Anand Prahlad,[96] the stultifying 'Gray Concrete'[97] of adult professional life, the 'Silver Town'[98] in Missouri where he becomes an academic, the 'copper mask'[99] he dons to perform that identity, the many 'yellow houses' that become beacons of belonging, and 'All the Green and Blue'[100] of laying one's 'burdens down'.[101] Some colours are literal, like the 'rubies, scarlets, carmines, crimsons, cerises, vermilions, rouges, russets, auburns, hennas, maroons ...'[102] worn by yogis at Rajneeshpuram. More often, the vivid palette of the text refutes both non-disabled and non-Black modes of organizing information. Moods have colour in *Black Aspie*; words may exit a person's mouth on an exhalation of hue.

Pickens argues that 'Black cultural production' evidences 'skepticism of linear progressive narratives that assume Western origins';[103] what she calls 'mad Blackness' 'disrupts ... the West's conception of space and time'.[104] Samuels writes similarly that 'crip time' 'extract[s] us from linear, progressive time with its normative life stages'.[105] Thus colour operates in *Black Aspie* as an unmetaphorical rendering of Prahlad's sense impressions as well as a specifically counter-discursive textual architecture that displaces normative conduits of sense-making, both a conventional visual epistemology and linearity. This may also account for the memoir's frequent mention of outer space, which simultaneously contests Western geocentrism, centres slave history as the memoir's origin story, and gestures at the estranging experience of neurodiversity in a culture profoundly ungenerous towards any whiff of insanity. Indeed, if the memoir has a textual antecedent, it's less the conventional autobiographies of white authors than the speculative fiction of Black writers who explicitly eschew patriarchal, racist and ableist realities by constructing new worlds (Prahlad's 'home planet' is not precisely terrestrial).[106] These philosophical implications are neatly encapsulated in *Black Aspie*'s final sentences, where the author describes 'Rule number 42': 'Take a few minutes. Let my eyes stop focusing so that I can see. Melt into the greens and the blues. The clouds. Look for the glimmer of spaceships.'[107] In these lines Prahlad gathers up the memoir's conceptual threads: its resistance to normative systems of time, the constraints of which he feels almost as a kind of bodily violence;[108] its explanation of an autist preference for ritual and pattern; and its escape from the strictures of realism through enactment of atypical processing and perception. The textual strategy of colour, then, goes well beyond illustrative detail to become a mode of interaction, a manifestation of knowing the world that exemplifies the memoir's warping of a reality we unknowingly, and uncritically, take for granted.

Indeed, when Prahlad explains his relationship to the object world, he bends the very physical laws. He does not just employ the objects in his house, for example; he talks to them, 'listen[s] to them whisper'.[109] 'Things come alive in the dark', he tells us, and 'move out of their forms'. He feels them 'reaching out to touch [him]', stays still so as to 'overhear their conversations'. In this fully animate world, very little stays put within normatively defined categories. What is 'space', after all, if it can be tasted on the tongue and measured in the murmurings of picture frames and teacups? When he describes the timber and beams of a building as wood 'still talking' as the forest it once was,[110] our conceptions of interiority, of nature, of demarcated space take on new identities. Learning is similarly written in terms of alternate reality: as a boy, Prahlad 'made up [his] own parallels' to what he finds out in school (67). Boys 'sometimes turned into girls'[111] in another kind of fluid transformation: 'Ruby' is 'a girl with slender hips' who lives in the 'mansions' within and 'come[s] out' when Prahlad is alone or feels safe.[112] Everything, in fact, is both 'nothing like' (80) anything else and subject to the author's habit of finding analogies and connections in unexpected ways. The memoir's kaleidoscopic effect,

I would argue, insists on the inherent legitimacy of things even as descriptions may defy the boundaries of ontology or the narrow expectations of social codes. Via this 'mad Black ... aesthetics', to quote Pickens once again,[113] a revisionary imagining of the world is effected.

Such liberatory effects must be understood, however, as a hard-won counter-force to the exhaustion of pretending 'that I was normal',[114] as Prahlad admits. When 'everyone's experiences and ways of looking at life were so different' from the author's own,[115] myriad 'small traumas'[116] are incurred over decades of confrontation with spaces rendered inhospitable through ableism, racism or both. An analogy to *Frankenstein* (1818), made several times in these pages, moves quickly past a common insult of disability as freakish monstrosity to confront the enduring damage of Enlightenment ideals. Mary Shelley's creature, cobbled together by a narcissistic, neglectful parent and rejected by a society horrified, alternately, by reproduction, the mobility of the lower classes, the dangers of education, lesbianism, impairment, the mutability of gender and race, and the unbridled hubris of science, wreaks his revenge in a display of self-righteous and justified anguish. Read this way, Prahlad-as-assemblage suggests that Black neurodiversity is shaped within a crucible of mad white science. That is, a Western ideology of ableism that cannot be uncoupled from racism and that inculcates in its subjects an expectation of progress and improvement so thorough as to '[tattoo] hatred ... across the most private parts of our bodies',[117] even as 'normalcy' – which Prahlad tells us he fiercely wants 'to believe' he can achieve[118] – would erase Blackness and madness alike.

The problem for Prahlad, as for Shelley's creature, is not self but system, which demands that differences stay hidden even as it directly benefits from their labor (I think of the creature gathering wood for the DeLacey family). As 'Frankenstein' cannot understand why he is shunned despite the gentility of his erudition, Prahlad struggles to 'be the black man role model', to 'learn to wear [his] professional man blackness like it was who [he] was'[119] – even though it wasn't, and at significant cost to his well-being. 'I was black, *and* I was "different"', the narrator declares. 'I was black. I was slow ... being black and slow in America was like being a caveman in a land of dinosaurs. Always hunted. Always hyper alert.'[120] But the imagery here demands notice, since in confusing a hierarchy of

predator and prey, of evolutionary progress and extinction, it calls
the order of things into question and so frustrates the very affective
response the simile seems to solicit – that is, fear (perhaps even pity)
for the 'sick' narrator. Instead, if being 'black and slow' is meant
to seem vulnerable, it is also a position of intellectual superiority,
outwitting threat. Prahlad strongly registers the dissociative cost
of the performance of academic identity: 'I was getting so good at
"passing" that I didn't even know anymore that I was doing it.'[121]
But in his final, adult iteration of 'black cyborg'[122] identity,[123] he
counters the very notion that selves should keep up some pretence
of unification.

Ultimately, and in a curious twist, these metaphors of composite
identity, gesturing at the pains and constrictions of multiple
expectations, also spotlight the limitations of Prahlad's title. For
though the end of passing seems to coincide with diagnosis and
accepting Asperger's as a way of accounting for the 'contradictions'[124]
of behaviour and attitude – thus allowing for a more holistic if not
singular sense of self – the memoir as a whole crafts an expansive
personhood that is much larger than the specifics of that diagnosis.
The text cannot neatly resolve the competing ideological strands
within which race, gender and disability become meaningful.
The nominalization of disability (and the insider slang of 'Aspie')
in Prahlad's title seems to guarantee the transparency of Autism
Spectrum Disorder and perhaps to predetermine readers' sense of
'knowing' the subject within. But at the same time, the memoir's
richly sensory aspect, its deliberate confusions of time and its
provocations of gender norms all exceed sedimented terminologies
of identity, which cannot sufficiently capture the totality of
the person who pilots a 'spaceship',[125] bound for the wilds of
imagination. Indeed 'spaceship' appears three times in the text's last
pages, as if in the very act of declaring himself known to us, Prahlad
would take flight and escape the bounds of his own definitional
efforts.

Garland-Thomson argues that 'the experience of misfitting'[126] is
not necessarily, or solely, one of exclusion and oppression; it can
also foster community, collaboration and heightened awareness of
both social injustice and the fullest range of human biodiversity.
My final example of cripistemological literature is Barbara
Neely's debut crime novel, *Blanche on the Lam* (1992),[127] which
brings Blackness and disability into conversation in just this way,

querying possible alliances across the threshold of difference. With an African American domestic worker as her amateur sleuth and an intellectually disabled white man as Blanche's sidekick in the solving of crime, Neely neatly upends some of the defining tropes of the genre, from the ratiocinative disembodied genius of men like Poe's Dupin and Conan Doyle's Holmes to the promised restoration of universal notions of civility and truth. The novel begins with Blanche White in North Carolina being charged with 30 days' jail time for writing a bad check, an offense that directly results from several of her employers having gone on vacation without paying her. Taking advantage of an uproar at the court house – the country commissioner has been charged with bribery – Blanche eludes the watch of a matron; she makes her way to a 'high end'[128] neighbourhood where she has recently cancelled a job and where she is mistaken at the gates of a front drive by a 'genteel Southern white wom[a]n'[129] who assumes she is Blanche's own replacement. The Hancock family is about to decamp to their beach house. Blanche goes along, exploiting these various dislocations (of geography, of recognition) to keep herself ahead of the law.

This premise indicts an obviously corrupt legal system and the racist logic of employment that assumes the interchangeability and 'stupidity'[130] of 'the help'.[131] Blanche moves exclusively in white spaces, from courthouse to private home, suggesting the ways in which whiteness infiltrates; Blanche is, sardonically, *named* by whiteness, interpellated by its operations. Racial injustice endures at the end of the novel because nothing systemically changes; the culprit Grace Hancock – who has killed (among others) her Black gardener Nate – is not incarcerated but quietly whisked off stage by the family lawyer, whereas Blanche's legal and financial position remains precarious. As an alternative locus of rectitude and eagerness for justice, however, Blanche also represents a 'radical' 'resistance fighter', in Frankie Y. Bailey's terms,[132] one who overtly defies white authority, often through a satiric performance of the very stereotypes that people impose on her. And the quality of Blanche's experience in white-dominated spaces is differentiated by economics. The novel insists that Blanche is a domestic worker by choice – 'she really was her own boss'[133] – so that her professional job counters what happens at court, subtly altering the balances of power.

The plot gets cripped in the person of Mumsfield (said to have mosaicism, a form of Down syndrome), who is integral to the interrogation of power and labor and of biased assumptions about the boundaries of humanity. As the primary heir of the family's fortune, Mumsfield represents money – the insular, dynastic mechanism of inheritance that sustains social inequality – and Blanche and Mumsfield clearly manifest the imbalances of racialized and gendered economic structures, just as Grace and others demonstrate the vastly unequal treatment of Black and white people by the legal system. Together, though, they also explode the brutal legacy of 'feeblemindedness' as a catch-all pathology linking so-called despised Others as the 'signifier[s] of tainted whiteness'.[134] Here again Neely makes strategic use of the crime template – implicated as it is in expectations of male supervisory control and analytical smarts – in 'detecting' the wrongdoings of social caste systems through the perspectives of a Black woman and cognitively disabled man.

Mumsfield initially enters the novel as a caricature of Faulkneresque Southern gothic: a pudgy, childish man with pants 'belted tightly above his belly', glasses strapped to his head, and 'an air of harmlessness about him that was puzzling in a white man'.[135] His impairment is mobilized by the plot as an easy way to gauge what's wrong with Grace and her husband Everett – since they don't take him 'seriously as a person'[136] and so exploit his 'innocence'[137] – and what's therefore pointedly more humane about Blanche. 'She was sure talking to him was *good for her*',[138] she thinks, in a common narrative move that turns the disabled character into a lesson to serve non-disabled betterment. Indeed, Blanche's first impression of Mumsfield, along with a tendency to accede to a minimizing of his 'ability … to understand',[139] has a significant pedagogical function because it stages a correction of sorts as Blanche comes to realize how much Mumsfield grasps of the nefarious goings-on around them. Anyone can be guilty of acquiescing to stereotypes.

But Mumsfield and Blanche quickly develop a kind of extrasensory connection, a 'wavelength' or 'frequency'[140] that lets Blanche sense Mumsfield's approach and facilitates a more genuine 'familiarity' that surprises her.[141] That their connection happens on an intuitive level similarly disrupts the empirical origins of the crime genre with its insistence on 'scientific', demonstrable conclusions. In this sense, Blanche and Mumsfield represent alternative epistemologies that move along pathways that skirt white male able-mindedness: the knowledge of 'wise women elders' of Black community,[142] for example, or the embodied 'feeling' that reveals important details to Mumsfield and helps Blanche to solve the case. As Blanche acknowledges, 'he could ... understand things. You only needed to get in step with his way of putting his thoughts and words together'.[143] Disability at first seems used to 'soften' Mumsfield, then, making him emotionally available to Blanche in a way that does not pertain to any of the other white men in the novel. But it is also rendered on its own terms, as a form of cognition that others must manoeuvre themselves into recognizing and understanding.

The novel does align disability and race as analogously disenfranchised subjectivities. Mumsfield's 'condition made him as invisible as [Blanche's] color and profession made her',[144] for example; not being taken seriously is 'something they shared',[145] and 'his Down's syndrome made him as recognizably different from the people who ran and owned the world as she'.[146] But as Nirmala Erevelles contends, the 'simplistic and problematic assertion' of analogy 'does nothing to engage the complex ways in which race and disability are imbricated in the construction of the pathological Other',[147] and *Blanche on the Lam* in fact precisely demonstrates why these identity markers must be carefully parsed. 'For all ... their seeming connectedness, Mumsfield was still a white man', Blanche thinks at the end of the text, when the case is closed and Mumsfield asks her to stay on, at a very generous salary;[148] she will 'stand firm against having her brain vanillaed'.[149] Warding off the insidious reach of whiteness prevails over any fear of disability in that last image, and something interesting happens in Blanche's uncoupling of whiteness *as* able-mindedness in her apprehension of Mumsfield. Blanche has tried 'to see the world the way he saw it',[150] and he seems to 'understand' her decision to leave almost as if he has 'leaped across the gap between them and truly knew what it meant to be a black woman trying to control her own life'.[151] In a genre defined by epistemological crisis – whodunnit? And what does it mean? – their collaboration suggests the necessity of bringing not just multiple but distinctly non-normative viewpoints to bear on questions of belonging, justice and respect.

The texts discussed in this chapter share a sense of empathy and radical interconnectedness, along with otherworldliness and outer space, disruptions of grammar and form, defamiliarized landscapes and remappings of space, the use of writing to defang the teratological 'monster' that is the disabled being, and disability as a way of shaping our investigations of human embodied experience. I have chosen to spotlight work that exemplifies the growing robustness of disability culture's archive (a tiny, idiosyncratic fraction), and I have taken my cues from other disability literary scholars in reading reparatively, following Eve Kosofsky Sedgwick in *Touching Feeling* (2003): to take assemblage, fragmentation and incoherence as the origins of hope and joy, and to esteem the experience of disability as a wholesale 'ecology of knowing'.[152]

Notes

1   G. Thomas Couser and Susannah Mintz, *Disability Experiences: Memoirs, Autobiographies and Other Personal Narratives* (Macmillan Reference: New York, 2019).

2   As just a few examples: *Beholding Disability in Renaissance England*, by Allison Hobgood; *Monstrous Kinds: Body, Space, and Narrative in Renaissance Representations of Disability*, by Elizabeth Bearden; *Recovering Disability in Early Modern England*, ed. Allison P. Hobgood and David Houston Wood; *The Idea of Disability in the Eighteenth Century*, ed. Chris Mounsey; *A Cultural History of Disability*, from the middle ages to the modern age, series ed. David Bolt and Robert McRuer.

3   Petra Kuppers, 'Literary Disability Culture Imaginations at Work: An Afterword', in *The Cambridge Companion to Literature and Disability*, ed. Clare Barker and Stuart Murray (Cambridge: Cambridge University Press, 2018), 227–32.

4   Kuppers, 'Afterword', 231.

5   Ibid., 232.

6   Eli Clare, *Brilliant Imperfection: Grappling with Cure* (Durham, NC: Duke University Press, 2017), 86.

7   Ibid., 88.

8   Tanya Titchkosky, *Reading & Writing Disability Differently: The Textured Life of Embodiment* (Toronto: University of Toronto Press, 2007), 131–2.

9   Riva Lehrer, *Golem Girl: A Memoir* (New York: One World, 2020).

10   Ibid., xv.

11   In her series *The Risk Pictures*, Lehrer strove to upend the power differential of portraiture by leaving her subjects alone with a work in progress and inviting them to intervene somehow – to leave their own mark on the canvas. Here, portraiture mimics but also refuses that imbalance of subject and object, gazer and gazed-upon, that has

a painful counterpart for disabled people in medical contexts: what Lehrer refers to as 'toxic staring'.

12 Rosemarie Garland-Thomson, 'Misfits: A Feminist Materialist Disability Concept', *Hypatia* 26, no. 3 (2011): 591–609.

13 Creative or 'disability gain' is a coinage derived from H-Dirksen L. Bauman and Joseph J. Murray's notion of 'Deaf-gain', articulated in 'Deaf Studies in the 21st Century: "Deaf-Gain" and the Future of Human Diversity', in *The Disability Studies Reader*, ed. Lennard J. Davis, 4th edn. (New York: Routledge, 2014), 246–60.

14 Laurie Lambeth, 'Reshaping the Outline' and 'Dysaesthesia', in *Beauty Is a Verb: The New Poetry of Disability*, ed. Jennifer Bartlett, Sheila Black, and Michael Northen (El Paso: Cinco Puntos Press, 2011), 174–82.

15 Ibid., 175.

16 Ibid., 176–7.

17 Lambeth, 'Dysaesthesia', 182.

18 Lambeth, 'Reshaping', 174.

19 Lambeth, 'Dysaesthesia', 182.

20 Ibid., italics in original.

21 Lambeth, 'Dysaesthesia', 182.

22 Lambeth, 'Reshaping', 176.

23 Michael Davidson, *Concerto for the Left Hand: Disability and the Defamiliar Body* (Ann Arbor: University of Michigan Press, 2008), 225.

24 Margrit Shildrick, *Dangerous Discourses of Disability, Subjectivity, and Sexuality* (London: Palgrave Macmillan, 2012), 33.

25 Lambeth, 'Reshaping', 174.

26 Petra Kuppers, *Gut Botany: Poems* (Detroit: Wayne State University Press, 2020).

27 See also Sarah Jaquette Ray and Jay Sibara, *Disability Studies and the Environmental Humanities: Toward an Eco-Crip Theory* (Lincoln: University of Nebraska Press, 2018).

28 Kuppers, *Gut Botany*, 11.

29 Ibid., 86.

30 Ibid., 47.

31 Ibid., 42.

32 Ibid., 45.

33 Ibid., 47.

34 Ibid., 46.

35 Ibid., 45.

36 Ellen Samuels, *Fantasies of Identification: Disability, Gender, Race* (New York: New York University Press, 2014), 14.

37 Ibid., 15.

38 Ibid., my italics.

39 Kuppers, *Gut Botany*, 59.

40 Tanya Titchkosky, 'Normal', in *Keywords for Disability Studies*, ed. Rachel Adams, Benjamin Reiss, and David Serlin (New York: New York University Press, 2015), 130–2.

41 Terese Marie Mailhot, *Heart Berries* (Berkeley: Counterpoint, 2018).

42 Ibid., 7.

43 Ibid., 12.

44 Ibid., 7.

45 Ibid., 15.

46 Ibid., 18–19.

47 Ibid., 17.

48 Jen Deerinwater argues that 'many of [the] health issues' experienced by Native people 'are a direct result of colonialism'. 'Healthcare is abysmal for Natives in urban areas', she writes, and 'historical and intergenerational trauma' accounts for much of the emotional and psychological impairment of indigenous people (50). 'The Erasure of Indigenous People in Chronic Illness', in *Disability Visibility: First-Person Stories from the Twenty-First Century*, ed. Alice Wong (New York: Vintage, 2020), 47–52, 50.

49 Garland-Thomson, 'Misfits', 597.

50 Mailhot, *Heart Berries*, 25.

51 Ibid., 31.

52 This phrase is attributed to Margaret Price, 'The Bodymind Problem and the Possibilities of Pain', *Hypatia* 30, no. 1 (2015): 269.

53 Mailhot, *Heart Berries*, 48.

54 Ibid., 42.

55 Ibid., 49.

56 Ibid., 111.

57 Ibid., 97.

58 Hilary N. Weaver, 'Disability through a Native American Lens: Examining Influences of Culture and Colonization', *Journal of Social Work in Disability and Rehabilitation* 14 (2015): 148–62.

59 Ibid., 114.

60 Mailhot, *Heart Berries*, 97.

61 Ibid., 92.

62 Ibid., 117.

63 Ibid., 18.

64 Ibid., 72.

65 Ibid., 79.

66 Ibid., 79.

67 Ibid., 114.

68 Weaver, 'Disability through a Native American Lens', 115.

69 Mailhot, *Heart Berries*, 69.

70 Ibid., 32.

71 Ibid., 69–70.

72 Ibid., 28.
73 See Clare, *Brilliant Imperfection*, on the ideology of cure.
74 Weaver, 'Disability through a Native American Lens', 151.
75 Mailhot, *Heart Berries*, 69.
76 Therí Alyce Pickens, *Black Madness:: Mad Blackness* (Durham, NC: Duke University Press, 2020), 30.
77 Anand Prahlad, *The Secret Life of a Black Aspie* (Fairbanks: University of Alaska Press, 2017), 7–8.
78 Pickens, *Black Madness*, 29.
79 Prahlad, *Black Aspie*, 8.
80 Ibid., 53.
81 Michelle Jarman, 'Race and Disability in US Literature', in *The Cambridge Companion to Literature and Disability*, ed. Clare Barker and Stuart Murray (Cambridge: Cambridge University Press, 2018), 16.
82 Ibid., 17. For more on drapetomania, see 'Diseases and Peculiarities of the Negro Race' from 1851, available online: https://www.pbs.org/wgbh/aia/part4/4h3106t.html
83 Prahlad, *Black Aspie*, 9.
84 Ibid., 22.
85 Prahlad, *Black Aspie*, 21.
86 Ibid., 20. Prahlad says that he 'loved tricking' because 'it broke the neurologically typical world apart and made it stop and look confused' (93). Tolson, writing about folklore, explains that 'for tricksters, adaptability is mandatory' (74).
87 Orlando Patterson, *Slavery and Social Death: A Comparative Study* (Cambridge, MA: Harvard University Press, 1982), 7, 5.
88 Ibid., 8.
89 Ibid., 10.
90 Prahlad, *Black Aspie*, 26–7.
91 Pickens, *Black Madness*, 4.
92 Prahlad, *Black Aspie*, 11.
93 Ibid., 10.
94 Ibid., 105.
95 Ibid., 139.
96 Prahlad gives glancing acknowledgement to the controversy about Bhagwan Shree Rahneesh (also called Osho): 'People outside were saying a lot of things about the Ranch, most of them not very good' (142). In fact, as Hugh Urban writes, the ashram was the site of 'a stunning array of criminal activities', including 'one of the largest wiretapping operations in U.S. history, the largest immigration fraud ever recorded, and – most shockingly – the largest bioterrorist attack on American soil', and is widely considered to have been a cult. See Hugh Urban, 'Rajneeshpuram Was More than a Utopia in the Desert. It Was a Mirror of the Time', *Humanities* 39, no. 2 (2018), and the Netflix documentary series *Wild Wild Country* from the same year.

97 Prahlad, *Black Aspie,* 166.
98 Ibid., 195.
99 Ibid., 202.
100 Ibid., 179.
101 Ibid., 183.
102 Ibid., 139.
103 Pickens, *Black Madness*, 29.
104 Ibid., 57.
105 Ellen Samuels, 'Six Ways of Looking at Crip Time', in *Disability Visibility: First-Person Stories from the Twenty-First Century*, ed. Alice Wong (New York: Vintage, 2020), 190. See also *Crip Temporalities*, a special issue of *South Atlantic Quarterly* 120, no. 2 (April 2021), co-edited by Samuels and Elizabeth Freeman.
106 Prahlad, *Black Aspie*, 187. For more on disability, race and the otherworldly, see Sami Schalk, *Bodyminds Reimagined: (Dis)ability, Race, and Gender in Black Women's Speculative Fiction* (Durham, NC: Duke University Press, 2008).
107 Prahlad, *Black Aspie*, 225.
108 On disability, academic productivity, and shame, see Janet Macarthur, 'Disrupting the Academic Self: Living with Lupus', in *Unfitting Stories: Narrative Approaches to Disease, Disability, and Trauma*, ed. Valerie Raoul, Connie Canam, Angela Henderson and Carla Paterson (Waterloo: Wilfred Laurier University Press, 2007), 171–9.
109 Prahlad, *Black Aspie*, 217.
110 Ibid., 141.
111 Ibid., 159.
112 Ibid., 85.
113 Pickens, *Black Madness*, 58.
114 Prahlad, *Black Aspie*, 166.
115 Ibid., 208.
116 Ibid., 166.
117 Ibid., 104.
118 Ibid., 110.
119 Ibid., 172.
120 Ibid., 122–3.
121 Ibid., 110.
122 Ibid., 107.
123 On the limitations of 'black cyborg', see Pickens, *Black Madness*, 19–20.
124 Prahlad, *Black Aspie*, 217.
125 Ibid., 221.
126 Garland-Thomson, 'Misfits', 597–8.
127 Barbara Neely, *Blanche on the Lam* (Leawood: Brash Books, 1992).
128 Ibid., 7.

129   Ibid., 4.
130   Ibid., 15.
131   Ibid., 12.
132   Frankie Y. Bailey, 'Blanche on the Lam, or the Invisible Woman Speaks', in *Diversity and Detective Fiction*, ed. Kathleen Gregory Klein (Bowling Green, OH: Bowling Green University Popular Press, 1999), 194–5.
133   Ibid., 76.
134   Anna Stubblefield, '"Beyond the Pale": Tainted Whiteness, Cognitive Disability and Eugenic Sterilization', *Hypatia* 22, no. 2 (2007): 162.
135   Ibid., 21.
136   Ibid., 73.
137   Ibid., 43.
138   Ibid., 93; my italics.
139   Ibid., 67.
140   Ibid., 40.
141   Ibid., 41.
142   Ibid., 102.
143   Ibid., 97.
144   Ibid., 91.
145   Ibid., 73.
146   Ibid., 192.
147   Nirmala Erevelles, 'Race', in *Keywords for Disability Studies*, ed. Rachel Adams, Benjamin Reiss, and David Serlin (New York: New York University Press, 2015), 147.
148   Neely, *Blanche*, 161.
149   Ibid., 192.
150   Ibid., 93.
151   Ibid., 192.
152   Eve Kosofsky Sedgwick, *Touching Feeling: Affect, Pedagogy, Performativity* (Durham, NC: Duke University Press, 2003), 145.

Bibliography

Bailey, Frankie Y. *'Blanche on the Lam, or the Invisible Woman Speaks'*. In *Diversity and Detective Fiction*, edited by Kathleen Gregory Klein, 186–204. Bowling Green, OH: Bowling Green University Popular Press, 1999.
Bauman, H-L. Dirksen, and Joseph J. Murray. 'Deaf Studies in the 21st Century: "Deaf-Gain" and the Future of Human Diversity'. In *The Disability Studies Reader*, edited by Lennard J. Davis, 4th edn., 246–60. New York: Routledge, 2013.

Clare, Eli. *Brilliant Imperfection: Grappling with Cure*. Durham,
NC: Duke University Press, 2017.

Couser, G. Thomas and Susannah Mintz. *Disability Experiences:
Memoirs, Autobiographies and Other Personal Narratives*. New York:
Macmillan Reference, 2019.

Davidson, Michael. *Concerto for the Left Hand: Disability and the
Defamiliar Body*. Ann Arbor: University of Michigan Press, 2008.

Deerinwater, Jen. 'The Erasure of Indigenous People in Chronic Illness'.
In *Disability Visibility: First-Person Stories from the Twenty-First
Century*, edited by Alice Wong, 47–52. New York: Vintage, 2020.

Erevelles, Nirmala. 'Race'. In *Keywords for Disability Studies*, edited by
Rachel Adams, Benjamin Reiss, and David Serlin, 145–8. New York:
New York University Press, 2015.

Kuppers, Petra. 'Literary Disability Culture Imaginations at Work:
An Afterword'. In *The Cambridge Companion to Literature and
Disability*, edited by Clare Barker and Stuart Murray, 227–32.
Cambridge: Cambridge University Press, 2018.

Kuppers, Petra. *Gut Botany: Poems*. Detroit: Wayne State University
Press, 2020.

Lehrer, Riva. *Golem Girl: A Memoir*. New York: One World, 2020.

Macarthur, Janet. 'Disrupting the Academic Self: Living with Lupus'. In
*Unfitting Stories: Narrative Approaches to Disease, Disability, and
Trauma*, edited by Valerie Raoul, Connie Canam, Angela Henderson and
Carla Paterson, 171–9. Waterloo: Wilfred Laurier University Press, 2007.

Mailhot, Terese Marie. *Heart Berries*. Berkeley: Counterpoint, 2018.

Neely, Barbara. *Blanche on the Lam*. Leawood: Brash Books, 1992.

Patterson, Orlando. *Slavery and Social Death: A Comparative Study*.
Cambridge, MA: Harvard University Press, 1982.

Pickens, Therí Alyce. *Black Madness :: Mad Blackness*. Durham, NC:
Duke University Press, 2019.

Prahlad, Anand. *The Secret Life of a Black Aspie*. Fairbanks: University of
Alaska Press, 2017.

Price, Margaret. 'The Bodymind Problem and the Possibilities of Pain'.
Hypatia 30, no. 1 (2015): 268–84.

Ray, Sarah Jaquette, and Jay Sibara. *Disability Studies and the
Environmental Humanities: Toward an Eco-Crip Theory*. Lincoln:
University of Nebraska Press, 2018.

Rekdal, Paisley. *Appropriate: A Provocation*. New York: W. W. Norton,
2021.

Samuels, Ellen. *Fantasies of Identification: Disability, Gender, Race*.
New York: New York University Press, 2014.

Samuels, Ellen. 'Six Ways of Looking at Crip Time'. In *Disability
Visibility: First-Person Stories from the Twenty-First Century*, edited by
Alice Wong, 189–96. New York: Vintage, 2020.

Schalk, Sami. *Bodyminds Reimagined: (Dis)ability, Race, and Gender in Black Women's Speculative Fiction*. Durham, NC: Duke University Press, 2008.

Sedgwick, Eve Kosofsky. *Touching Feeling: Affect, Pedagogy, Performativity*. Durham, NC: Duke University Press, 2003.

Shildrick, Margrit. *Dangerous Discourses of Disability, Subjectivity, and Sexuality*. London: Palgrave Macmillan, 2012.

Stubblefield, Anna. '"Beyond the Pale": Tainted Whiteness, Cognitive Disability and Eugenic Sterilization'. *Hypatia* 22, no. 2 (2007): 162–81.

Titchkosky, Tanya. *Reading & Writing Disability Differently: The Textured Life of Embodiment*. Toronto: University of Toronto Press, 2007.

Titchkosky, Tanya. 'Normal'. In *Keywords for Disability Studies*, edited by Rachel Adams, Benjamin Reiss, and David Serlin, 130–2. New York: New York University Press, 2015.

Tolson, Nancy D. 'The Butler Didn't Do It So Now They're Blaming the Maid: Defining a Black Feminist Trickster through the Novels of Barbara Neely'. *South Central Review* 18, nos. 3–4 (2001): 72–85.

Urban, Hugh. 'Rajneeshpuram Was More than a Utopia in the Desert. It Was a Mirror of the Time'. *Humanities* 39, no. 2 (2018). Available online: https://www.neh.gov/humanities/2018/spring/feature/rajneeshpuram-was-more-utopia-desert-it-was-mirror

8

Aging and Old Age

J. Brooks Bouson

'What does a woman of a certain age see when she looks at herself in time's mirror?' asks feminist scholar and literary critic Nancy K. Miller as she reflects on the aging process.[1] Describing aging as a 'project of coming to terms with a face and a body in process' and as 'an emotional effort, an oscillation that moves between the mirrored poles of acceptance and refusal', Miller writes that for many aging women 'an archaic but tenacious private shame haunts our vision'.[2] An older and self-aware feminist, Miller wants to resist the shame that accompanies the aging process, but she still finds it difficult to embrace her identity as an older woman. In a similar way, feminist scholar Lynne Segal confesses to her own reluctance to discuss her age.

> How old am I? Don't ask; don't tell. The question frightens me. It is maddening, all the more so for those like me, feminists on the left, approaching our sixth or seventh decade, who like to feel we have spent much of our time trying to combat prejudice on all sides. Yet fears of revealing our age ... are hard to smother.[3]

Why can it be so difficult, as Miller and Segal admit, for older women – and aging feminists – to resist ageism and embrace their identities as aging women or even to admit their age to others? And why has it been so difficult for feminist scholars to break the social and academic silence surrounding the plight of older women in our greying culture?

Because women in general live longer than men, we live in a society, as Margaret Cruikshank has remarked, where '"old" means "women,"' and where old women bear 'the brunt of ageism'.[4] Even as society continues to grey in the twenty-first century and more women live into advanced old age, old age remains deeply stigmatized. Indeed, the increase in life span has 'amplified rather than diminished social antipathy' towards the aging population even at a time in which there is an 'aversion towards the very topic of ageing'.[5] Because women 'have learned to watch, control and where necessary censor their bodies from the moment they are made conscious of their gender', as women's studies scholar Jeannette King observes, the 'coming into consciousness of the ageing body is ... in a sense nothing new'.[6] For women, the 'coming into consciousness of the aging body' in our appearance-driven culture is a painful process in which old women are 'equated with declining bodies' and are systematically devalued[7] and thus women learn to reject and feel ashamed of their age-altered appearance as they get older. Indeed, shame about the visible signs of aging is a cultural burden inherited by women in our culture. But because shame can breed silence and a hiding response and because the exposure of shame can cause even more shame, all too often older women live alone with their cultural wounds as they come to internalize society's harsh and shaming judgements against them – that they are physically unattractive and socially unimportant people.

'Shame, which is antithetical to the central value of human dignity, the heart of our ethical vision', writes Martha Holstein, 'is nonetheless a familiar experience for many aging women'.[8] The responses of aging second-wave feminists to the aging process offers troubling evidence of the insidious and shaming power of the master narrative of old age as decline and the accompanying social devaluation and body shaming of older women. Despite the wide dissemination of feminist critiques of cultural representations of femininity and the female body, many contemporary women's studies and age studies scholars have noted that ageism is deeply entrenched in feminism and that many older second-wave feminists are deeply ageist. For example, in their analysis of the 'inadvertent but pernicious ageism' found in much contemporary women's studies scholarship, age study scholars Toni Calasanti, Kathleen Slevin and Neal King write that, while feminists 'have contributed to the literature on bodies, discussion of old bodies is sorely lacking'.[9] Moreover, even as feminists have recently begun to show more concern about aging, perhaps because they themselves are aging, they 'do not often question the stigma affixed to old age' nor do they 'ask why it seems denigrating to label someone old'.[10] In a similar way, Margaret Cruikshank points to the impact of ageism on women's studies scholarship. 'We in women's studies have averted our gaze from women over sixty, even if we are over sixty ourselves', comments Cruikshank.[11] Noting the lack of scholarly interest in age studies, Cruikshank speculates that women's studies scholars 'may unconsciously avoid the topic, knowing that old people, especially women, are stigmatized. Internalized ageism may afflict us, in other words. Like others, feminists resist physical changes and the diminishment of our social power, and thus aging has not seemed to be a promising subject for study'.[12]

Because of what age critic Kathleen Woodward calls the 'youthful structure of the look – that is, the culturally induced tendency to degrade and reduce an older person to the prejudicial category of old age'[13] – older women may go to great lengths to pass as younger, and they may reject both their own aging bodies and the bodies of their age peers who show their age. As society greys in the twenty-first century, the pressures on older women to avoid the stigma of an age-marked appearance have only intensified under the so-called successful or positive aging paradigm, which promulgates the idea that a younger-looking appearance in middle and even old age is a sign of successful aging. Influenced by the 'healthist discourses that hold individuals personally responsible' for both the health and appearance of their bodies, which are presumed to be 'one and the same thing', older women have felt increasingly that they have a 'moral responsibility to fight the onset of an aged appearance'.[14] Those who 'look old and, therefore, ugly and unhealthy' are harshly judged as people who have 'morally, socially, and physically failed in their clash with the never-ending advancement of time'.[15] Because older women feel more pressured than ever to retain a younger-looking appearance as long as possible, they may use anti-aging non-surgical cosmetic interventions or products (such as Botox or laser skin treatments) or surgical cosmetic procedures (such as face lifts or liposuction) in order to keep up a more youthful appearance. The fact that the contemporary preferred way to age successfully is to maintain a younger-looking appearance or to minimize the physical signs of aging calls attention to the deep shame and disgust attached to old age and to the age-altered (therefore 'ugly') bodies of older women.

Just as feminist age studies scholars have noted how 'lethal' ageism can be for women in our society where 'ageism is entrenched within feminism' – where feminists, too, have internalized the culture's 'prejudices against aging and old age'[16] – so they have worried about the generational divide that has long existed within the feminist movement. Like the second-wave feminism of the 1960s and 1970s, the third-wave feminism that arose in the 1990s has been 'predominantly a young woman's movement with little interest in the problems facing the older woman', as Jeannette King has remarked.[17] The persistence of a generational divide within the evolving late-twentieth- and twenty-first-century feminist movements reveals how difficult it is to confront and find a solution to feminism's deeply entrenched and generational ageism. Shame theory, as I will show, helps us understand the affective roots of this feminist response to aging by revealing the impact of 'learned cultural shame' on aging women – that is, the internalized sexageist shame that grows out of ageist decline ideology and the social denigration of the bodies and identities of aging and especially elderly women in contemporary culture. Thus, one of my central goals is to bring together shame theory and the work of feminist age study scholars in order to expose how gendered ageism wounds older women and makes them ashamed of their age. I also offer exemplary scenes of shame drawn from the growing body of post-1960 literary works by North American and British women writers focused on the aging woman as I show how women writers have responded to the shaming of older women by publicly exposing the myriad ways our culture devalues and humiliates older women in our age-phobic contemporary culture.

Learned cultural shame: The mask of aging and the older woman

Sexageism functions as a deeply entrenched and persistent shaming ideology that oppresses women – even aging feminists – in our greying twenty-first-century culture.[18] But even though many women experience shame as they grow older, they feel that they 'must be silent about the vagaries of their aging bodies lest they collaborate in their own devaluation', observe co-authors Martha Holstein, Jennifer Parks and Mark Waymack.[19] Although older women 'inhabit and live in and through culturally stigmatized bodies' and are 'aware of how others judge their bodies', the 'meanings attached to living and functioning with and through bodies that are not culturally esteemed' have received 'almost no public attention'.[20]

'To feel shame is to feel *seen* in a painfully diminished sense' and to be 'revealed as lesser', writes shame theorist Gershen Kaufman.[21] The 'affect of indignity', shame is of vital importance to the individual because no other affect 'is closer to the experienced self' or is 'more central for the sense of identity'.[22] Individuals need to feel 'valued and respected' in their daily relations with others and when this need is not provided for, 'shame will inevitably ensue'.[23] In a similar way, shame theorist Paul Gilbert, in his work on 'body shame', describes the experience of shame as an 'inner experience of self as an unattractive social agent', and an 'involuntary response to an awareness that one has lost status and is devalued'.[24] Gilbert states that in 'body shame' such an experience of social devaluation may be reflected in negative assessments of the body – 'I hate, or am disgusted by, my body.'[25] As many women succumb to the shaming ideology of sexageism as they get older and experience 'body shame', they become subjected to what shame theorist Andrew Morrison calls 'learned cultural shame'[26] as they, internalizing the contemptuous gaze of others, come to see themselves as physically unattractive and socially devalued people. Indeed, to bear the visible bodily marks of aging and old age is to take on a socially devalued, stigmatized identity in our age-phobic society where 'being old is a stigma and reflects a spoiled self'.[27] But while the social and body shaming of older women is commonplace in our society, many older women, rather than revealing their shame – and thereby risking the intensification of their feelings of shameful exposure – remain silent about the indignities they confront in their daily lives. Thus, it is not surprising that many older women attempt to conceal the aging process – that is, hide their shame – by dyeing their hair and using cosmetics and plastic surgery as they try to minimize or eliminate the signs of aging on their faces. Many older women who feel good about their appearance do so on the basis of looking younger.

As women age and so find it increasingly difficult to pass as younger and to hide the visible signs of bodily aging, they may experience the stigmatizing process called the 'mask of aging' as they come to view their aging appearance as a 'mask or disguise concealing the essentially youthful self beneath'.[28] The fact that older women often see the 'aging mask' of their grey hair and wrinkles and other signs of aging as 'pathological or deviant' while the youthful inner self is 'normal'[29] reveals how the age-altered body is pathologized in our appearance-driven culture. Given the focus on women's physical appearance, it is not surprising that the 'mask of aging' experience of aging – the feeling of being a young person trapped in an old (and therefore pathological and deviant) face and body – is so commonplace in the lives of many older women and even aging feminists. 'A friend's mother', writes feminist philosopher Sandra Bartky, 'described to me her sense of alienation when she would glimpse herself in a mirror. She felt young inside, she said, but her face was crisscrossed with deep lines of age. I myself have the same experience, but with fewer lines; I am shocked by the aging of my body, not just my face'.[30] While Nancy Miller insists that aging women need to 'resist the narrative of decline' and its assumption that women are at their 'most beautiful or desirable at a youthful moment and the rest is downhill',[31] she, too, has had unsettling encounters with the stranger in the mirror:

> On a good day, when I forget who and where I am, and find myself completely absorbed in what I'm doing, if I turn and see myself in the mirror, I often have the shock of misrecognition … Who is that yenta in the mirror, that matron walking down Broadway? It's … my mother, but it's also *me*. How did I get there? When did I stop being twenty-eight?[32]

Feminist philosopher Diana Tietjens Meyers similarly describes the experience many older women have when they confront an 'alien image' – a 'stranger'– in the mirror.[33] While Meyers seeks ways for older women to 'salvage' their 'face-esteem' and thus 'embrace the stranger in the mirror', she also understands why so many older women want to hide the signs of aging in a culture in which 'women's aging features have been shanghaied as figurative vehicles for decline and demise'.[34]

The self-alienating encounter with the aging stranger in the mirror described by Barky, Miller and Meyers is a scene of shame that is repeated, again and again, in the works of recent and contemporary women writers. The 65-year-old Stella Brentwood in Penelope Lively's novel *Spiderweb* (1998), who associates aging with decline and the 'awful tyranny of the body', is aware of the undeniable fact that she is bodily aging: 'The face in the mirror – at which she gave only the most perfunctory glances these days – seemed like some disturbing distortion of her real face. These jowls, those pouches. The backs of her hands were brocaded with brown blotches beneath which twined the thick grey worms of veins.'[35] While the nearly seventy-year-old Fay Langdon in Anita Brookner's *Brief Lives* (1990) appears 'attractive' for her age, she is aware that her body is aging 'quite comprehensively' and that she looks her age: 'there was no danger of my being mistaken for somebody younger … Behind the daytime mask the cruel body goes its way, breeding its own destruction, signaling – blatantly – its own decay. I knew all this'. [36] For May Sarton's 76-year-old character, Caro Spencer, in the novel *As We Are Now* (1973), old age is a 'disguise'[37] that only the old can penetrate. Exposing her own learned cultural shame, Caro, in a classic invocation of the mask of aging experience of the aging process, views her age-marked body as a deviant or pathological mask that conceals her youthful inner self: 'I feel exactly as I always did, as young inside as when I was twenty-one, but the outward shell conceals the real me – sometimes even from itself – and betrays that person deep down inside, under wrinkles and liver spots and all the horrors of decay.'[38] In a similar way, Margaret Laurence's ninety-year-old Hagar Shipley in the novel *The Stone Angel* (1964) views her old face as an ugly mask that conceals her essential – and youthful – identity: 'When I look in my mirror and beyond the changing shell that houses me, I see the eyes of Hagar Currie, the same dark eyes as when I first began to remember and to notice myself', Hagar reflects at one point, thinking that if she were to look in the mirror and take herself by surprise, she might catch sight of her younger self.[39] Instead, when the elderly Hagar glances at herself in the mirror, she sees her

> puffed face purpled with veins as though someone had scribbled over the skin with an indelible pencil … Below the eyes the shadows bloom as though two soft black petals had been stuck there. The hair which should by rights be black is yellowed white, like damask stored too long in a damp basement. Well, Hagar Shipley, you are a sight for sore eyes, all right.[40]

Dealing in an open way with the dread of old age and with the fear and loathing of the age-altered female body that permeate contemporary culture, authors like Lively, Brookner, Sarton and Laurence acknowledge the insidious ways in which 'women's aging features have been shanghaied as figurative vehicles for decline and demise'.[41] That older women have reported in interviews that they view aging as 'an inevitable, undesirable and uncontrollable status passage in which the true self becomes less visible in the aged shell of the body' and that they may react to their old-woman appearance with 'angst, bewilderment and even despair'[42] reveals just how distressing and bewildering the bodily changes associated with the aging process can be for many older women as they age into old age.

The hypervisible and socially invisible aging woman

'Many older women have given up even the possibility that they can satisfy the requirements of ideal embodied femininity and believe they are now supposed to become invisible, to dwindle away', writes Sandra Bartky.[43] If aging women are rendered hypervisible because they bear the physical signs of age – which publicly mark them as socially undesirable older women with spoiled identities – they are also socially invisible, for others ignore or shun them or even treat them in an openly hostile way in the public sphere. The plight of the hypervisible and socially invisible older woman in our culture points to the hidden shame script that governs the lives of so many older women. For just as shame about appearance can lead to the defensive desire to hide or disappear, it can also lead to the fear of disappearing; to the experience of social invisibility that is the consequence of social rejection; and to the social death that occurs when one is ignored or openly treated as an object of contempt in public spaces. Describing the annihilating force of contempt, shame theorist Léon Wurmser writes: 'Contempt says: "You should disappear as such a being as you have shown yourself to be – failing, weak, flawed, and dirty. Get out of my sight: Disappear!"'[44] To be exposed as one who fails someone else's or one's own expectations causes shame, and to 'disappear into nothing is the punishment for such failure'.[45] In his account of the contempt-disappear scenario, Wurmser calls attention to the punishing aspects of contempt, a 'strong form of rejection' that wants 'to eliminate' the other person: 'If it is appearance (exposure) that is central in shame, disappearance is the logical outcome of shame – and contempt is the affect that brings this aim about.'[46] The phenomenon of the hypervisible but also socially invisible – and disappearing – older woman reveals how contemptuously aging women are treated in our age-phobic culture as they are subjected in their daily lives to the contempt that says, in effect, get out of sight and disappear. In a more sinister version of a contempt-disappear scenario, those who are old and disabled or ill may end up 'disappearing' into nursing homes.

Remarking that the 'embodied experiences of older women and their perceptions of beauty work have been largely unexplored', sociologists and gerontological researchers Laura Hurd Clarke and Meridith Griffin have investigated, through in-depth interviews with women ranging in age from fifty to seventy years old, contemporary women's experiences of and responses to their aging appearances.[47] Subjected to gendered ageism because they are both aging and female, the women in Hurd Clarke and Griffin's study feel deeply distressed about and damaged by the loss of a younger-looking appearance. 'I've felt for the last 10 years that I'm completely invisible to men ... Nobody even sees me ... I am invisible. I am not there', comments a 52-year-old woman.[48] 'Our attitude towards older people, particularly older women, is that they've lost their power and they're insignificant and, taken to an extreme, they're of no value any more', states a 65-year-old woman in the study.[49] Aware that when she walks down the street next to her daughter, she 'might as well be bloody invisible' because people look at her daughter, not her, a 55-year-old woman asks why youth but not age is 'beautiful' in our society.[50] Noticing that when her hair turned grey she 'became invisible' when walking down the street, another woman, who is sixty-eight, admits that when people 'just about walk into' her, she feels 'not-so-confident' and 'put down and demeaned'.[51] 'I know that essentially the world thinks old things and old people are kind of like garbage ... and when I look like a piece of garbage, it's probably how I'll be treated', confesses yet another 65year-old woman.[52] Again and again in the narratives of the women they interviewed, Hurd Clarke and Griffin note a central irony: that the women's 'perceptions of invisibility' derive from their possession of 'the visible markers of gray hair, wrinkles, and sagging skin' and thus are 'grounded in their acute visibility as old women'.[53] Aware of the 'various social perils of looking old', older women feel pressured 'to mask, if not alter, the physical signs of ageing with the use of beauty work interventions such as hair dye, make-up, and non-surgical and surgical cosmetic procedures, all in order to maintain their social power and visibility'.[54]

Noting that feminists 'do not often question the stigma affixed to old age', Calasanti, Slevin and King state that by accepting the new dictate for old women to 'age successfully', feminists end up reinforcing ageism.[55] As they point out: 'Successful aging assumes a "feminine" aspect in the ideal that the good, elderly woman be healthy, slim, discreetly sexy, and independent ... Suffice it to say, our standard constructions of old age contain little that is positive. Fear of and disgust with growing old are widespread; people stigmatize it and associate it with personal failure, with "letting yourself go."'[56] The successful aging paradigm, as Martha Holstein observes, has created a new model of aging, one that stresses a kind of 'endless middle age' extending into later life.[57] To Holstein, the affirmations of agelessness voiced in commonplace sayings – sixty is the new forty and seventy is the new fifty; aging is not inevitable; you are only as old as you feel – are evidence of 'age denial'. 'If one can't change the power of binaries – young is better than old – then claiming to belong to the valued category is a sensible, albeit problematic, strategy', writes Holstein, since the struggle to be 'not old' is 'a struggle in opposition to our probable future selves'.[58]

Aware of the damage our culture does to aging women who are both hypervisible because of their age-marked bodies but also socially invisible, Doris Lessing, in her novels *The Summer Before the Dark* (1973) and *Love, Again* (1995), exposes the kind of angst that accompanies the aging process. Lessing's character, Kate Brown, in *The Summer before the Dark*,[59] is a 45-year-old woman who has long worked to keep up a stylish, attractive and youthful appearance only to experience in a 'shortened, heightened, concentrated' time[60] the process of growing older when she becomes ill. During her illness, which is presented as both a debilitating physical illness and a mid-life crisis, Kate becomes the image of the socially marginalized older woman. Looking in the mirror as she begins to recover from her illness, she becomes painfully aware of her visibly aging appearance: 'She stood in front of a glass ... She saw a woman all bones and big elbows, with large knees above lanky calves; she had small dark anxious eyes in a white sagging face around which was a rough mat of brassy hair.'[61] A woman who has long attracted positive attention by sending out the signal, 'I am accustomed to being noticed',[62] Kate becomes acutely aware of her social devaluation – and invisibility – as a visibly aging woman. 'I'm here, can't you see? Why don't you look at me?' Kate wants to cry out when men totally ignore her when she walks down the street, making her feel 'invisible.'[63] As Kate consciously experiments with her younger-looking and old-woman identities by alternately dressing as the younger-looking, stylish and sexually attractive Mrs. Brown and as an invisible, sagging, old woman, she realizes that feels dislocated when she assumes her invisible, old-woman identity: she is 'floating, without ballast', her head is 'chaotic, her feelings numbed with confusion'.[64] Like the middle-aged Kate Brown, the 65-year-old Sarah Durham in Lessing's novel *Love, Again*[65] becomes aware of her own invisibility as an older woman. A woman who has aged successfully and so initially looks twenty years younger than her actual age, Sarah, in a short period of time, takes on the appearance of an old woman. As Sarah comes to acknowledge the shameful bodily realities of her aging appearance, she perceives herself to be 'drying out',[66] and she becomes aware of the 'irrevocableness' of the aging process as she observes the 'subtle disintegration' of her aging body.[67] As an older woman, Sarah is 'in exactly the same situation as the innumerable people of the world who are ugly, deformed, or crippled, or who have horrible skin disorders' – socially stigmatized individuals, who 'spend their lives behind ugly masks, longing for the simplicities of love known to attractive people'.[68] If Sarah once belonged to 'a privileged class sexually' when she was young and attractive and thus sexually sought after, she has now entered 'a desert of deprivation', and, as a socially invisible and sexually disqualified older woman, she feels like 'a miserable old ghost at a feast'.[69]

In a similar way, the unnamed woman in Eva Figes's novel *Waking* (1981)[70] feels a deep sense of self-alienation when she starts to get old. As an aging woman, she is aware that 'nothing will bring back' the young woman she once was; instead, she is 'doomed to drag' about in a body that fills her with 'disgust' and that others ignore as they 'glance past or look straight through' her as if she does not 'exist'.[71] When she walks down the street, she is invisible to others, and when she catches sight of her reflection, she is a stranger to herself: 'Outside I have become invisible in the dull stone light of winter, until I suddenly catch a glimpse ... of a woman wrapped up against the cold. Her eyes light up, hurt and twisted, seeing them peer helplessly through two holes of pinched wintry flesh in the vivid patch of mottled mirror.'[72] As Figes recounts the old woman's experiences of loss and diminishment, she draws on the idea that there is a ghostly and uncanny quality to the lived experience of old age as her unnamed woman becomes an invisible 'ghost in a faded photograph' and spends her final days in solitude and silence.[73] Commenting on the hypervisibility and invisibility of the older female body in our contemporary visual mass culture, Woodward remarks: 'It would seem that the wish of our visual culture is to erase the older female body from view. The logic of the disappearing female body would seem to be this: first we see it, then we don't.'[74] Cognizant of the connection between a woman's aging appearance and her decreasing social value and erasure from view, Figes, like Lessing, shows how sexageism wounds and shames older women as they come to experience the social exclusion and invisibility that accompany women as they grow visibly older in our youth-obsessed culture.

The rejected body and the nursing home spectre

Because of our culture's 'overemphasis on bodily decline' in our view of the aging process, the 'entire meaning of old age' becomes associated with physical loss and as a consequence of this, old people end up being 'reduced to deteriorating bodies'.[75] If the new focus on what is called successful or healthy aging is said to offer a 'refreshing contrast' to the 'decline and loss' view of aging, it also serves to reinforce 'prejudice against disabled elders which often is shared by the elderly themselves', even though chronic illness and disability remain a 'continuing reality' for many older people.[76] By assuming that individuals can remain healthy and active into advanced old age, the successful aging model actively promotes ageism by reinforcing prejudice against the disabled or chronically ill elderly, especially the dependent elderly who end up in nursing homes because they suffer from debilitating illnesses and/or functional impairments. In her trenchant analysis of the new binary that has emerged in recent years – the third and fourth ages – Martha Holstein explains that 'ageism is simply displaced' in this new division of late life, which relegates 'a time of progressive disablement' to the fourth age and associates the positive features of successful aging with the third age.[77] Not only does the successful, anti-aging model promote ageism but it also poses a special burden for aging women, whose social worth is largely based on their appearance. If women experience shame because they inhabit bodies visibly marked by the signs of age, they experience even more shame if they suffer from the chronic illnesses or functional limitations or physical disabilities that accompany the aging process. Yet while the experiences of aging – 'of being ill, of being in pain, of physical and intellectual limitations' – are part of the natural aging process and while disability and old age are 'aspects of identity with which gender is very much entwined', the identities of older and disabled women have been largely 'ignored' by feminist writers.[78]

Because feminist writers have long been focused on female empowerment and on the physically strong and controlled body, they have tended to avoid the bodily experiences of women as they age into old age, which is associated in our cultural imagination with the stigma and shame of physical decline and disability. As feminist philosopher Susan Wendell writes, cultural demands that women 'control' and 'attempt to perfect' their bodies 'create rejection, shame, and fear in relation to both failures to control the body and deviations from body ideals'.[79] Wendell uses the term 'rejected body', as she explains, 'to refer to those aspects of bodily life (such as illness, disability, weakness, and dying), bodily appearance (usually deviations from the cultural ideals of the body), and bodily experience (including most forms of body suffering) that are feared, ignored, despised, and/or rejected in a society and its culture'.[80] Those with 'rejected' bodies become 'devalued people because of their devalued bodies' and serve as reminders of 'what the "normal" are trying to avoid, forget, and ignore'.[81] The rejected body is shunned not only from 'fear of being or becoming abnormal' but also from 'fear of pain, illness, limitation, suffering, and dying'.[82] And yet, as Wendell points out, '[u]nless we die suddenly, we are all disabled eventually. Most of us will live part of our lives with bodies that hurt, that move with difficulty or not at all, that deprive us of activities we once took for granted, or that others take for granted'.[83] Drawing on Wendell's notion of the rejected body, Carolyn Morell has argued that in order to challenge the notion of 'successful aging', feminists must reclaim the rejected body and 'develop a more body-sensitive and thus age-sensitive model of empowerment', one that destigmatizes the rejected body and accepts the disabling aspects of aging and thus transforms disability and death into 'acceptable and respectable human experiences'.[84]

Feminists also need to grapple with what Betty Friedan has called 'the nursing home specter'.[85] Admitting to her own dread of nursing homes, Friedan refers to nursing homes as 'death sentences, the final interment from which there is no exit but death'.[86] In a culture in which aging is viewed as 'a falling away, a failure to be young' and the old are contemptuously 'evaluated as "less than,"'[87] the dependent and sick elderly are further devalued by being relegated to the fourth age, removed from mainstream society, and segregated in nursing homes. Because the new emphasis on successful aging serves to reinforce 'the moral failings of dependency', admission to a nursing home 'denotes a kind of moral/personal failure'.[88] Living as we do in a society in which the 'constant quest for youth' stigmatizes the old and sick as 'human failures', Andrew Blaikie speculates that just as 'deep old age' may become the 'great prohibition' in the twenty-first century, so the old may 'un-become persons (hence become un-persons)' if they undergo physical or cognitive decline.[89] Treated with contempt by society and obeying the social message conveyed by contempt – to get out of sight and disappear – the elderly, in a classic contempt/disappear scenario, literally become socially invisible as they disappear into geriatric hospital wards and nursing homes.

In works of women authors who deal with the nursing home spectre and the bodily indignities suffered by women in old age, we find powerful indictments of our ageist culture. Pat Barker's story of Alice Bell in the novel *Union Street* (1982)[90] illuminates the social shaming endured by the infirm elderly. Left severely impaired after suffering a stroke – half of her body is 'useless, dragged along by the rest' and the sounds that 'glugged out of her mouth' barely resemble speech[91] – Alice feels deeply unworthy in her encounter with the social services representative who comes at the behest of her son and daughter-in-law to place her in a nursing home. Seeing herself through his contemptuous gaze, she views herself as an object of contempt – as '[r]ubbish. Ready for the tip'.[92] As she reflects on the 'not-seeing' eyes of the stranger from social services, she understands 'the full indignity of rape' and feels herself dwindling, becoming 'a heap of old garbage waiting for the pit'.[93] In a similar way, Thea Astley's Kathleen Hackendorf in the novel *Coda* (1994)[94] resists placement in a nursing home. 'Flat, care, coffin', Kathleen says of the nursing home, where her daughter and son-in-law place her after they use their power of attorney to sell Kathleen's house and empty it of all its furnishings.[95] 'Charnel number 5', Kathleen remarks when she is escorted to her room.[96] 'Corpsed', she thinks as she falls asleep on her first night in 'the coffin room' of the nursing home.[97] When Margaret Laurence's Hagar Shipley in the novel *The Stone Angel* (1964) is told by her son and daughter-in-law that they want to place her in a nursing home because they find it difficult to care for her, she feels that she is being treated with utter contempt. 'If you make me go there, you're only signing my death warrant', Hagar tells them, feeling that they want to 'crate' her up and deliver her 'like a parcel of old clothes' to the nursing home.[98] Like Laurence's Hagar Shipley, May Sarton's Caro Spencer in the novel *As We Are Now* (1973) becomes aware of the power of ageist contempt when she ends up in a nursing home, 'a concentration camp for the old, a place where people dump their parents or relatives exactly as though it were an ash can'.[99] 'Stowed away in an old people's home' and 'denuded of everything that might make life livable', Caro finds herself 'breaking into pieces with shame and misery' and becoming 'sick with fear and disgust' by her experience of confinement in an 'ash heap for the moribund'.[100] In a culture that stigmatizes old age and consigns older women to invisibility and silence, authors like Barker, Astley, Laurence and Sarton bring visibility to the plight of those who, in a contempt/disappear scenario, are removed from mainstream society and become socially invisible and silenced old women or even 'un-persons' as they disappear into nursing homes. As these authors reflect on what Friedan called the 'nursing home specter', they affirm the value of the lives of their old women characters and make a moral claim on their readers by insisting that we should honour the dignity and respect the humanity of old people who end up spending their final days in nursing homes instead of viewing them as personal and moral failures or, worse, as un-persons.

Women's stories of aging in a culture of shame

Long concerned about the impact of internalized ageism on aging women, feminist gerontologist Martha Holstein calls for older women to 'age consciously' and to define and give meaning to old age 'not by denying but by embracing it'.[101] For Holstein, storytelling is central to this process, and thus she urges older women to 'shape' their own stories and 'claim' their voices in order to be viewed 'in ways that transcend appearance' and to be known as 'the multidimensional people' that they are.[102] Holstein also feels that the stories told by women living with chronic illnesses and impairments that 'challenge their taken-for-granted lifeworlds' deserve both 'visibility' and 'respect'.[103] Like Holstein, Kathleen Woodward calls attention to the importance of storytelling in the lives of older women. 'As with the history of feminism, social consciousness of aging has needed to be reinvented time and again throughout the twentieth century', writes Woodward, who is 'hopeful' that we have begun in the twenty-first century to develop 'a broad social consciousness' of aging.[104] Arguing that it is necessary to change the 'affect script' for aging people, Woodward feels that this can be accomplished 'in great part by telling stories'.[105] In a similar way, feminist gerontologist Ruth Ray, who argues that gerontologists have 'an ethical responsibility to function as social-change agents', calls for a 'narrative for social change', which involves 'telling countercultural stories about aging and old age' and 'celebrating the unexpected and the inexplicable in these stories'.[106]

Aware of how difficult it is for older women to 'insulate' themselves from the 'cultural pressures that often abet self-devaluation and lead to heroic efforts to be not old', Holstein, like others, finds deep value in the affirmation women can gain through acts of resistance: 'I, and many others like me, as lifelong activists, must struggle to wear our bodies proudly and to affirm their unique qualities while accepting their nearly universal age markings, as we confront the rhetoric of agelessness and eternal youth.'[107] Yet even as feminist age scholars emphasize the need for alternate stories about women's aging, they are also aware of the myriad ways that sexageism shames aging women, even aging feminists, in our culture. Despite the successes of the women's movement, women today 'face an escalating set of expectations' about their bodies as the culture of consumerism 'markets a certain aesthetic to the new gray market'.[108] Arguing that anti-aging interventions work to devalue old age, Holstein states: 'I would prefer cultural norms that valued what I am becoming as I try to come to terms with a face and a body in process.'[109] Instead, becoming old is associated with 'failure' and the aged are 'a painful reminder, an embarrassment, a sort of obscenity that the rest of society would prefer not to see', a shaming attitude that damages the 'self-respect' of the aged.[110]

'The natural response to shame is hiding, and hiding breeds silence which further deepens shame', as shame theorist Gershen Kaufman tells us.[111] Refusing to be silent, feminist scholars and women authors publicly expose in their writings the insidious and relentless ways in which our culture wounds and shames older women. While the exposure of shame can be very painful, it is a necessary first step if we are to challenge the shame script that diminishes the lives of so many older women in our contemporary youth-centric and age-hating culture.

Notes

1   Nancy K. Miller, 'The Marks of Time', in *Figuring Age: Women, Bodies, Generations*, ed. Kathleen Woodward (Bloomington: Indiana University Press, 1999), 3.

2   Ibid., 4.

3   Lynne Segal, *Out of Time: The Pleasures and Perils of Ageing* (London: Verso, 2013), 1.

4   Margaret Cruikshank, *Learning to Be Old: Gender, Culture, and Aging*, 2nd edn. (2003; New York: Rowman and Littlefield, 2009), x, 142.

5   Segal, *Out of Time*, 2.

6   Jeannette King, *Discourses of Ageing in Fiction and Feminism: The Invisible Woman* (New York: Palgrave Macmillan, 2013), 148.

7   Cruikshank, *Learning to Be Old*, 4.

8   Martha Holstein, 'On Being an Aging Woman', in *Age Matters: Realigning Feminist Thinking*, ed. Toni M. Calasanti and Kathleen F. Slevin (New York: Routledge, 2006), 321.

9   Toni Calasanti, Kathleen Slevin, and Neal King, 'Ageism and Feminism: From "Et Cetera" to Center', *NWSA Journal* 18, no. 1 (Spring 2006): 13, 14.

10 Ibid., 15.
11 Cruikshank, *Learning to Be Old*, 181.
12 Ibid.
13 Kathleen Woodward, 'Performing Age, Performing Gender', *NWSA Journal* 18, no. 1 (Spring 2006): 164.
14 Laura Hurd Clarke, *Facing Age: Women Growing Older in Anti-aging Culture* (Lanham, MD: Rowman and Littlefield, 2011), 133, 127.
15 Ibid., 135.
16 Kathleen Woodward, 'Introduction', in *Figuring Age: Women, Bodies, Generations,* ed. Kathleen Woodward (Bloomington: Indiana University Press, 1999), xi.
17 King, *Discourses of Ageing in Fiction and Feminism,* 138.
18 The term 'sexagism' brings together two oppressive and shaming ideologies – 'sexism' and 'ageism' – to describe the ageism experienced by older women. In her 1996 essay 'Female Grotesques in Academia', women studies scholar Mary Carpenter used this term to describe the plight of aging academic women when she stated that 'ageism for the academic woman is always sexagism' (Mary Wilson Carpenter, 'Female Grotesques in Academia: Ageism, Antifeminism, and Feminists on the Faculty', in *Antifeminism in the Academy,* ed. VèVè Clark, Shirley Nelson Garner, Margaret Higonnet, and Ketu H. Katrak [New York: Routledge, 1996], 151). In more recent years, other women studies scholars have found the terms 'sexageism' or 'gendered ageism' useful in their analysis of the damaging impact of our sexist and ageist culture on older women in our greying society.
19 Martha B. Holstein, Jennifer A. Parks, and Mark H. Waymack, *Ethics, Aging, and Society: The Critical Turn* (New York: Springer, 2011), 54.
20 Ibid., 47.
21 Gershen Kaufman, *Shame: The Power of Caring,* 3rd edn. (1980, 1985; Rochester, VT: Schenkman Books, 1992), 195.
22 Ibid., xix, xx.
23 Ibid., 201. While the shame experience is deeply familiar to many older women in our culture, only in recent years has shame – the so-called master emotion – become the subject of intense psychoanalytic and psychological scrutiny, most notably in the work of affect and shame theorists, such as Silvan Tomkins, Helen Block Lewis, Donald Nathanson, Andrew Morrison, Paul Gilbert, Gershen Kaufman, Thomas Scheff and Léon Wurmser. In a similar way, 'the recent turn to the emotions in the humanities has brought shame out of hiding and made it subject to critical reassessment' within both literary and cultural studies (Sinéad McDermott, 'The Double Wound: Shame

and Trauma in Joy Kogawa's *Obasan'*, in *Sexed Sentiments: Interdisciplinary Perspectives on Gender and Emotion*, ed. Willemijn Ruberg and Kristine Steenbergh [Amsterdam: Rodopi, 2010], 144).

24 Paul Gilbert, 'What Is Shame? Some Core Issues and Controversies', in *Shame: Interpersonal Behavior, Psychopathology, and Culture*, ed. Paul Gilbert and Bernice Andrews (New York: Oxford University Press, 1998), 22.

25 Paul Gilbert, 'Body Shame: A Biopsychosocial Conceptualisation and Overview, with Treatment Implications', in *Body Shame: Conceptualisation, Research and Treatment*, ed. Paul Gilbert and Jeremy Miles (New York: Brunner-Routledge, 2002), 10.

26 Andrew Morrison, *The Culture of Shame* (New York: Ballantine-Random House, 1996), see 35–8.

27 Michael Lewis, *Shame: The Exposed Self* (1992; New York: Free Press-Simon and Schuster, 1995), 197. Lewis draws a connection between shame and stigma. Viewed by others as being 'deviant, flawed, limited, spoiled, or generally undesirable', the stigmatized individual, as Lewis explains, suffers from a 'spoiled identity', and so 'the very act of stigmatization is shame-inducing' (*Shame: The Exposed Self,* 194, 207). The fact that 'people with stigmas are thought to be not quite human' reveals the lethal power of ageism in our contemporary culture (*Shame: The Exposed Self,* 194).

28 Mike Featherstone and Mike Hepworth, 'The Mask of Ageing and the Postmodern Life Course', in *The Body: Social Process and Cultural Theory*, ed. Mike Featherstone, Mike Hepworth, and Bryan Turner (London: Sage Publications, 1991), 379.

29 Ibid.

30 Sandra Bartky, 'Unplanned Obsolescence: Some Reflections on Aging', in *Mother Time: Women, Aging, and Ethics*, ed. Margaret Urban Walker (New York: Rowman and Littlefield, 1999), 71–2.

31 Miller, 'The Marks of Time', 7.

32 Ibid., 14.

33 Diana Tietjens Meyers, 'Miroir, Mémoire, Mirage: Appearance, Aging, and Women', in *Mother Time: Women, Aging, and Ethics*, ed. Margaret Urban Walker (New York: Rowman and Littlefield, 1999), 24.

34 Ibid., 24, 38.

35 Penelope Lively, *Spiderweb* (1998; New York: HarperCollins-Perennial, 2000), 85, 132.

36 Anita Brookner, *Brief Lives* (New York: Random House, 1990), 192.

37 May Sarton, *As We Are Now* (1973; New York: W.W. Norton, 1992), 80.

38 Ibid.

39 Margaret Laurence, *The Stone Angel* (1964; Chicago: University of Chicago Press, 1993), 38.
40 Ibid., 79.
41 Meyers, '*Miroir, Mémoire, Mirage*', 38.
42 Laura Hurd Clarke, 'Older Women's Bodies and the Self: The Construction of Identity in Later Life', *CRSA/RCSA* 38, no. 4 (2001): 459, 460.
43 Bartky, 'Unplanned Obsolescence', 72.
44 Léon Wurmser, 'Shame: The Veiled Companion of Narcissism', in *The Many Faces of Shame*, ed. Donald Nathanson (New York: Guilford Press, 1987), 67.
45 Ibid.
46 Léon Wurmser, *The Mask of Shame* (1981; Northvale, NJ: Jason Aronson, 1994), 81, 80, 81.
47 Laura Hurd Clarke and Meridith Griffin, 'Visible and Invisible Ageing: Beauty Work as a Response to Ageism', *Ageing and Society* 28 (2008): 654.
48 Ibid., 661.
49 Ibid., 662.
50 Ibid., 667.
51 Ibid., 664.
52 Ibid., 662.
53 Ibid., 669.
54 Ibid., 656.
55 Calasanti, Slevin, and King, 'Ageism and Feminism', 15.
56 Ibid.
57 Martha Holstein, *Women in Late Life: Critical Perspectives on Gender and Age* (Lanham, MD: Rowman and Littlefield, 2015), 110.
58 Ibid., 82.
59 Doris Lessing, *The Summer before the Dark* (1973; New York: Vintage-Random House, 1983).
60 Ibid., 5.
61 Ibid., 141.
62 Ibid., 180.
63 Ibid., 180, 179.
64 Ibid., 179.
65 Doris Lessing, *Love, Again* (New York: HarperCollins, 1997).
66 Ibid., 97.
67 Ibid., 243.
68 Ibid., 141.
69 Ibid.
70 Eva Figes, *Waking* (New York: Pantheon Books, 1981).
71 Ibid., 70.
72 Ibid., 73.

73 Ibid., 77.
74 Woodward, 'Performing Age, Performing Gender', 163.
75 Cruikshank, *Learning to Be Old,* 37.
76 Meredith Minkler, 'Aging and Disability: Behind and Beyond the Stereotypes', *Journal of Aging Studies* 4, no. 3 (1990): 256.
77 Holstein, *Women in Late Life,* 138.
78 Jenny Morris, 'Feminism and Disability', *Feminist Review* 43 (Spring 1993): 68, 58.
79 Susan Wendell, *The Rejected Body: Feminist Philosophical Reflections on Disability* (New York: Routledge, 1996), 85.
80 Ibid.
81 Ibid., 91.
82 Ibid.
83 Ibid., 18.
84 Carolyn M. Morell, 'Empowerment and Long-Living Women: Return to the Rejected Body', *Journal of Aging Studies* 17 (2003): 80, 69, 83.
85 Betty Friedan, *The Fountain of Age* (1993; New York: Simon and Schuster, 2006), see 500–37.
86 Ibid., 510.
87 Julia Twigg, 'The Body and Bathing: Help with Personal Care at Home', in *Aging Bodies: Images and Everyday Experience*, ed. Christopher Faircloth (Walnut Creek, CA: Rowman and Littlefield/ Altamira Press, 2003), 154.
88 Holstein, Parks, and Waymack, *Ethics, Aging, and Society,* 166.
89 Andrew Blaikie, *Ageing and Popular Culture* (Cambridge, UK: Cambridge University Press, 1999), 109, 193.
90 Pat Barker, *Union Street* (1982; London: Virago Press, 2011).
91 Ibid., 247, 245.
92 Ibid., 259.
93 Ibid., 260.
94 Thea Astley, *Coda* (London: Secker and Warburg, 1994).
95 Ibid., 135.
96 Ibid., 140.
97 Ibid., 141.
98 Laurence, *The Stone Angel,* 76, 185.
99 Sarton, *As We Are Now,* 9.
100 Ibid., 40, 28, 35, 49.
101 Holstein, *Women in Late Life.* 89, 17.
102 Ibid., 259.
103 Ibid., 119, 122.
104 Kathleen Woodward, 'Against Wisdom: The Social Politics of Anger and Aging', *Cultural Critique* 51 (Spring 2002): 188.
105 Ibid., 207.

106   Ruth Ray, *Endnotes: An Intimate Look at the End of Life*
        (New York: Columbia University Press, 2008), xi.
107   Holstein, 'On Being an Aging Woman', 323, 327–8.
108   Ibid., 320.
109   Martha Holstein, 'A Feminist Perspective on Anti-aging Medicine',
        Generations 25, no. 4 (Winter 2001–2002): 42.
110   Holstein, Parks, and Waymack, *Ethics, Aging, and Society*, 99.
111   Kaufman, *Shame*, 231.

Bibliography

Astley, Thea. *Coda*. London: Secker and Warburg, 1994.

Barker, Pat. *Union Street*. 1982. London: Virago Press, 2011.

Bartky, Sandra. 'Unplanned Obsolescence: Some Reflections on Aging'. In
    Mother Time: Women, Aging, and Ethics, edited by Margaret Urban
    Walker, 61–74. New York: Rowman and Littlefield, 1999.

Blaikie, Andrew. *Ageing and Popular Culture*. Cambridge, UK: Cambridge
    University Press, 1999.

Brookner, Anita. *Brief Lives*. New York: Random House, 1990.

Calasanti, Toni, Kathleen Slevin, and Neal King. 'Ageism and Feminism:
    From "Et Cetera" to Center'. *NWSA Journal* 18, no. 1 (Spring 2006):
    13–30.

Carpenter, Mary Wilson. 'Female Grotesques in Academia: Ageism,
    Antifeminism, and Feminists on the Faculty'. In *Antifeminism in the
    Academy*, edited by VèVè Clark, Shirley Nelson Garner, Margaret
    Higonnet, and Ketu H. Katrak, 141–65. New York: Routledge, 1996.

Cruikshank, Margaret. *Learning to Be Old: Gender, Culture, and Aging*.
    2003. 2nd edn. New York: Rowman and Littlefield, 2009.

Featherstone, Mike, and Mike Hepworth. In 'The Mask of Ageing and
    the Postmodern Life Course'. *The Body: Social Process and Cultural
    Theory*, edited by Mike Featherstone, Mike Hepworth, and Bryan
    Turner, 371–89. London: Sage Publications, 1991.

Figes, Eva. *Waking*. New York: Pantheon Books, 1981.

Friedan, Betty. *The Fountain of Age*. 1993. New York: Simon and
    Schuster, 2006.

Gilbert, Paul. 'Body Shame: A Biopsychosocial Conceptualisation
    and Overview, with Treatment Implications'. In *Body Shame:
    Conceptualisation, Research and Treatment*, edited by Paul Gilbert and
    Jeremy Miles, 3–54. New York: Brunner-Routledge, 2002.

Gilbert, Paul. 'What Is Shame? Some Core Issues and Controversies'.
    In *Shame: Interpersonal Behavior, Psychopathology, and Culture*,

edited by Paul Gilbert and Bernice Andrews, 3–38. New York: Oxford University Press, 1998.

Holstein, Martha. 'A Feminist Perspective on Anti-aging Medicine'. *Generations* 25, no.4 (Winter 2001–2002): 38–43.

Holstein, Martha. 'On Being an Aging Woman'. In *Age Matters: Realigning Feminist Thinking*, edited by Toni M. Calasanti and Kathleen F. Slevin, 313–34. New York: Routledge, 2006.

Holstein, Martha. *Women in Late Life: Critical Perspectives on Gender and Age*. Lanham, MD: Rowman and Littlefield, 2015.

Holstein, Martha B., Jennifer A. Parks, and Mark H. Waymack. *Ethics, Aging, and Society: The Critical Turn*. New York: Springer, 2011.

Hurd Clarke, Laura. *Facing Age: Women Growing Older in Anti-aging Culture*. Lanham, MD: Rowman and Littlefield, 2011.

Hurd Clarke, Laura. 'Older Women's Bodies and the Self: The Construction of Identity in Later Life'. *CRSA/RCSA* 38, no. 4 (2001): 441–64.

Hurd Clarke, Laura, and Meridith Griffin. 'Visible and Invisible Ageing: Beauty Work as a Response to Ageism'. *Ageing and Society* 28 (2008): 653–74.

Kaufman, Gershen. *Shame: The Power of Caring*. 1980, 1985, 3rd edn. Rochester, VT: Schenkman Books, 1992.

King, Jeannette. *Discourses of Ageing in Fiction and Feminism: The Invisible Woman*. New York: Palgrave Macmillan, 2013.

Laurence, Margaret. *The Stone Angel*. 1964. Chicago: University of Chicago Press, 1993.

Lessing, Doris. *Love, Again*. 1995. New York: HarperCollins, 1997.

Lessing, Doris. *The Summer before the Dark*. 1973. New York: Vintage-Random House, 1983.

Lewis, Michael. *Shame: The Exposed Self*. 1992. New York: Free Press-Simon and Schuster, 1995.

Lively, Penelope. *Spiderweb*. 1998. New York: HarperCollins-Perennial, 2000.

McDermott, Sinéad. 'The Double Wound: Shame and Trauma in Joy Kogawa's *Obasan*'. In *Sexed Sentiments: Interdisciplinary Perspectives on Gender and Emotion*, edited by Willemijn Ruberg and Kristine Steenbergh, 141–63. Amsterdam: Rodopi, 2010.

Meyers, Diana Tietjens. '*Miroir, Mémoire, Mirage: Appearance, Aging, and Women*'. In *Mother Time: Women, Aging, and Ethics*, edited by Margaret Urban Walker, 23–41. New York: Rowman and Littlefield, 1999.

Miller, Nancy K. 'The Marks of Time'. In *Figuring Age: Women, Bodies, Generations*, edited by Kathleen Woodward, 3–19. Bloomington: Indiana University Press, 1999.

Minkler, Meredith. 'Aging and Disability: Behind and Beyond the Stereotypes'. *Journal of Aging Studies* 4, no. 3 (1990): 245–60.

Morell, Carolyn M. 'Empowerment and Long-Living Women: Return to the Rejected Body'. *Journal of Aging Studies* 17 (2003): 69–85.

Morris, Jenny. 'Feminism and Disability'. *Feminist Review* 43 (Spring 1993): 57–70.

Morrison, Andrew. *The Culture of Shame*. New York: Ballantine-Random House, 1996.

Ray, Ruth. *Endnotes: An Intimate Look at the End of Life*. New York: Columbia University Press, 2008.

Sarton, May. *As We Are Now*. 1973. New York: W.W. Norton, 1992.

Segal, Lynne. *Out of Time: The Pleasures and Perils of Ageing*. London: Verso, 2013.

Twigg, Julia. 'The Body and Bathing: Help with Personal Care at Home'. In *Aging Bodies: Images and Everyday Experience*, edited by Christopher Faircloth, 143–69. Walnut Creek, CA: Rowman and Littlefield/Altamira Press, 2003.

Wendell, Susan. *The Rejected Body: Feminist Philosophical Reflections on Disability*. New York: Routledge, 1996.

Woodward, Kathleen. 'Introduction'. In *Figuring Age: Women, Bodies, Generations*, edited by Kathleen Woodward, ix–xxix. Bloomington: Indiana University Press, 1999.

Woodward, Kathleen. 'Against Wisdom: The Social Politics of Anger and Aging'. *Cultural Critique* 51 (Spring 2002): 186–218.

Woodward, Kathleen. 'Performing Age, Performing Gender'. *NWSA Journal* 18, no. 1 (Spring 2006): 162–89.

Wurmser, Léon. *The Mask of Shame*. 1981. Northvale, NJ: Jason Aronson, 1994.

Wurmser, Léon. 'Shame: The Veiled Companion of Narcissism'. In *The Many Faces of Shame*, edited by Donald Nathanson, 64–92. New York: Guilford Press, 1987.

9

The Posthuman

Luna Dolezal and Amelia DeFalco

'Posthuman' is a multivalent and multidisciplinary term that references a complex, sometimes conflicted reconceptualization of the body and subjectivity resulting from developments in biology, technology and ecology, which highlight human animals as fundamentally relational and mutable. Biotechnology, genomic and transplantation sciences, microbiome research, climate science, cybernetics and a host of other research areas have effectively cast doubt on the integrity and unity of 'the human' as a discrete material and conceptual entity. The posthuman and its attendant philosophies emerge out of this reconceptualization of the human as a malleable material entity interconnected and inter-related with a whole host of 'others', human, animal, environmental and technological.

In cultural texts, posthuman bodies are frequently represented as those that have been enhanced and augmented, both functionally and aesthetically, by prostheses, implants or other assistive technologies. Posthuman bodies abound in contemporary literature and film, where the posthuman imaginary of the cyborg figure – 'a hybrid of machine and organism', to use Haraway's formulation[1] – enacts two visions of posthuman discourse. First, a transgressive and liberatory vision, via thinkers such as Haraway, where entanglements with 'others' – machines, animals, technologies, etc. – overthrow limiting categories of humanism and a 'way out of the maze of dualisms' that categorize Western thought.[2] And second, a transhuman vision, where entanglements with others – primarily enhancement technologies – produce posthuman beings who have overcome the limiting realities of flesh-and-blood human bodies.

In this chapter, we explore the tensions and contradictions between these competing visions and discourses of posthumanism through an exploration of how the posthuman frequently converges with two embodied motifs: the hyper-sexualized female body and the 'supercrip', a 'disabled' body which has overcome impairment to achieve mastery and 'success'.[3] The sexualized representation of female 'supercrips', such as athlete and model Aimee Mullins and pop singer Viktoria Modesta, has become commonplace; visual culture is replete with images of attractive and accomplished women sporting their prostheses as part of a broader assemblage of aesthetic choices.[4] The public fascination with attractive women who are also prosthesis users produces multiple effects (often all at once), empowering, normalizing and fetishizing prosthetics and their users.[5]

A more recent twist in these representations of 'cyborgian sex-kittens', to use Marquard Smith's phrase,[6] is the incorporation of deadly weapons into prosthetic limbs, transforming cyborg sex kittens into sexualized cyborg assassins. In this chapter we take a feminist and disability studies approach to examine a particular imaginary of the posthuman cyborg. We explore cultural imaginaries of the posthuman hyper-sexualized supercrip as expressed in two contemporary films, *Kingsman: The Secret Service* (2014) and *Planet Terror* (2007), which feature deadly weaponized lower limb prostheses.[7] Exploring the posthuman through the intersection of the prosthesis and the military-industrial complex in these contemporary representations of deadly female cyborgs, we argue that these characters embody the posthuman cyborg's ambivalent and sometimes contradictory position, at once radical and regressive.

The posthuman body

The concept of the 'posthuman' has enjoyed prominence in academic research and popular culture for several decades. It is frequently deployed as a means to understand how interactions with technology can modify the human condition and put into question what counts as 'human'.[8] At the core of the posthuman position is an unsettling and decentring of the self-contained, sovereign subject that characterizes the liberal humanist position. The central posthuman revelation – that human bodies and ontologies are not fixed, contained or reliable – destabilizes the unity of the liberal human subject as a singular, sovereign, self-contained consciousness that operates with rationality and mastery over its world and environment. Instead, the posthuman subject is conceived of as radically relational – with technology, with the environment, with other humans, and with other species – and, as a result, has fluid and multiple identities.[9] In other words, a refiguring of the human body is central to the posthuman position. The posthuman body is not a self-contained and discrete entity controlled by an autonomous, self-governing and rational subject. Instead, the posthuman body is relational, fluid and multiple, characterized by multiplicity, assemblage and becoming.[10]

Under the paradigm of the posthuman, two diverging imaginaries and discourses of posthuman bodies have emerged. The first can be characterized as 'transhuman', which aligns with the intellectual and social movement of 'transhumanism'. Transhumanism sees engagement with technology coupled with aspirations to 'morphological freedom'[11] as a means to 'evolve' beyond our current 'limitations': 'overcoming aging, cognitive shortcomings, involuntary suffering, and [ultimately] our confinement to planet Earth'.[12] The central aim of the transhuman position is to create posthumans that are invulnerable to illness, frailty and aging and who use technologies – such as implants, nano-technology, prostheses, genetic engineering, surgery, uploading – to transcend the ordinary limitations of human bodies. While recognizing the human body as technologically malleable, the transhuman position ultimately reinforces the liberal humanist idea of the sovereign subject being characterized by self-determination, individuality and self-mastery and engaged in projects of self-improvement, self-actualization and enhancement.[13] As the 'Transhumanist FAQ, version 2.1', summarizes, the transhumanist position 'affirms the possibility and desirability of fundamentally improving the human condition ... especially by developing and making widely available technologies to eliminate aging and to greatly enhance human intellectual, physical and psychological capacities'.[14] The aim of the transhumanist conception of the posthuman body is to use augmentation, via the incorporation of technology into the body, to ensure both invulnerability and superhuman capability.

In contrast to this transhuman vision of posthuman bodies is Donna Haraway's conception of the 'cyborg', a 'hybrid of machine and organism'.[15] As a portmanteau of 'cybernetic organism', the term 'cyborg' invokes a biotechnological fabrication that accentuates the deep imbrication of organic and machine bodies. In Haraway's enduringly provocative manifesto, she treats the cyborg as the posthuman figure par excellence, a perpetually emerging 'naturalcultural' assemblage that challenges and rejects the limiting binaries that traditionally define femininity and embodiment.[16] In short, Haraway uses the cyborg to illustrate the malleability, affectivity and radical relationality of the posthuman body. In contrast to the transhumanist position, which reinforces the sovereign, self-contained subject, Haraway's posthuman conception of the body as expressed in the cyborg figure offers 'enthralling promises of possible re-embodiments'.[17] As Rosi Braidotti argues, cyborgs as '[m]ultiple, heterogeneous, uncivilized ... show the way to multiple virtual possibilities ... the classical "other than" the human are thus emancipated from the category of pejorative difference and shown forth in a more positive light'.[18] In other words, for Haraway the cyborg offers a transgressive potential for feminist politics. Rather than positioning technology and the posthuman as oppressive and limiting patriarchal structures, feminist thinkers like Haraway reconceive them as a means to redefine and liberate the sociopolitical meaning and significance of the category 'woman'.

In contrast to Haraway's feminist and transgressive reconception of the cyborg, the prototypical cyborg figure in popular culture has frequently embodied a stereotypically heteronormative masculine identity aligned more closely with the transhuman paradigm, using technological enhancement to ensure invulnerability and superhuman capabilities. As Sara Shabot Cohen notes, '[s]ince its first apparitions in fiction ... the cyborg is not intrinsically challenging or liberating'.[19] Cohen argues that the cyborg has served to reinforce 'traditional categories of gender' and 'stereotypes of masculinity and femininity', which ultimately limit and disadvantage women and other marginalized subjects, rather than serving any sort of transgressive or liberatory potential.[20] Prototypical fictional cyborgs, such as Robocop, Terminator and the Six Million Dollar

Man, embody this patriarchal and transhuman cyborgian imaginary, where technological prosthetics have been incorporated into a flesh and blood human body, extending and enhancing its capabilities, usually for the purposes of law enforcement or military combat.[21]

Haraway herself acknowledges the cyborg's doubleness, which maps on to the two diverging imaginaries of the posthuman body: first, the transhuman position which aspires to an invulnerable masculine body, crystallized in the cultural imaginary through impervious militarized cyborgs, and second, the radically transgressive posthuman body which is deeply relational, contradictory, impartial and imperfect. As Haraway writes:

> From one perspective, a cyborg world is about the final imposition of a grid of control on the planet, about the final abstraction embodied in a Star Wars apocalypse waged in the name of defense, about the final appropriation of women's bodies in a masculinist orgy of war. From another perspective, a cyborg world might be about lived social and bodily realities in which people are not afraid of their joint kinship with animals and machines, not afraid of permanently partial identities and contradictory standpoints. The political struggle is to see from both perspectives at once because each reveals dominations and possibilities unimaginable from the other vantage point. Single vision produces worse illusions than double vision or many-headed monsters.[22]

Haraway's invocation of the (often overlooked) patriarchal and militaristic origins of the cyborg figure draws attention to another, often unspoken, progenitor of the posthuman body, namely disability. Many militarized cyborg figures are rendered cyborg, or man-machine hybrids, through the incorporation of prostheses and other technologies of disability: Robocop is transformed into a cyborg law enforcement officer through the use of what is essentially a complex exoskeleton, a technology that has been developed to restore mobility for those with stroke or spinal cord injuries; the Terminator is a robotic assassin that uses prosthetic eyes to enable his sight; the Six Million Dollar Man is an injured astronaut rebuilt with bionic implants and prostheses which replace his legs, left eye and right arm. These cyborg figures are far from unique in their reliance on prostheses and other technologies of disability. However, the relation between the posthuman, cyborgs and disability often remains elided in both theory and popular culture.

Stuart Murray has highlighted this surprising omission in posthuman discourses in his book *Disability and the Posthuman* (2020), arguing that disability is the site where the origins of the posthuman cyborg body come into focus – these are bodies that are intertwined with prostheses and technologies and demonstrate a wide range of physical diversity in terms of appearance and ability. Indeed, Haraway herself points to disability as a site of cyborg experience: '[p]erhaps paraplegics and other severely handicapped people can (and sometimes do) have the most intense experiences of complex hybridization' because of their use and reliance on technologies.[23] Indeed, it is through the integration of prostheses, a technology of disability, that many transhuman imaginaries of cyborgs, such as Robocop and Terminator, enact their potential, transforming vulnerable, incomplete bodies into posthuman uber-beings. In what follows we discuss the intertwined histories of the prosthesis and the military-industrial complex as a means to elucidate some of the enduring imaginaries that coalesce in transhuman-inflected posthuman cyborg figures.

The military-industrial complex and prostheses

The military-industrial complex is one of the primary sites of the technological realization of the posthuman body through limb prostheses, implants, exoskeletons and other assistive technologies. The innovation and development of these typically 'posthuman' technologies have a long history of entanglement with military efforts.[24] Throughout the twentieth century, returning war veteran amputees drove the development and technologization of prosthetic technologies, where innovations in prostheses during the immediate post-war period of the 1940s and 1950s were intrinsically tied to restoring the male body to engage in productive labour, ensuring self-worth and employment for disabled veterans.[25] Hence, throughout the latter part of the twentieth century, military agencies and military-funded enterprises developed prosthetic technology to 'repair' returnee soldiers in an effort to restore them to 'ordinary'

citizens who can return to employment and daily family life
through rehabilitating their bodies, their masculinity and their
social identities.

The development of prostheses by the military has arguably
intensified in the twenty-first century as a result of an increasing
number of returnee soldiers in the United States, the UK and
other developed countries surviving combat with grave injuries
that result in arm, hand and lower limb amputations.[26] As such,
limb loss injuries, in military and combat contexts, are directly
correlated to technological innovation in the field of prosthetics and
other embodied technologies. The US military's Defense Advanced
Research Project Agency (DARPA) has been a pioneer in limb
prostheses development and also in the development of human
exoskeletons in recent decades.[27] Former soldiers are often the first to
trial and receive high-tech limb prostheses, whose prohibitive costs
often render them inaccessible to civilian populations. Furthermore,
while limb loss for soldiers previously heralded a discharge from
active service, advancements to prosthetic technologies have meant
that some amputee service members have been able to remain on
active duty.[28] At present, the US Army has dozens of soldiers who
have suffered major limb amputation (complete loss of an arm, leg,
foot or hand) that have remained on active duty in combat and
support roles.

Ongoing developments in a range of prosthetic technologies
(involving techniques such as osseointegration, the process of
attaching prosthetics directly to the skeleton; re-routing nerve
endings for so-called mind-controlled limbs; and brain-computer
interfaces (BCI) or neural implants for the telepresence control of
robotic limbs and exoskeletons) are heralding an age of military
'enhancement' that will potentially allow combat soldiers to be faster,
stronger and more durable than their peers. Exoskeletons, while
having a variety of uses in medical contexts, are being developed
by DARPA and other military-funded agencies to give soldiers the
capacity for increased stamina, strength and productivity. Ocular
implants and auditory enhancement are predicted to give soldiers
heightened sensory capacity. In 2016, DARPA announced a research
project Neural Engineering System Design (NESD) which aims to
develop an implantable chip that would act as a neural interface,
connecting humans directly to computers, which would result in
a range of technological enhancements including the ability to

control and move robotic limbs remotely. As Cristina Masters argues, 'the twenty-first century cyborg land soldier will be outfitted with technology that in essence replace his "senses" through technological prostheses that replicate biological senses while circumventing human biological limitations: poor eyesight, hearing and discernment'.[29] Through prosthetic enhancement, creating transhuman 'cyborg soldiers' has become an explicit aim of the US military with a recent Department of Defense Report, 'Cyborg Soldier 2050', detailing how implants and other technologies have the potential to create the 'cybernetically enhanced super soldier' within thirty years.[30]

In short, military innovations in prostheses are no longer merely about repairing returnee soldiers to reintegrate into a productive civilian life but instead about creating more efficient and effective transhuman soldiers and weapons *through* prostheses. This trend in prosthetic weapons harks back to a history of rudimentary limb prostheses (such as peg legs) used as improvised bludgeons in nineteenth- and twentieth-century literature. As Ryan Sweet argues, 'prosthetic body parts were conceptualised as devices that were not necessarily capable of restoring the appearance and function of a lost body part but were able to provide their user with a close-to-hand deadly weapon'.[31] Following this long history of weapon prostheses, the contemporary intertwining of disability, cyborg bodies and 'prostheticized, posthumanist military capability'[32] creates a particular form of the contemporary 'supercrip' figure: one that is glamorized, enhanced, militarized and gender-coded.[33] As Masters notes, the 'cyborg soldier has blurred particular distinctions between machine and man, where *technology* embodies *masculinity*'.[34] These militarized cyborgs embody transhuman fantasies of superhuman invulnerability.

The development of transhuman 'cyborg soldiers' manifests Haraway's warnings about cyborg ancestry. As the 'illegitimate offspring'[35] of violence, militarism and patriarchal capitalism, the cyborg inevitably carries traces of its patriarchal legacy. Haraway's reimagining of the cyborg signifies a break with this patriarchal, militaristic, anthropocentric legacy. As described above, her 'cyborg world' is instead 'about lived social and bodily realities in which people are not afraid of their joint kinship with animals and machines, not afraid of permanently partial identities'.[36] In contrast, the real-life development of posthuman cyborgs via the military-industrial complex advances patriarchal domination: the 'tele-thanatological machines created by our own advanced technology' enable posthuman wars that 'breed new forms of inhumanity'.[37] Through the 'post-anthropocentric weaponry' and technologies reshaping contemporary warfare,[38] the transhuman cyborg soldier is not radically relational to the 'other' (other people, machines, animals, the environment) but instead effects 'a distance and disassociation from the other so that it can engage in practices of domination, subordination and subjugation'.[39] Violence becomes 'insourced', so to speak, incorporated into the sphere of personal embodiment through the creation of weapons that are literally incorporated into transhuman bodies, or bodies are literally transformed into weapons.

We analyse fictional 'post-anthropocentric weaponry' in the guise of machine guns and sabres as prosthetic body parts, weapons incorporated into the posthuman cyborg bodies that employ them. The particular (and particularly heightened) gendering and sexualization of these deadly, weaponized bodies lead to additional insights regarding both the patriarchal transhuman and transgressive posthuman potential of cyborg figures. Following Haraway's intuition that the 'illegitimate [cyborg] offspring are often exceedingly unfaithful to their origins. Their fathers, after all, are inessential',[40] we explore how contemporary cultural imaginaries of the posthuman cyborg have abandoned their 'inessential fathers', namely the impenetrable transhuman militarized masculine figure, in favour of the vulnerable civilian female. Exploring the trope of the hyper-attractive female 'cyborgian sex-kitten', our analysis focuses primarily on the characters of Gazelle, from Matthew Vaughn's 2014 film *Kingsman: The Secret Service*, and Cherry, from Robert Rodriguez's 2007 film *Planet Terror*.

In *Planet Terror* and *Kingsman*, prosthetics and the posthuman paradigm function not as a means to restore damaged masculinity but as a means to exoticize and sexualize a potentially violated and wounded femininity. The posthuman potential, hence, is radically undermined by the 'spectacle of excess' through which these characters and their prostheses are portrayed.[41] The empowerment and agency generated for the disabled female characters 'accompan[y] militaristic and gangster- style violence where prostheses – and disabled bodies – become contemporary fetishizations of violence as power'.[42] Our own reading transposes

Ewart's analysis into a posthuman register in order to suggest the two films enact a perverse and problematic literalization of the cyborg's heritage – the militarism and patriarchal capitalist legacy described by Haraway – discarding any illusion of the feminist potential inherent in these cyborg figure.

Sexy cyborg killers

Planet Terror and *Kingsman: The Secret Service* feature female characters whose bodies have been transformed into efficient killing machines via prosthetic augmentation. Both films are self-aware, yet nostalgic re-creations of genres that flourished in the 1970s and 1980s – 'grindhouse' exploitation films in the case of *Planet Terror* and Bond-style gentleman spy films in the case of *Kingsman* – genres that, despite their contrasting aesthetics, depend on violence and sexualized female bodies for their thrilling appeal. In Rodriguez and Vaughn's reinventions, the titillating power of hypersexualized bodies and violent destruction are combined in the figures of Cherry Darling (played by Rose McGowan) and Gazelle (played by Sofia Boutella).[43] In *Planet Terror*, Cherry is a stripper and go-go dancer who loses a leg after a flesh-eating zombie attack. The stolen leg is eventually replaced by a high-powered machine gun, which she wields as a deadly weapon in the war between humans and zombies. In *Kingsman*, Gazelle is billionaire villain Richmond Valentine's (played by Samuel L Jackson) deadly sidekick. Gazelle's lower legs have been replaced by blade prostheses reminiscent of the 'cheetah legs' used by elite athletes. However, Gazelle's prosthetic legs are literal blades, which she uses to slice enemies and adversaries into pieces, killing loyally to serve Valentine's evil plan for global domination. While both characters are disabled women reliant on lower limb prostheses, their disability is unsettled by the incorporation of technology, in this case deadly weapons, into their bodies. Ultimately, Cherry and Gazelle are not presented as disabled characters but as posthuman figures whose more-than-human power is enabled through their technological enhancement.

Planet Terror oscillates between glorifying the transhuman power of prosthetic enhancement and hinting at the transgressive 'cyborg' potential of posthuman bodies. When Cherry first wakes in the hospital to find her right leg amputated above the knee, the film highlights her distress at the discovery through a series of close-ups of her shaking, gagging, crying face. The film's opening credit sequence features Cherry's titillating pole dancing; without her leg, her mobility and desirability are disabled. 'I have no leg', Cherry shouts at her boyfriend Wray when he urges her to flee the hospital, which is under zombie attack, and he responds by smashing a table and roughly thrusting its wooden leg onto the metal stud protruding from Cherry's stump. Though it provides limited mobility, this improvised peg leg begins the process of Cherry's posthuman weaponization: after escaping the hospital, Cherry is held hostage by psychopathic military operatives and her improvised prosthetic proves not only enabling but triumphantly lethal. When one of her captors forces her to dance at gunpoint, Cherry bashes her abuser's head with her prosthetic before using the splintered remains to stab him in the eye. The symbolism of the triumphant vengeance is obvious: his ogling eye is literally penetrated by her prosthesis and this prosthesis-enabled act of revenge is clearly coded as a victory to be relished. When Wray arrives to rescue Cherry, he provides another, more unconventional prosthesis: a customized machine gun that is somehow engineered so Cherry can fire it at will. As he shoves the new prosthesis onto Cherry's stump, Wray looks into her eyes: 'I believe in you, I always have ... right now I need you to become who you were meant to be', he tells her, before commanding her to 'stand' and 'open that door will you baby?' Cherry rises triumphantly on her new limb and blasts her attacker's disintegrating body through the locked doors with her machine gun prosthetic. She marches proudly through the open doors, head held high, before using the gun to kill the remaining military personnel who have been holding her hostage. The narrative message is clear: Cherry is enabled and empowered by this new weapon prosthesis, which, unlike the improvised peg leg, is specifically designed for violence. Cherry is no longer 'disabled' by her limb loss and no longer at the mercy of the men (whether human or zombie) around her; she has become a transhuman killer who no longer needs to suffer the degradation of dancing for leering men.

In the film's final scene, Cherry employs her machine gun prosthetic to help a few remaining humans to escape from the zombie-infested military compound. She marches out amidst gun fire, arms pumping before using the propulsion of her prosthetic's gunfire to propel her body into an optimal position from which to eliminate her enemies with acrobatic gusto. The scene is celebratory, triumphant; Cherry's augmented body has made her a militarized cyborg more powerful than her (primarily male) human counterparts. In short, the film's over-the-top, gory, sexualized satire reproduces familiar supercrip narratives and 'inspiration porn' in its deployment of disability as a means to super-human transformation.[44] Cherry's disability is overcome via militaristic augmentation. The film's treatment of Cherry's disability and prosthetic enhancement evokes the doubleness Haraway identifies as endemic to the cyborg: on the one hand, Cherry appears to embody the transgressive, playful, posthuman cyborg figure that overturns the usual limiting categories of patriarchy and ableism, a manifestation of the 'enthralling promises of possible re-embodiment'.[45] On the other hand, her weaponized prosthesis, which renders her invulnerable, powerful, deadly, invokes the transhuman potential of the posthuman.

Though less gory, *Kingsman* is similarly preoccupied with over-the-top violence. For example, the audience first meets Gazelle after she slices a man from the crown of his head to his groin, the two pieces of his body remaining upright before falling away in a comically delayed parting to reveal Gazelle in medium close-up. As the body parts fall away, the camera tilts down her body, resting briefly on her prosthetic blades before travelling back up to her face. While this is the first time the audience sees Gazelle's entire body, we have already glimpsed her in the fleeting image of her blades, a blur of glinting steel slicing a man in two. However, it is only in the camera's lingering perusal of Gazelle's body, at once unveiled and framed by the peeling away of the bisected body of her victim, that her form becomes fully visible and recognizable as human. As a result, much like *Planet Terror*, *Kingsman* introduces viewers to the film's central female warrior by immediately objectifying her; however, Gazelle's sexualized objectification incorporates, indeed highlights, her deadly prostheses from the outset. The camera's slow tilt up and down her body, which compels viewers to take in the details of her form in a series of fragmented close-ups (a long-standing visual tactic that communicates the desirability of the cinematic object), lingers on her blades before returning to her face, indicating the erotic significance of her prostheses. In other words, the prosthetic blades (and their gruesome effects) are integral to Gazelle's power (she has just sliced a man in two) and sexual appeal (the camera treats the prosthetic blades with the same caressing gaze it directs towards Gazelle's more conventionally sexual physical features).

Gazelle is a perfected, weaponized transhuman, the apotheosis of beauty and power, but her power remains at the service of her male master. She rarely speaks in the film. Her primary role is as a talented helpmate, providing both domestic and homicidal services for her male master, Valentine. In every scene she wears a sleek black uniform with white collar and cuffs – a reference to traditional black-and-white housemaid's dress – that underscores her domestic position. When, after violently eliminating all threats, Gazelle welcomes Valentine into an alpine chalet by offering him a glass of whiskey and the assurance that 'everything is to clean' (having covered a slew of dead bodies with sheets and towels), Gazelle's dual role as both maid and killer is especially conspicuous. Like Cherry, Gazelle is enhanced by her weaponized prosthetics, enabled and empowered in ways that make her uniquely useful to her male commander. While her feminine, costumed body performs domestic tasks, such as serving Valentine dinner from a silver cart with notably silent elegance, her blades enable virtuosic, acrobatic violence. In her final, spectacular battle with the film's hero, Eggsy (played by Taron Egerton), Gazelle spins, leaps, flips and kicks. The threat of Gazelle's impressive dexterity is demonstrated in her quick decimation of each of the improvised weapons that her opponent wields against her. When she is finally bested, cut with a poisoned dagger, Eggsy rips the prosthetic blade from her body and hurls it at Valentine, destroying the villain and saving the world. Unlike Gazelle, the film's male hero *wields*, rather than *merges* with the blade. In his hands, it is only a weapon, not a prosthetic; he is whole with or without it. Cherry and Gazelle, on the other hand, do not employ but *become* weapons, incorporating guns and blades into their very bodies to become militarized cyborgs, made more powerful, more desirable, more deadly via prosthetic enhancement.

Both Cherry and Gazelle are disabled women reliant on lower limb prostheses. Their disability is unsettled by the incorporation of technology – in this case deadly weapons – into their bodies in ways that evoke the transgressive posthuman paradigm offered by Haraway, their impairments offering exciting possibilities for re-embodiment. In addition, although both figures are hyper-sexualized and objectified, their powerful weaponized bodies suggest feminist empowerment, enabling them to overthrow (some) attempts at masculine domination. By replacing their missing legs with deadly weapons, their desirability, their power and their threat seemingly 'overwrite' their disability and their passive femininity.[46] However, the specific weaponization of their cyborg re-embodiment also lends them transhuman power and significance, a triumphant invulnerability, a surmounting of the 'limitations' of flesh-and-blood bodies that renders them efficient, self-contained super-human killers. The interplay of transgressive and transhuman posthuman imagery in these films provides a complex and, at times, contradictory symbolic landscape – one that is very familiar in both feminism and disability studies, where hypersexualized attractiveness can be both empowering and disempowering for women, and where imaginaries of technology, enhancement and posthumanism hold both liberatory and limiting potentials (often at the same time) for individuals living with disabilities.

Conclusions: Problematic posthumanism?

In both *Kingsman* and *Planet Terror* the celebration of the posthuman cyborg is overlaid with a tongue-in-cheek post-feminist hyper-sexualization of female bodies – where the 'fantasy of female sexuality as a threatening weapon'[47] is moved from the metaphorical to the literal. Cherry and Gazelle are not merely 'bombshells' or *'femme fatales'* with their sex imagined *like* a deadly weapon, but instead their hyper-sexualized, attractive bodies have *literally become* weapons that kill, maim and harm men. Both Cherry and Gazelle appear empowered by their augmentations, their transformation into powerfully, violently transhuman cyborgs who eliminate would-be predators. They are presented as radically empowered women made malleable through their engagement with technology. They are hypersexualized (both visually and narratively), yet able to evade, rebuff and punish the male violence that so frequently accompanies such hypersexualization. However, the feminist potential of their augmentation and malleability remains inhibited by their militarism. Through the incorporation of weapons into their bodies, Cherry and Gazelle invoke the dominating, closed-off, transhuman, militarized imaginary, one which is limiting, and reactionary in its efforts at violent invulnerability. In both films, posthuman and transhuman possibilities remain in tension, invoking both the 'enthralling possibilities' and the 'traditional categories' and 'stereotypes'[48] associated with the cyborg. As a result, the films demand the 'double vision' which Haraway suggests is key to recognizing the 'dominations and possibilities' of each vantage point.[49]

Celebrating the posthuman potential, whether transgressive or transhuman, of Cherry and Gazelle can only come from a rather superficial reading of these films. In both films, the competing and conflicting narratives of the cyborg parallel competing and conflicting narratives of disability and gender, which the films self-consciously engage via satire, exaggeration and parody. The satirical bent of these films results in retro posthuman cyborgs that at once reproduce and subvert both the feminist and militarist potential of their augmentations, as outlined above. Indeed, Cherry and Gazelle are seemingly empowered: their vulnerability as disabled women is ostensibly overcome through weaponized prostheses. Overturning conventional associations between disability and vulnerability or helplessness, figures like Cherry and Gazelle appear powerful, even invulnerable in their cyborgian hybridity. However, their empowerment is facilitated by and for a legitimized masculine violence against women: they are both sexually objectified and physically assaulted. Their ostensible power as sexy cyborgian assassins is undermined by the overt patriarchal domination of their bodies. As Masters argues, 'while the figure of the cyborg may provide new grounds upon which to reveal gender representations as contingent and historically grounded social constructs, we need also attend to the ways in which the figure of the cyborg may continue to represent a desire for total masculinist control and domination'.[50]

The posthuman cyborg's ambivalent position as both radically relational and hybrid, while also militaristic and patriarchal, is a reminder of the contradictions inherent in the ideas and discourses of the posthuman; like the cyborg, the posthuman is ambivalent, even contradictory in its theory and signification. The posthuman cyborg can frequently reify and sustain classic humanist and patriarchal tendencies in its reproduction of its militaristic ancestry (where subjects are invulnerable, self-contained and gender-coded as masculine). However, at the same time, the posthuman is mobilized as a conceptual framework which destabilizes the human exceptionalism and uncovers our radical relationality to human and non-human others (subjects are permeable, vulnerable, intercorporeal and intertwined with the 'other': other humans, animals, technology, the environment).[51]

Notes

1   Donna Haraway, 'A Manifesto for Cyborgs: Science, Technology, and Socialist Feminism in the 1980s', in *The Postmodern Turn: New Perspectives on Social Theory*, ed. Steven Seidman (Cambridge: Cambridge University Press, 1994), 83.

2   Alison Kafer, *Queer Feminist Crip* (Bloomington: Indiana University Press, 2013), 103.

3   Amit Kama 'Supercrips versus the Pitiful Handicapped: Reception of Disabling Images by Disabled Audience Members', *Communications* 29, no. 4 (2004): 447–66.
    Carla Filomena Silva and P. David Howe, 'The (In)validity of *Supercrip* Representation of Paralympian Athletes', *Journal of Sport and Social Issues* 36, no. 2 (2012): 174–94.

4   Aimee Mullins has become an iconic prosthetic user since her shift into high-profiling modelling in 1999, when she appeared in hand-carved prosthetic legs designed by Alexander McQueen. Pop star Viktoria Modesta is a similarly high-profile figure, creating music, videos and live performances that highlight her wide range of custom prosthetics, promoting her posthuman body as 'the model of the future', as the lyrics of her most popular single, 'Prototype', proclaim. Mullins and Modesta's fashionably aesthetic prosthetics, what Olga Vainshtein (2013) calls 'proaesthetics', have made them iconic emblems of contemporary cyborgian mutability. Both have sported imposing, even fetishistic prosthetics, including a spike that Modesta refers to as 'a giant stiletto heel' and describes as 'a new level of power dressing' (qtd. in Burton and Melkumova-Reynolds 200), and images of their fashion-model physiques are frequently reproduced as aspirational representations of empowerment (Dolezal 2017). Marquard Smith goes so far as to calls Mullins's public and media persona 'a quintessential Cyborgian sex kitten rather than an amputee' Marquard Smith, 'The Vulnerable Articulate: James Gillingham, Aimee Mullins and Matthew Barney', in *The Prosthetic Impulse: From a Posthuman Present to a Biocultural Future*, ed. Marquand Smith and Joanna Morra (Cambridge, MA: MIT Press, 2006), 58, invoking a bizarre either/or logic that

prohibits amputees from inhabiting a sexualized role. Despite Smith's overstatement, the underlying point – that culture demands the body of the amputee be amended via prosthetic augmentation in order to be acceptable and desirable – stands. In the cases of Mullins and Modesta, and even more so in the films we discuss below, weaponized prosthetics – spikes, blades, guns – produce cyborgs as 'contemporary fetishizations of violence and power' Chris Ewart. 'An Arm Up or a Leg Down?: Grounding the Prosthesis and Other Instabilities', in *The Matters of Disability: Materiality, Biopolitics, Crip Affect*, ed. D.T. Mitchell, Susan Antebi and Sharon L. Snyder (Ann Arbor: University of Michigan Press, 2019), 161, a titillating posthumanism in which disability is not disguised but instead 'overwritten' as a site of danger and desire Sarah S. Jain, 'The Prosthetic Imagination: Enabling and Disabling the Prosthesis Trope', *Technology and Human Values* 24, no. 1 (1999): 49. The material reality of the disabled body is obscured by images of sexual, sometimes deadly 'proaesthetics', the celebration of prosthetics that 'empower[s]' the cyborg user according to a very narrow remit and frequently impede or even prohibit ambulation. For Mullins and Modesta (much like Cherry and Gazelle below), the prosthetic is an aesthetic, symbolic feature that perpetuates the metaphorization of disability and the prosthetic even as it draws attention to the material specificity of these extraordinary augmentations. While both celebrity prosthetic users 'frame their prosthetic body parts as fashion accessories, or as interfaces between their bodies and fashion' Burton, Laini and Jana Melkumova-Reynolds. '"My Leg Is a Giant Stiletto Heel": Fashioning the Prosthetised Body'. *Fashion Theory: The Journal of Dress, Body and Culture* 23, no. 2 (2019): 203., Modesta pushes this interface towards weaponization; the video for 'Prototype' includes multiple prosthetics that threaten the malevolent government operatives that seeks to incarcerate her, including a crystal encrusted limb that redirects lasers back at her persecutors, and the aforementioned 'stiletto' leg. These weaponized posthuman bodies are reminders of the prosthesis' military origins.

5 Luna Dolezal, 'Representing Posthuman Embodiment: Considering Disability and the Case of Aimee Mullins', *Women's Studies* 46, no. 1 (2017): 60–75.
P.D. Howe, 'Cyborg and Supercrip: The Paralympics Technology and the (Dis)empowerment of Disabled Athletes', *Sociology* 45, no. 5 (2011): 868–82.

6 Smith, 'The Vulnerable Articulate', 58.

7 While our analysis focuses on *Planet Terror* and *Kingsman: A Secret Service*, there are a number of other films that feature attractive

weapon who have weaponized prostheses, including Furiosa (played
by Charlize Theron) in *Mad Max: Fury Road* (2015), Ami (played
by Minase Yashiro) in *The Machine Girl* (2008), Red Harrington
(played by Helena Bonham Carter) in *The Lone Ranger* (2013). This
is also a trope that has long featured in Anime.

8   Pramod K. Nayar, *Posthumanism* (Cambridge: Polity Press, 2014).
9   Rosi Braidotti, *The Posthuman* (Maldan, MA: Polity, 2013).
10 Jack Halberstam and Ira Livingstone, 'Introduction: Posthuman
    Bodies', in *Posthuman Bodies*, ed. Jack Halberstam and Ira
    Livingston (Bloomington: Indiana University Press, 1995), 1–22.
11 Anders Sandberg, 'Morphological Freedom – Why We Not Just
    Want It, but Need It', in *The Transhumanist Reader: Classic and
    Contemporary Essays on the Science, Technology and Philosophy of
    the Human Future*, ed. Max More and Natasha Vita-More (Oxford:
    Wiley–Blackwell, 2013), 56–64.
12 'Transhumanist Declaration (2012)', in *The Transhumanist Reader:
    Classic and Contemporary Essays on the Science, Technology and
    Philosophy of the Human Future*, ed. Max More and Natasha Vita-
    More (Oxford: Wiley–Blackwell, 2013), 54–5.
13 Luna Dolezal, 'Morphological Freedom and Medicine: Constructing
    the Posthuman Body', in *The Edinburgh Companion to the Critical
    Medical Humanities*, ed. Anne Whitehead, Angela Woods, Sarah
    Atkinson, Jane Macnaughton, and Jennifer Richards (Edinburgh:
    Edinburgh University Press, 2016), 310–24.
14 Nick Bostrom, 'Transhumanist F.A.Q.: A General Introduction,
    Version 2.1 – World Trans-humanist Association' (2003). Available
    online: http://www.transhumanism.org/resources/FAQv21.pdf.
15 Haraway 'A Manifesto for Cyborgs', 83.
16 Donna Haraway, *The Haraway Reader* (New York: Routledge,
    2004), 2.
17 Rosi Braidotti, 'Posthuman, All Too Human', *Theory, Culture and
    Society* 23, no. 7/8 (2006): 204.
18 Braidotti, 'Posthuman, All Too Human', 204.
19 Sara Cohen Shabot, 'Grotesque Bodies: A Response to Disembodied
    Cyborgs', *Journal of Gender Studies* 15, no. 3 (2006): 224.
20 Shabot, 'Grotesque Bodies', 224, 226.
21 There are additional positive readings of prosthetic cyborgs and their
    potential to undermine what Rosemarie Garland Thomson terms 'the
    normate' body (1997: 8), exposing the 'natural' as always already
    cultural and technological. As Margrit Shildrick explains,

> prostheses contest our faith in corporeal integrity even as they
> are intended to restore the clean and proper body. They not only
> demonstrate the inherent plasticity of the body, but, in the very

process of incorporating non-self matter, point to the multiple
possibilities of co-corporeality, where bodies are not just
contiguous and mutually reliant but entwined with one another.
Against a modernist convention of fully bounded bodies,
separate and distinct from one another, such modes of corporeal
transformation comprehensively undo the limits of the embodied
self. (2015: 16)

According to such perspectives, exposing human embodiment as
mutable, contingent, technological – in short, 'prosthetic' – assists in
destabilizing the unity of the 'normate' human as a unified discursive
and material category. From this perspective, embodiment itself is
prosthetic (Haraway 1988): manufactured, technological, 'unnatural'.
Many have argued that late capitalist technoscience turns 'more and
more people into posthuman bodies, eroding the putatively bounded,
self-determined, and supreme category "Man" and offering humanity
in-stead a prosthetic existence, a "cyborg subjectivity" which is
perpetually under (de)construction' (Manuela Rossini 2016: 153).
Disability studies scholars Mitchell and Snyder similarly stress the
ubiquity of embodiment's plasticity, indeterminacy and technicity; as
they explain, 'the prostheticized body is the rule, not the exception'
(2000: 7).

22 Haraway, 'A Manifesto for Cyborgs', 90.
23 Quoted in Kafer, *Queer Feminist Crip*, 105.
24 Katherine Ott, 'Carnage Remembered: Prosthetics in the US Military since the 1860s', in *Materializing the Military*, ed. Bernard Finn and Barton C. Hacker (London: Science Museum, 2005), 47–64.
25 David Serlin, *Replaceable You: Engineering the Body in Postwar America* (Chicago: University of Chicago Press, 2004).
26 Ott, 'Carnage Remembered'.
27 Robert Bogue, 'Exoskeletons and Robotic Prosthetics: A Review of Recent Developments', *Industrial Robot* 36, no. 5 (2009): 421–7.
28 Whitney Delbridge Nichels, 'Soldier Amputees Have More Options than Ever for Redeployment', *US Army*, 27 July 2018.
29 Cristina Masters, 'Bodies of Technology: Cyborg Soldiers and Militarized Masculinities', *International Feminist Journal of Politics* 7, no. 1 (2005): 122.
30 Kyle Mizokami, 'The U.S. Army Expects to Field Cyborg Soldiers by 2050', *Popular Mechanics*, 26 November 2019.
31 Ryan Sweet, 'Prosthetic Body Parts in Literature and Culture, 1832 to 1908' (PhD Dissertation, University of Exeter, 2016), 119.
32 Stuart Murray, *Disability and the Posthuman: Bodies, Technology and Cultural Futures* (Liverpool: Liverpool University Press, 2020), 156.

33 David McGillivray, Hugh O'Donnell, Gayle McPherson, and Laura
    Misener, 'Repurposing the (Super)Crip: Media Representations of
    Disability at the Rio 2016 Paralympic Games', *Communication and
    Sport* 9, no. 1 (2021): 3–32.
34 Masters, 'Bodies of Technology', 115.
35 Haraway, 'A Manifesto for Cyborgs', 85.
36 Ibid., 90.
37 Rosi Braidotti, *The Posthuman* (Maldan, MA: Polity, 2013), 9, 122.
38 Braidotti, *The Posthuman*, 127.
39 Masters, 'Bodies of Technology', 125.
40 Haraway, 'A Manifesto for Cyborgs', 85.
41 Ewart. 'An Arm Up or a Leg Down?', 161.
42 Ibid., 161.
43 It is worth noting that the actresses who play the characters of
    Gazelle (Sofia Boutella) and Cherry (Rose McGowan) in *Kingsman*
    and *Planet Terror* are not prosthesis users, and their prosthetic limbs
    were inserted using digital special effects. In *Kingsman*, Boutella
    wore green leggings while the film was shooting, which were then
    digitally replaced by blades in post-production. In *Planet Terror*
    digital special effects were used to remove McGowan's right leg from
    the footage and replace it with computer-generated props, a table leg
    and then a high-powered machine gun. McGowan wore a cast on
    her leg which restricted her movement to give the effect of using a
    prosthetic limb.
44 The term 'inspiration porn' was coined by disability activist Stella
    Young (Young, 'We're not here for your inspiration'. *ABC News*. 3
    July 2012. Online at: https://www.abc.net.au/news/2012-07-03/
    young-inspiration-porn/4107006).
45 Braidotti, 'Posthuman, All Too Human', 204.
46 Jain, 'The Prosthetic Imagination', 31–54.
47 Kelly Oliver, *Women as Weapons of War: Iraq, Sex and the Media*
    (New York: Columbia University Press, 2007), 5.
48 Shabot, 'Grotesque Bodies', 224, 226.
49 Haraway, 'A Manifesto for Cyborgs', 90.
50 Cristina Masters, 'Cyborg Soldiers and Militarized Masculinity',
    Eurozine, 2010.
51 Acknowledgments: This research was funded in whole, or in part,
    by the Wellcome Trust [214963/B/18/Z] and [214963/Z/18/Z]. For
    the purpose of Open Access, the authors have applied a CC BY
    public copyright licence to any Author Accepted Manuscript version
    arising from this submission. LD would also like to acknowledge
    the Wellcome Centre for Cultures and Environments of Health
    (WCCEH), University of Exeter, for its support during this research.

Bibliography

Bogue, Robert. 'Exoskeletons and Robotic Prosthetics: A Review of Recent Developments'. *Industrial Robot* 36, no. 5 (2009): 421–7.

Bostrom, Nick. 'Transhumanist F.A.Q.: A General Introduction, Version 2.1 – World Trans-humanist Association' (2003). Available online: <http://www.transhumanism.org/resources/FAQv21.pdf> (accessed 30 March 2015).

Braidotti, Rosi. 'Posthuman, All Too Human'. *Theory, Culture and Society* 23, no. 7/8 (2006): 197–208.

Braidotti, Rosi. *The Posthuman*. Maldan, MA: Polity, 2013.

Burton, Laini and Jana Melkumova-Reynolds. '"My Leg Is a Giant Stiletto Heel": Fashioning the Prosthetised Body'. *Fashion Theory: The Journal of Dress, Body and Culture* 23, no. 2 (2019): 195–218.

Dolezal, Luna. 'Morphological Freedom and Medicine: Constructing the Posthuman Body'. In *The Edinburgh Companion to the Critical Medical Humanities*, edited by Anne Whitehead, Angela Woods, Sarah Atkinson, Jane Macnaughton, and Jennifer Richards, 310–24. Edinburgh: Edinburgh University Press, 2016.

Dolezal, Luna. 'Representing Posthuman Embodiment: Considering Disability and the Case of Aimee Mullins'. *Women's Studies* 46, no. 1 (2017): 60–75.

Dolezal, Luna. 'Disability as Malleability: The Prosthetic Metaphor, Merleau-Ponty and the Case of Aimee Mullins'. In *Medial Bodies Between Fiction and Faction: Reinventing Corporeality*, edited by Denisa Butnaru, 123–44. Bielefeld: Transcript-Verlag, 2020.

Ewart, Chris. 'An Arm Up or a Leg Down?: Grounding the Prosthesis and Other Instabilities'. In *The Matters of Disability: Materiality, Biopolitics, Crip Affect*, edited by David T. Mitchell, Susan Antebi and Sharon L. Snyder, 160–81. Ann Arbor: University of Michigan Press, 2019.

Garland Thomson, Rosemarie. *Extraordinary Bodies: Figuring Physical Disability in American Culture and Literature*. New York: Columbia University Press, 1997.

Halberstam, Jack, and Ira Livingstone. 'Introduction: Posthuman Bodies'. In *Posthuman Bodies*, edited by Jack Halberstam and Ira Livingston, 1–22. Bloomington: Indiana University Press, 1995.

Haraway Donna. 'Situated Knowledges: The Science Question in Feminism and the Privilege of Partial Perspective'. *Feminist Studies* 14, no. 3 (1988): 575–99.

Haraway Donna. 'A Manifesto for Cyborgs: Science, Technology, and Socialist Feminism in the 1980s'. In *The Postmodern Turn: New Perspectives on Social Theory*, edited by Steven Seidman, 82–116. Cambridge: Cambridge University Press, 1994.

Haraway Donna. *The Haraway Reader*. New York: Routledge, 2004.

Howe, P. David. 'Cyborg and Supercrip: The Paralympics Technology and the (Dis)empowerment of Disabled Athletes'. *Sociology* 45, no. 5 (2011): 868–82.

Jain, Sarah S. 'The Prosthetic Imagination: Enabling and Disabling the Prosthesis Trope'. *Technology and Human Values* 24, no. 1 (1999): 31–54.

Kafer, Alison. *Queer Feminist Crip*. Bloomington: Indiana University Press, 2013.

Kama, Amit. 'Supercrips versus the Pitiful Handicapped: Reception of Disabling Images by Disabled Audience Members'. *Communications* 29, no. 4 (2004): 447–66.

Kingsman: The Secret Service. [Film] Dir. Matthew Vaughn, USA: 20th Century Fox, 2014.

Masters, Cristina. 'Bodies of Technology: Cyborg Soldiers and Militarized Masculinities'. *International Feminist Journal of Politics* 7, no. 1 (2005): 112–32.

Masters, Cristina. *Eurozine*, 2010. Available online: https://www.eurozine.com/cyborg-soldiers-and-militarised-masculinities/

McGillivray, David, Hugh O'Donnell, Gayle McPherson, and Laura Misener. 'Repurposing the (Super)Crip: Media Representations of Disability at the Rio 2016 Paralympic Games'. *Communication and Sport* 9, no. 1 (2021): 3–32.

Middleton, Karen. 'The Invictus Games Will Show Us What Is Possible through Rehabilitation'. *The Huffington Post*, 20 August 2014. Available online: https://www.huffingtonpost.co.uk/professor-karen-middleton/invictus-games_b_5691133.html

Mitchell, David T., and Sharon L. Snyder, eds. *The Body and Physical Difference: Discourses of Disability*. Ann Arbor: University of Michigan Press, 1997.

Mizokami, Kyle. 'The U.S. Army Expects to Field Cyborg Soldiers by 2050'. *Popular Mechanics*, 26 November, 2019. Available online: https://www.popularmechanics.com/military/research/a29963287/us-army-cyborgs/

Murray, Stuart. *Disability and the Posthuman: Bodies, Technology and Cultural Futures*. Liverpool: Liverpool University Press, 2020.

Nayar, Pramod K. *Posthumanism*. Cambridge: Polity Press, 2014.

Nichels, Whitney Delbridge. 'Soldier Amputees Have More Options than Ever for Redeployment'. *US Army*, 27 July 2018. Available online: https://www.army.mil/article/209083/soldier_amputees_have_more_options_than_ever_for_redeployment

Oliver, Kelly. *Women as Weapons of War: Iraq, Sex and the Media*. New York: Columbia University Press, 2007.

Ott, Katherine. 'Carnage Remembered: Prosthetics in the US Military since the 1860s'. In *Materializing the Military*, edited by Bernard Finn and Barton C. Hacker, 47–64. London: Science Museum, 2005.

Planet Terror., [Film] Dir. Robert Rodriguez, USA: Dimension Films, 2007.

Rossini, Manuela. 'Bodies'. In *The Cambridge Companion to Literature and the Posthuman*, edited by Bruce Clarke and Manuela Rossini, 154–69. Cambridge: Cambridge University Press, 2016.

Sandberg, Anders. 'Morphological Freedom – Why We Not Just Want It, but Need It'. In *The Transhumanist Reader: Classic and Contemporary Essays on the Science, Technology and Philosophy of the Human Future*, edited by Max More and Natasha Vita-More, 56–64. Oxford: Wiley–Blackwell, 2013.

Serlin, David. *Replaceable You: Engineering the Body in Postwar America*. Chicago: University of Chicago Press, 2004.

Shabot, Sara Cohen. 'Grotesque Bodies: A Response to Disembodied Cyborgs'. *Journal of Gender Studies* 15, no. 3 (2006): 223–35.

Silva, Carla Filomena and P. David Howe. 'The (In)validity of Supercrip Representation of Paralympian Athletes'. *Journal of Sport and Social Issues* 36, no. 2 (2012): 174–94.

Smith, Marquand. 'The Vulnerable Articulate: James Gillingham, Aimee Mullins and Matthew Barney'. In *The Prosthetic Impulse: From a Posthuman Present to a Biocultural Future*, edited by Marquand Smith and Joanna Morra, 43–72. Cambridge, MA: MIT Press, 2006.

Sweet, Ryan. 'Prosthetic Body Parts in Literature and Culture, 1832 to 1908'. PhD Dissertation, University of Exeter, 2016.

'Transhumanist Declaration (2012)'. In *The Transhumanist Reader: Classic and Contemporary Essays on the Science, Technology and Philosophy of the Human Future*, edited by Max More and Natasha Vita-More, 54–5. Oxford: Wiley–Blackwell, 2013.

Vainshtein, Olga. 'Developing ProAesthetics: Disability as Fashion Discourse'. In *Fashion-Wise*, edited by Maria Vaccerella and Jacquelyn Foltyn,103–11. Leiden: Brill, 2013.

Young, Stella. 'We're Not Here for Your Inspiration'. *ABC News*. 3 July 2012. Available Online: https://www.abc.net.au/news/2012-07-03/ young-inspiration-porn/4107006.

INDEX